D1714457

LINCOLN'S ADVOCATE

The Life of Judge Joseph HOLT

SUSAN B. DYER

Preface by JAMES C. KLOTTER

Acclaim Press
MORLEY, MISSOURI

P.O. Box 238
Morley, MO 63767
(573) 472-9800
www.acclaimpress.com

Designer: M. Frene Melton
Cover Design: M. Frene Melton

Library of Congress Cataloging-in-Publication Data

Dyer, Susan B.
Lincoln's advocate: the life of Judge Joseph Holt / by Susan B. Dyer.
p. cm.
Includes index.
ISBN-13: 978-1-935001-26-3 (alk. paper)
ISBN-10: 1-935001-26-4 (alk. paper)
1. Holt, Joseph, 1807-1894. 2. Judges--United States--Biography I. Title.
KF368.H586D94 2009
347.73'14092--dc22
[B]

2009030161

Second Printing: 2010
Printed in the United States of America
10 9 8 7 6 5 4 3 2

Contents

Dedication

To my husband, Eddie
whose support and love
helped complete the dream
of writing the book.

Preface

Joseph Holt's story has long needed to be told. A few scholarly studies have explored various aspects of the man, but few indepth works have appeared. Now Susan Dyer has sought to change all that and give voice to Joseph Holt once more. Combining good research in the sources with her creativity, she has crafted a book that explores the spirit and the heart of Joseph Holt.

Holt has languished in almost obscurity for much too long. But why? After all, here was a man who was a successful attorney and loving husband, a person who served as Postmaster General and then Secretary of War under President James Buchanan. When Abraham Lincoln followed in office, he recognized Holt's talents and would make him Judge Advocate General. Holt, who did so much to keep the key state of Kentucky in the Union, would also gain the rank of Major General during the conflict.

After the assassination of the president, Holt played an important part in the trials of the conspirators. In that role, he became involved in much controversy, which has caused some students of history to shy away from a study of his life and career. The fact that Kentucky turned pro-southern in sympathy after the war also contributed to Holt's fall from historical grace. His unionism did not sit well with the next several generations of mostly pro-southern writers and he remained covered in the mists of historical forgetfulness.

He deserves better than history has given him. Now, Susan Dyer has brought Holt back to center stage. By focusing on his personal side, on his life and his loves, she shows aspects of Holt that have largely been hidden from the accounts. When the record is silent, she has used her knowledge of the man to recreate aspects of his life. Hers is a story worth reading.

But there is more to the story than just this book. Her interest in the person took her to his home. There the ghosts of history could be heard; there the abandoned walls cried out for help. Due to her efforts, and the efforts of so many others, the Holt House has been saved. If this book sparked that effort, it remains an ongoing fight, with battles yet to be fought.

In short, the author has done her homework, has given Holt's story a new hearing, and has given his home a new lease on life. Such effort would have made Holt proud.

James C. Klotter
The State Historian of Kentucky and Professor of History
Georgetown College

Acknowledgements

Thanks to the following for their time and willingness with the contributions in the Holt story.

First, I thank God, who put this idea on my heart.

To Dr. James C. Klotter, The State Historian of Kentucky and a professor of history at Georgetown College, author and editor who invested time, guidance, editing, and mentoring in assisting the author.

To Douglas W. Sikes, the publisher who recognized the importance of publishing the work, and sharing with the nation, while helping promote the Holt Project to save Judge Holt's Kentucky home.

To Etta Wilson, publisher and author who made a contact with John Edgerton.

To John Edgerton, author who made a connection to Dr. James C. Klotter.

To Kenneth L. Tabb, Hardin County Clerk, who introduced Douglas W. Sikes, publisher to the author.

To Mr. and Mrs. John P. Behen, for giving advice and ideas about topics in the book, encouraging massive reading, loaning wonderful collections from the period, and listening to the chapters throughout the project.

To a departed friend, George Triplett III, former judge and lawyer who shared stories about his ancestor, Governor Charles Anderson Wickliffe of Kentucky, in numerous interviews.

To a departed lady, Marguerite Bennett, whose fellowship endures and who kindly gave an interview about the Holt House.

To James L. Wimsatt, for using his beautiful drawing of the Holt House for the book cover.

To the students whom I have taught, from my heart I have given my best, and kept my promise in writing a book telling the untold story of Judge Joseph Holt in efforts of saving his home.

To Bruce Kirby, at the Library of Congress, Manuscript Division who assisted numerous times and helped me locate important materials and pictures needed to tell the Holt story.

To Bonnie Coles, at the Library of Congress, who worked diligently finding pictures.

To Sarah L. Robinson, who assisted with locating numerous letters, diaries, and scrapbooks from the Library of Congress.

To my sons Quince and Justin, grand-daughter Jaydyn, and family who have heard numerous times the chapters as they were written, edited and revised.

To Aaron Glenn, who assisted numerous times with computer tasks.

To two church ladies Norma Rae Butler and Jean Robinson who listened to the chapters as they were written sometimes out of sequence, but always available for listening.

To Ints Kampars, who read the rough draft of the book and gave his opinion.

To Jackie Butler, who proofread the edited version.

To Mr. Dan Snodgrass, for empowering the author to do more than she could dream of and still keep working to give her best.

To Brother Ken Jesse, who said, "You need to tell about the project in the book so the people will know the massiveness of this community project, and for the many prayers said.

To Bryon Crawford, for doing a story in the *Courier-Journal* about the Holt project and book.

To local editor David Hayes, for writing a featured story about the project and the book.

For the prayers of three ministers Reverend J. A. Lawhorn, Reverend Ken Jesse, and Reverend Janet Carden.

Thanks and appreciation for the support of family, friends, church family, and community.

To Representative Dwight D. Butler, for his prayers and confidence.

To the numerous organizations who have invited the author to speak about the wonderful journey of writing the book.

Introduction

The Holt House has been empty since 1960, waiting, perhaps to be rescued, and to re-create the life it once knew, when kings and queens visited. On a Sunday afternoon in 1997, a teacher out for a long Sunday afternoon drive suddenly stopped in the middle of the road, and stared at the house. It touched her heart. It was as if the house was speaking out, seeking her help. Its latest visitor decided that if she wrote a book, then maybe, just maybe, it would bring attention to the house and it would be possible to save this irreplaceable home for children who did not know about their Lincoln connection.

Believing in a dream, and never giving up, brought results. State Representatives, Senators, the Kentucky Heritage Council Preservation Office, the Kentucky Lincoln Bicentennial Commission, the Kentucky Historical Society, Preservation Kentucky, local citizens, county judges, and the people all helped the Holt House win acknowledgements from Preservation Kentucky as One of the Most Endangered Historic Places in Kentucky. It has become a Legacy Project of the Kentucky Lincoln Bicentennial Commission, and was named by the Kentucky Historical Society and the Kentucky Heritage Preservation Office as being on the Kentucky Lincoln Heritage Trail and an official Lincoln Site in Kentucky.

With the acquisition complete, Breckinridge County now owns the Holt House, in partnership with the Kentucky Heritage Council Preservation Office. But what will the future bring for the house? Will the nation help restore this Lincoln connection, this place nestled along the Ohio River in an unspoiled region, looking much the same as when Judge Holt walked the river bottoms as a young farm boy growing, pursuing his dreams of serving his country?

Joseph Holt's spirit will rest when the nation and Kentucky honor him by restoring and preserving his Kentucky home. The long walks up and down the stairs, the pacing, the feelings within his heart, can be finally released.

Joseph Holt can once again be happy and content about the stately home he so loved; the mansion can be rescued from the present-day conditions of neglect. Once again the home can have laughter ringing in the halls, Christmas balls, spreading cheer and red velvet drapes decorating the walls. Judge Holt's last wish was for his family to celebrate the centennial celebration of the Holt Plantation in 1911, and for the land to always stay in the family. The 200th anniversary of the Holt Family Plantation homesteading occurs in 2011. The home continues to seek the life it once knew when it stood as the showplace of Breckinridge County.

The Day of Execution

Along Washington's wharf the old capital prison sat silent like a casket, as it housed the prisoners of the Lincoln Conspiracy Trial. On June 29, 1865, Mary Surratt, Lewis Powell (alias Paine/Payne), George Atzerodt, and David Herold were found guilty of being involved in the conspiracy to murder Abraham Lincoln. They remained in their cells after the trial ended, not knowing their fate, for a week, until two days after the Fourth of July. What thoughts ran through their minds as Major General Winfield Scott Hancock walked into the cells of Atzerodt, Herold, Powell and Surratt around noon? Would it be life or death? He read them their sentences to be hanged until dead. Powell was shaken by the rushed methods in which the four were to be executed. Mrs. Surratt burst into violent grief, asking for Father Walter, Father Wiget, her daughter Anna, and John P. Brophy, a friend. She begged for a reprieve.

With only twenty-four hours left, what could be done to save them? Mrs. Surratt's attorney, John Clampitt remembered, "So sudden was the shock, so unexpected the result, amazed beyond expression at the celerity of the order, we hardly knew how to proceed."

However, everyone tried, with hope. Anna Surratt and Clampitt tried to see President Andrew Johnson, who turned them away, and the following morning Anna scurried back again to the White House to try to save the life of her dear mother, but was barred by Preston King, and James Lane, who later both committed suicide. One last chance existed to get Judge Alexander Wyler to issue a writ of habeas corpus early into the morning hours from a civil court, ordering Mrs. Surratt's release from military custody. But General Hancock and Attorney General James Speed rushed to court with an executive order from the president, suspending the writ. However, five of the judges had signed a document, suggesting President Johnson should commute her sentence to life in prison. As these developments transpired, Major General John Hartranft, in charge of the prisoners remained at the prison waiting. Rumors spread that Mary had been pardoned by the president or that General

Hancock was going to be arrested by civil authorities or that Mrs. Surratt would be rescued.

On that fateful day, the crowd in the courtyard outside the Washington Arsenal was limited to members of the press, necessary witnesses, and a few officers. Only one photographer, Alexander Gardner, photographed the historical event. President Johnson had requested Gardner, and Lincoln had liked him. As people waited, their patience soon grew thin as many expected Mary Surratt to be spared, thus the delay. Captain Christian Rath, the hangman, also thought Mrs. Surratt would escape the sentence, and only put five knots in her rope.

That scorching Friday would be under fire for the next century and a half as doubts began to be heard before the execution even ended. While waiting in her cell, Mrs. Surratt thought, "The first day I remember being brought into the first floor and placed in cell number 153. It was two and one half feet by eight feet with only a straw pallet and one bucket to set upon. Is this how my life is to end; a well-educated, devoted Christian, kind, affectionate and charitable lady who attended church and did all her duties to God and man? If only I could have testified in my own behalf." However, that would have only been possible if the trial had been in Maine. And the law would not be passed until March 16, 1878 to testify in one's own behalf. So the ruling of the commission was not unduly or legally harsh.

Mrs. Surratt's health worsened after she was arrested. She had a diseased womb and her lawyer believed she was mortally ill at the time she was to be hanged. Her treatment proved no worse than other political prisoners at the time. She was never hooded, though Secretary of War Edwin M. Stanton seemed to be vindictive toward the woman prisoner. Taking suggestions from Dr. John T. Gray's recommendations on June 20, 1865, the men had been given a box or stool, but Mrs. Surratt had been supplied with a chair. Later she enjoyed extra privileges, such as a large, airy cell with windows, visitors, and any food she desired. Her leg irons were removed as the trial progressed and as her health worsened.

An endless night for Mrs. Surratt lengthened as she heard the commotion outside the south yard of the building. Echoes of hammering reached her third floor, as Captain Rath instructed prison carpenters on how to build the scaffold. As she tried to rest, visioning Surratt did not know what had transpired that day surrounding her daughter, and home on H

Street. At dusk Anna arrived at home after spending an exhausting day with her mother. Sobbing, heart-torn, she managed to ascend from her buggy assisted by two gentlemen. As the curious public watched, only a single, dim light shown from one silent room.

The *Evening Star* marked that spectators attending the public execution would require a signed pass from Major General Hancock and that would not be easy to acquire because of only standing room in the courtyard. People fled to the Metropolitan Hotel, where Hancock stayed requesting passes to witness the most degrading occurrence. People began a dance with death, as the nation waited.

Daylight arrived, and as the four prepared to die, Mrs. Surratt asked John Brophy to try and clear her name of the crime, and he promised he would do everything possible. She spent the entire morning praying with Father Wiget and Father Walter. At noon, Herold's seven sisters left the cell of their brother, telling him goodbye until eternity, weeping rivers of tears. Atzerodt was counseled by the Reverend Dr. Butler; the last visitors were his mother and wife. Powell listened attentively, sitting firmly in his prison cell.

Final touches had been made to the gallows that morning by 11:00, and a test drop with a bag of shot at 11:25. The noise brought Mrs. Surratt back into reality. Workmen around the prison were superstitious, so soldiers dug the shallow graves. White boxes from the Navy Yard would be used as coffins.

The afternoon heat became suffocating as the crowd waited anticipating that a reprieve was causing the delay.

Time passed. Washington had changed from a city of happiness, with rockets blasting now to a city who had mourned a dead President as horror had darkened the nation with agony, and apprehension of not knowing what was next. What would the future say of this fateful day on July 7, 1865? Mrs. Surratt was quoted as saying to Father Walter, "Holy Father, can I not tell these people that I am ignorant of the crime for which I have been condemned to death?" Father Walter replied, "No, my child, the world and all that it is in it has now receded forever." Clampitt thought that this "should forever set the question of the guilt or innocence of this poor woman." However, all newspapers wrote of her guilt and involvement with Booth and the three meetings of the two on the day of the assassination. Seventy-five years after the trial, Louis

J. Weichmann's manuscript was published and, in referring to Mrs. Surratt and her son, he said, "Their whole course of action towards me from the time they became acquainted with Booth was of lying ingratitude and treachery."

Judge Advocate General Joseph Holt, the setting judge of the Lincoln Conspiracy Trial, wanted his friends to know that he had conducted the trial fairly, and for the rest of his life he worked for the honor of his name. He would never be able to remove the scene from his memory.

The scorching heat beat down burning the faces of those present. Only umbrellas offered protection from the blazing sun. Soldiers lined the walls, with their guns close by their sides, as if sealing this grimly day from the world. Guards watched the courtyard, lined with old, young, male, and female for any unexpected movements, on the windless, miserable day. As Judge Holt waited, he remembered the scene in the courtroom, with its whitewashed walls and new carpet, and how the days had also been extremely hot and stuffy there. The male prisoners of the conspiracy had been led in, hooded and with leg irons, and remained hooded during the completion of the trial. However, Mrs. Surratt wore a veil, not putting light on her face. As reporters tried to catch her features, none did her covered face justice, for they did not know her appearance. But those who once knew her remembered how she had been considered a belle in her youth and had rather pleasant features of dark gray eyes and brown hair. Historians to this day question why Alexander Grandy did not photograph Mrs. Surratt and Dr. Mudd.

Judge Holt thought about the rules governing the Commission, and how two-thirds of the members had to vote for the death penalty. In Mrs. Surratt's case, that had been done only after a plea for clemency had been written to the president, asking him, in consideration of the age and sex of Mrs. Surratt, to commute her sentence to life imprisonment, "if he could find it consistent with his sense of duty to the country."

Holt's eyes guarded each moment as proceedings began. General Hancock appeared from the building at 1:00, acknowledging the guards. Four chairs emerged on the scaffold, two on each side. Gardner placed photographic equipment at the windows to capture the view from the west yard, taking numerous photographs of the vivid scene as the living stage progressed. At 1:02 the prisoners arrived at the door, with Mrs. Surratt's steady step leading them to the platform of the scaffold. A heavy veil covered her face. She led the others, supported by an officer and non-commissioned officer.

Witnesses saw a dreary scene as the prisoners came into the courtyard. The prisoners had been confined in small spaces in very uncomfortable conditions. The condemned carried cannon balls attached to heavy shackles between their ankles. While in their cells they remained hooded with only a small hole to eat through. Bathing had been scarce, and they had lived a life of misery since being arrested for conspiracy to assassinate President Lincoln.

To live without taking a bath, without having the right to speak to their attorneys when they wanted, to be hooded during all of the trial for fifty-two days in extreme temperatures, to have cannon balls attached to heavy shackles between their ankles (except for Mrs. Surratt) and to have a military trial instead of a civil one, was the price for being charged with conspiring to murder Lincoln.

Now judgment time had come, prisoners walking their last walk. Anna Surratt watched with tearstained eyes as the four condemned prisoners took each fateful step closer to the scaffold. Mrs. Surratt, weakened by the heavy irons, could barely walk. Anna now breathless, watching this dreaded scene as the small group proceeded past the freshly dug graves that were to be theirs. The prisoners smelled the new earth, felt the hot breeze, and listened in pain as they began ascending the fifteen, creaking, railed steps. Mrs. Surratt, faltering somewhat, mounted the fifteen-feet wide, ten-feet high platform and was placed in the chair on the right, the location of "honor" facing west. Her spiritual advisor directed her thoughts to eternity. Stacked pine boxes that were to be their coffins awaited them. Standing beside three men, with final minutes approaching, Mrs. Surratt hoped for notice of rescue, while the dangling rope reminded her of the alternative. Would she be spared, remembering every day for the rest of her natural life the tragedy that had brought her this horror? The hangman started adjusting the ropes. Atzerodt was placed by Mrs. Surratt, with Reverend Butler by his side. Bareheaded, with worn clothes seen many days during the trial, he was seated in a chair with a white handkerchief resting on his head. Herold, the third would-be assassin, looked most miserable, wearing a rusty black coat and checked pants with a black hat turned all around. He sat right of Atzerodt. Powell, last of the party, accompanied by Reverend Gillette, continued looking up at the heavens. Wearing a straw hat, sailor-blue shirt and pants, he strolled with head erect, understanding the consequences of his guilt. All four muttered prayers to be rescued from this terrible fate. The condemned watched as the four were hooded one at a time. Mrs. Surratt hoped and waited for loud shouts, "Stop! Stop!, Stop!," and a messenger from the White House. Then the hush would become unfrozen from the trance, waiting for instructions of what would occur.

Judge Holt, now realizing the reality of the condemned, turned in all directions waiting for the final call, the final curtain for this horrendous performance delivered by the United States of America. Had the officers of the commission been too ruthless pursuing the assassins? The officers composing the commission had been faithful to duty. Seventy–five years after the trial Louis J. Weichmann's published manuscript quoted him saying, "Right is Right and God is God, American people will stand by a man who knows he is right who has courage to stand by the right who only asks for fair play and honest treatment." Lincoln's assassination was a violated crime against mankind.

Soldiers positioned beneath the scaffold waited for closure to the death of the late president. Only recently had the Union troops marched down Pennsylvania Avenue with the most grandest and mournful pageant in that city. Thousands had given their approval and applause there but now officer's swords were wrapped in crepe and all flags and wreaths in black. Lincoln could not rejoice in the victory for his countrymen.

Judge Holt thought, "I prosecuted these people for their involvement in the killing of my president, Abraham Lincoln. I did it. What would history say?"

After General Hartranft read the death warrant, General Hancock appeared on the scaffold, ordering the executioner to proceed. General Hancock stationed himself at the east end of the building, still waiting for a reprieve. Judge Holt watched the hangman approach Mrs. Surratt and put the white hood over her face. She murmured, "Please don't let me fall, please don't let me fall." The silent crowd knew death was near them. Would Mrs. Surratt be saved in time? The hangman continued covering the heads of the others. Will the White House rider arrive in time with President Johnson's signature on the clemency papers? Will shouts be heard ringing across the courtyard stop the execution? Only seconds remained. Holt watched. Mrs. Surratt waited.

Truth Is Lost

The halls of the Holt House have heard the silent echoes of the sounds when queens and kings entered its doors. They arrived by passenger boat from the Ohio River. The house saw ladies arrive wearing expensive, elegant dresses, and saw gentlemen displaying their manners, helping the women exit the boats to the carriages bringing guests to the massive mansion.

Later, in the 1890's, visitors came by rail. Not far from the back of the house, guests exited the trains at the depot. Throughout the years, by whatever made them proud, important people came to social events where servants greeted the visitors as they approached. The foyer sparkled, with the sight of beautiful gas chandeliers and red velvet drapery with gold tiebacks adored the walls.

What the guests saw dazzled them! Stairwells, freestanding with cases, making a complete circle to the third floor. Under the stairs was a door. Was it a secret passageway leading to a private room, or was it used to hide slaves traveling to reach freedom across the Ohio River? Handrails made of walnut graced the spindles of oak trim, and guests looked out the double windows of the upper porch over the 10,000 acres making up the grand estate.

The home had a blue room, and a green room in which elegant mirrors decorated the huge walls. Elaborate furniture from New York made the home stand out with style as the Oriental rugs accented beautiful walnut floors.

In the rear of the mansion, a carriage house made life more comfortable by having the carriages close at hand. There was a grand line of valuable horses used to pull the carriages in style. Plenty of space made the carriage house roomy to house the horses of visitors and important guests as their visits lingered. Some guest enjoyed gathering by the beautiful trees next to the decorative porch.

In later years, Joseph Holt built a small church in honor of his beloved mother, Eleanor. Looking from the front view of the home the chapel could be seen and was a short walking distance from the home.

Southern ladies and belles of the ball walked down the magnificent stairs making their entrance. The sounds of fun and laughter filled the halls, musicians played the violins, and the double parlors opened for those who liked waltzing. Those not dancing strolled in the scenic flower gardens, and enjoyed conversations on comfortable benches close by the house. Food, in abundance with great wines, made the celebration even merrier.

Whispered words and quiet conversations told how long ago in the early 1800's, Richard Stephens' daughter, Eleanor, acquired the land to build her first home, and how it burned to the ground in the 1830's only to be rebuilt. Eleanor and her husband Colonel John Washington Holt raised five sons and one daughter in this house.

The second son, Joseph, became Commissioner of Patents, Post Master General, and Secretary of War under President James Buchanan in Washington D.C. Joseph, as the Judge Advocate General in Lincoln's cabinet, also conducted the trial of the accused who planned and committed the assassination of the sixteenth president, Abraham Lincoln. After the trial, Joseph lived a sad, secluded and lonely life in Washington. Many times Joseph returned for comfort to his childhood safehaven in Breckinridge County, Kentucky. Sadly, Joseph lost both wives to tuberculosis, and had no heirs to care and support him as an old man. He died in Washington D.C., and afterwards his body traveled home by train. A second funeral conducted there was the most famous funeral in the county's history. In honor of his mother, Joseph had earlier built the little church where now his body lay in respect. In the Holt family cemetery he now sleeps his final sleep.

As the years have passed, so have the caretakers of the century, and of his house. But will the building's unique architecture, landscape, and story be saved? Will the stately home become what it use to be? Will the grand home sparkle in the night again, with the circular drive and long, straight lawn of different species of exotic trees? Will the ginkgo, white oak, sugar maple, red beech, and many plants adoring the grounds and fill the garden? Will eyes welcome the sights of a well-kept garden with a devoted gardener caring for the grounds of the home place?

Will visitors once again smell fresh paint, as the walls recover from dull and dirty to clean and adorable? Will stencils above windows and iron fireplaces return to their original location in the home and complete the Nineteenth Century grandeur? Will steps, now grimy from years of soil, be reworked and brought back to where reflections can be seen from the natural wood?

Will the green shutters, product of the talented work of a trusted, skilled craftsman of woodworking, be remounted? Will the two urns sold dating 1852 be returned? Will the exterior walls of brick made not far from the house and painted white two centuries ago be refurbished? Will the original roof of heavy metal be resurfaced?

Time is running out! The Holt Mansion could add charm, and delight to Kentucky's list of finely preserved southern homes. Yet, since 1894, the Holt family's connection to the home has been absent. Locals say his ghost still walks the halls of his lonely, old home calling out for help. With hope reborn and the mansion saved, chandeliers once again could illumine the vast darkness, and the sounds of logs crackling on a long winter's night might give peace to many years of neglect, and to the ghost of a haunted Joseph Holt.

The moon shinning on the soft fallen snow could give contentment once again and the house could once more provide comfort, peace, relaxation, and enjoyment for the good life of beautiful Breckinridge County. It could balance its great, rich heritage of yesterday with the technology of the twenty-first century.

The Holt Mansion has been waiting since 1894, begging to be restored to its glorious days when it entertained the most distinguished people in America and Europe. Future historians must make it what it once was, so that again voices can be heard of people living, and being merry in the pleasant environment of the river amid the long, rolling fields of green and the sweet smell of goldenrods in the south.

And so the legacy begins with a home. It holds fast to memories of life as its owners.

Eleanor

Eleanor Stephens Holt was Joseph Holt's mother. Her father had been the youngest captain of George Washington's army, and he served under him during the Revolutionary War for the Virginia Continental Line. After the war, the country paid its soldiers with land grants for their services. Due to this Joseph's maternal grandfather, Richard Stephens, received 93,000 acres of land expanding from Louisville, along the Ohio River, to the south to a little village later named after Eleanor's father (Stephensport, Kentucky).

Because fathers want the best for their children, Stephens built all of his daughters a home. Two white framed homes of great majestic endure for Eleanor's two sisters, Nancy and Sara. Her father offered her the land where the Holt House is today for her first home, out of brick.

Being young and having a free spirit, Eleanor was carefully chaperoned by her family. Young lovers had few moments to hold hands, have a mellow soft touch, or kiss without the company of others raising their brows. Etiquette played importance in the Stephens family. Choosing suitable callers for a vigorous, youthful lady meant the guidance of a cousin, or aunt or parents. Sometimes they selected gentlemen a young girl despised or one old enough to be her father. The family's acceptance of the desired beau might depend on the acquired estate, land, and money he would bring into the marriage.

Young Eleanor fully loved life. Passion touched her heart as she fell in love at first sight. She had returned home by riverboat after visiting the South and while the boat was docking, she glanced over the wet deck. A sudden thunderstorm had caused the atmosphere to become humid. Across the soaked deck, on the riverbank, sat a gallant, young gentleman sitting tall in the saddle, dressed in a suit of fine cloth. His light hair with brown eyes made her notice him. Suddenly, their eyes met. She realized her blushing face caused her to appear as a school girl without experience. Eleanor, frozen for the moment, hoped she would become his wife.

Excited and delighted, Eleanor believed she had finally discovered someone who met her expectations. Pretending not to be a bit interested, she sent forth a radiant smile. The young man approached and offered his hand to assist her in reaching the bank of the river safely. "May I help you young lady?" said the handsome, young gentlemen?

"No thank you kind sir. I can manage on my own," Eleanor said with a gentle nod and walked straight to the carriage waiting for her. Her heart started beating rapidly and she wondered if she would see him again. Was he some stranger passing by on business? Was he leaving on the boat to go to Louisiana? Would they ever be properly introduced?

As the carriage came closer to the house, Eleanor saw her mother standing on the edge of the terrace waving. Finally she was home, where she was safe and sheltered. A servant, Mammy, a woman of color, had escorted her to New Orleans and was with her as well.

Eleanor waited to get her mother alone to ask about the handsome, young man, but her father taking high steps toward the carriage changed her thoughts. Her father's beaming smile made Eleanor happy realizing just how much she had missed him and her home. Later Eleanor would inquire about the mysterious gentleman.

"And how was your trip sweetheart?" her father asked.

"Better than I expected and even more father." I had the best time ever, tasting new foods, traveling the busy streets, and shopping for presents for the whole family. I can't wait to show you what I brought back for everyone. Of course, I bought a few new dresses, father. I don't get the opportunity to go on a shopping trip such as this too often."

"That's splendid, Eleanor come in and tell us all about your trip," father continued.

"Father, I know everyone wants to hear the stories, adventures, and details about the voyage, the garden parties, who was there, what they wore, what was in style, and catch me up on all of the local gossip, but may we wait until supper time?" begged Eleanor.

"All right, my girl," said father. "You know it is difficult for me to say no to you. I can wait like everyone else. Now, give your mother a huge hug because she worried so much and fussed at me for letting you venture out on your own, even with Mammy accompanying you."

Sooner than expected, Sara completed the evening meal. After lying down for a short nap, Eleanor was refreshed from the long river journey. At supper, plans for Eleanor's homecoming would surface for discussion.

As she reached the bottom of the stairs, she saw before her the young man she had seen earlier in the day. He was dinning with the family! Eleanor seemed barely able to swallow or to get oxygen necessary for breathing. However, her father was soon at her side and with his special mannerisms introduced her to Colonel John Holt, who had also served under George Washington.

Eleanor blushed once again as her father introduced her as his daughter, Eleanor. Soon they were all enjoying a wonderful feast of wild venison with sweet potatoes, tomatoes, and spinach, and for dessert they consumed one entire chocolate cake.

After supper Colonel Holt asked Eleanor's father permission to take a walk in the garden with her. To her surprise, her father said, "Of course." This left Eleanor wondering what would she say to the Colonel? Even though she had not known the Colonel was to be a guest for the evening, she had still dressed in a stunning way, though the blue taffeta dress purchased in New Orleans still hung in the closet.

John said to Eleanor, "Your pink dress with beige lace moves so dramatically on you in the light of this most unique garden of beautiful, red, and yellow roses." The brightness of the moon and the radiant shine of the stars made the night memorable. With the gentle breeze blowing, they could smell the new blossoms. As they spoke causally about traveling, they moved closer to the front porch chairs.

They discussed the new country, difficult ways to travel, and Eleanor's experiences in New Orleans. Time went by fast and Colonel Holt looked in Eleanor's deep, brown eyes, and asked if she cared to accompany him on a picnic after church the following Sunday. He told her he would take care of all the food supply, if it was all right with her father and mother. Eleanor, who was only eighteen years old, was still abiding by custom to ask permission from her parents to court. Colonel Holt walked her back to the smoking room where her father enjoyed his favorite type of cigar. "I enjoyed the company of your daughter Eleanor greatly tonight. She is knowledgeable about the ways of the world. With your permission I would like to escort her on a picnic after church on Sunday. Another couple will accompany us for proper chaperoning, and I promise Eleanor's arrival home at a very early hour before sunset." Colonel Holt said. After careful consideration, Eleanor's father agreed. She couldn't believe her ears. Did father actually say yes? Was she dreaming? Was father paying attention? Was he intrigued with John, or did he think he was suitable for her?

Over the next few days, Eleanor thought about little except Sunday. She thought about the day, that moment in her life, when she would experience her first real date. She tried everything on in her wardrobe at least twice. Being nervous and wondering what to wear, she called to her sister, "Nancy, Nancy where are you?" When you need their advice older sisters never seem available. "How will I wear my hair? What shade of rouge and lip color should I use?"

The day approached slowly. As Eleanor glanced at the image in the mirror, she wondered if she was beautiful enough. What about her figure? Most women tried to impress gentleman callers with a low bust line. Eleanor thought her attire must be simple, yet elegant. She decided on a lavender dress with many ruffles of white lace and puffy sleeves. Her light brown hair falling long and loose would touch her pale shoulders. Pearls belonging to her grandmother accented her gracefulness.

Wanting to impress Colonel Holt, Eleanor ate lightly all week so her dress fit smoothly, and her small waist would accent her figure. Only one day left to wait. Saturday approached so slowly. Restless as a bear, she watched Sara prepare breakfast in the kitchen next to the big house. Sara insisted she take a walk and breakfast would be ready when she returned. Reluctantly, Eleanor took a brisk walk. Daydreaming, she wondered how she rated with Mr. Holt. Should I call him Colonel or would he insist I call him John?

Sunday arrived as everyone prepared for church services. The Reverend Robert Williams conducted Sunday service and the congregation witnessed one sinner saved. However, that caused the service to be longer than usual. As church dismissed families gathered around the front doors enjoying the fellowship of visiting and sharing with their neighbors.

Colonel Holt walked over to Eleanor's father and mother and briefly spoke as everyone started getting their teams of horses and buggies ready to go home. Mr. Holt, smiling, as he trotted across the grass, reached for Eleanor's hand. They walked slowly together to the nice couple, Levi and Elizabeth, accompanying them on the picnic.

The top of the buggy helped protect their faces from the reflections of the sun. John raised Eleanor aboard the stylish buggy and seated her in front. They traveled down the small dirt road five or six miles to a clearing. They passed the river and long, straight fields of tall, flowing grass around the river bank.

The couples celebrated a most beautiful picnic of fried chicken, creamy potatoes with a thick sauce, fresh baked bread, green beans, and cheesecake for desert. A cool glass of cider completed the meal. With everything packed and put away, John asked Eleanor to take a walk along the banks of the calm, flowing Ohio River. As the walk continued, John reached down grabbing small leaves from a nearby bush. Eleanor stood amazed, wondering why John was picking leaves. As she walked over to the bush, he started tossing leaves one at a time in her hair, flirting with her. "I bet you have had a lot of beaus," John smiled. Not wanting John to know she hadn't had a steady beau she said, "Well, most of the boys do like me and I have been asked for dates many times."

As the walk continued, Colonel Holt said, "Eleanor, you are knowledgeable beyond your years and with your permission I would like to be called your beau and get to know you better."

Barely able to control herself Eleanor answered, "Certainly, Colonel Holt, it's agreeable for you to be my beau."

"Please call me John. Colonel Holt sounds so old, and I prefer John."

Eleanor said, "If that's what you want, I will be glad to call you John."

Eleanor felt like her friend Elizabeth now. Realizing for the first time her dream was happening. But what would father say? Would he be as strict as he had been, and would he allow her to date a man several years older? Eleanor tried to stay calm, but felt shaky.

The young couple strolled together hand in hand, his hand squeezing hers softly to let her know he felt warmth for her. She liked John's gentle touch because he was a gentleman. Eleanor witnessed so much firmness with her father, it relaxed her to experience the gentleness John portrayed in the brief time she had known him.

The days seemed endless thinking about John and the few moments they encountered together. Eleanor wondered where this would lead, but she felt in her heart she had met the person she wanted to spend the rest of her life with sharing her most precious thoughts and dreams.

Eleanor did not take happiness for granted, because she felt in life each moment should be celebrated with a smile, a laugh, a hug, or a friendly hello. She wanted happiness more than anything, and to be loved by a passionate, considerate man who always loved her not just for beauty and youth, but for the grand qualities of loving life and living it to the fullest extent. When her beauty started to fade, Eleanor wanted a man who saw the beauty deep in her soul. She craved her life to be exciting, and adventurous.

Eleanor desired her husband to enjoy her personality, and expected him to love only one woman in his lifetime. She honored the principle to stand by his side with pride and strong belief that anything was possible if you believed in each other.

With Christmas soon approaching, a bustling movement transformed the atmosphere. Everything was meticulously cleaned. The talented gardener loaned his expertise advice on how to rake, and tidy the grounds. The yard surrounding the house included huge primitive oak trees. Guests felt as if they were explorers in a tropical rainforest when looking at the canopy above them.

Each year Eleanor's parents gave a Christmas Ball for friends and family. They hired musicians to play the violin, or fiddle, as the locals called them. The practice times helped her with the confidence she needed to lead the first dance of the ball. In her mind she heard her father announcing the first dance.

With servants busy preparing the house, it left little time to gather decorations. Eleanor and her sisters scouted the plantation for in-season garland or, glorious, red holly, or mistletoe from the high tree tops, to decorate two adjoining front rooms connecting to the impressively large foyer. With invitations sent, food prepared, and decorations completed the house passed inspection. The most decorative red bows and ribbons with candles lined the ten foot pine tree visitors eyed as arriving in the front entrance of the beloved home.

Richard, Eleanor's father, ordered the finest of cigars to pass out in the smoking room for the gentleman. Taking a break from the dancing, eating, and visiting, the gentlemen enjoyed smoking and talking of politics. The ladies discussed the church socials, the needs of the community, the work load of trying to teach the young children, and keeping the slaves in proper training method of the etiquette of entertaining and housekeeping.

December 23 arrived and with it came three inches of snow. It started to turn cold and Eleanor worried that folks might not get their teams and buggies through the inclement weather of the season. "Oh mother what if the weather gets so terrible no one comes?" She asked. "I don't know what I would do if I don't get to see John again."

"Eleanor K. Stephens, you know exactly what I have taught you," mother scorned.

"Be patient and see how things turn for the better. Sometimes it adds a small flavor with a covered landscape decorated by the divine, and if it is meant for us to have the annual Christmas Ball then by golly we will, and your Mr. Holt, if fate has it, will walk through the front foyer searching for you, my dear."

"Mother, how do you always know everything?" asked Eleanor.

"It's easy, just looking at you reminds me of myself twenty years earlier," smiled her mother.

The landscape covered with snow gave stillness with fresh and misty air and the stars in the sky seemed like diamonds sparkling. Earlier candles placed in the overextended jars helped to lead the lighted path, even though the wind blew fiercely.

Gabe, a young Negro slave, helped guests exit their buggies and wagons while two other young slaves, Tom and Ned, led the horses to the barn for sweet oats and a warm, dry place to rest. The wind howled and the snow pounded on a cold winter's night.

Father introduced Eleanor to the guests while her younger sisters Sara and Elizabeth watched from the stairs. They were not old enough to stay at the ball, and left early to go to bed.

Oh, it seemed such a marvelous time to be alive, to live, to dream, and to think of pleasing yourself, thought Eleanor. But what would destiny deal her in life and what path would she take? Would it be the right one or would obstacles cause her to go a different route, taking her longer than expected to follow the dreams of her heart?

As Eleanor stood beside the fireplace, logs flickered as their dim light cast a silhouette of her pale face with large, brown eyes and high cheekbones lined with pointed lips and a smile capturing the attention of those present. At that moment, Eleanor saw John Holt approaching her slowly with an enormous smile. As the musicians started playing a familiar waltz, her father approached them and asked if they would be the couple to begin the waltzing so others would join. When John took her hand, she melted into his arms. She looked so naive, so innocent, but yet so secure and in perfect place as they stepped highly to the merry music being made.

Eleanor stood five foot seven inches while John was a quite tall six foot two inches. She glided so gracefully within his arms in her red velvet Christmas dress. Others cut in from time to time to take a swirl, but none could compare with John's embrace. His smile and eyes seemed to watch her in a teasing way. They danced long into the night, as friends enjoyed celebrating the season of love and giving. At one time the violinists took a short break and some of those present sang Christmas carols around the piano. Time advanced quickly. Guests, a few at a time, said their goodbys and left in the damp and blustery evening to prepare for Christmas with their families. John said his goodbye inside the house. He smiled and said, "See you again soon," and winked at Eleanor.

Eleanor, excited from the day and the Christmas Ball, undressed put on her warm nightgown, and fell asleep, to dream. In what only seemed minutes she awoke to the sound of children running and Elizabeth, her mother, calling her name. Eleanor dressed quickly and ran down the stairs. Christmas Eve arrived and the house was busy again. The servants were cleaning from the ball and planning Christmas dinner for the immediate family.

As Eleanor entered the dinning room her mother handed her a sealed note with her name on the front. She opened it slowly and read, "Dear Eleanor, you took my breath away last night. Please take a sleigh ride with me this afternoon at 3:00. Affectionately Yours, John."

Precisely at 3:00 a sleigh arrived at the entrance of the house. John knocked on the front door, and Eleanor answering, told him she would only be a minute. She chose her riding boots, long wool coat with muff and mittens to keep the cold from her face.

No sooner had Eleanor and John sped away on the sleigh when Father entered the house. "Where was Eleanor headed?" spoke Mr. Stephens in a coarse voice.

"She was going for an afternoon adventure in the snow, my dear." said Mother.

"Without a proper chaperone?" stated Father.

"Do you really think it necessary to have a chaperone in broad daylight, and she is eighteen years old?" said Mother with confidence.

"It is not proper for her to take off with a gentleman we hardly know," voiced Father.

"We have to trust our daughter and believe in her judgment," said Mother.

"Maybe so," said Father. "But it is hard getting use to the idea she is a woman."

John drove the sleigh down to the river where they first met. It seemed so different today with no sounds except the distant falcons. The wind was making large waves and ripples along the water's edge as they looked at each other.

John uncovered a small package hidden stashed away in a tiny compartment in the sleigh. Eleanor's face lightened with surprise and her heart raced, wondering what was inside. "Had he bought me a nice bracelet or a pretty broach?"

Her thoughts raced, "I wondered why John winked at me last night. I prayed he really enjoyed being with me because we were alone in our own world." John's face met her's with a passionate smile as he took off his glove taking hold of her hand looking straight into her deep set eyes saying, "Do you ever want to marry me?"

Eleanor quickly responded, "Yes." Carefully she opened the rectangle-shaped box made of crush, green, velvet trimmed on the inside with white satin. Inside was the most pleasing gift she had ever received. A beautiful solitaire diamond ring signifying purity for maintaining peace, and dispersing storms. It sparkled brightly in the mist of the snow hurting her eyes to glance at it. "Am I dreaming? Was this reality, real life, the way people really lived?" Eleanor, excited, hugged John for the first time. "Oh John, I love you so much. I always want to be with you, and do everything together, and enjoy the brightest of all the days that we have as a gift from God." On Christmas Eve 1804, John and Eleanor became engaged. John would next approach her father to ask for his blessings.

Eleanor said to John, "You are invited for Christmas dinner. Mother expects me to ask you for dinner, but father, on the other hand, will be totally unprepared for the news."

"Leave your father to me Eleanor," said John calmly.

"All right, but be prepared for the unexpected. Father has no idea we are this serious about each other."

As always, Father asked the guests if they would like to ask the blessing before dinning. John stood to give the blessing and when he was finished he said, "I have an announcement to make before all of you. With your permission and blessing, I want to marry Eleanor. I pray sir you will give her hand because I am very much in love with your daughter."

Mr. Stephens, more than a little surprised, said, "I knew you two liked each other, but I did not expect it to be this soon. Eleanor is of age and has always had good intelligence, so her mother and I give our blessing. As a wedding gift, I will give you a lot of 500 acres, next to the Ohio River, for a suitable place to build a home."

"Oh thank you father," said Eleanor with an enormous smile, almost lighting the room. The rest of the family joined in clapping for the glorious news.

Construction began on the new home in early March. With much help from the Stephens and John, the home was completed by late December, in time for the young couple to move in after the wedding.

"Marriage is a blessing," said John.

"We will be so happy here, I can feel the warmth of love surrounding us," Eleanor sighed.

Exactly one year from the engagement, John W. Holt and Eleanor K. Stephens accepted each other's love for a life commitment. The couple married in the presence of family, friends, and neighbors at Eleanor's new home. The celebration continued way into the night.

After the ceremony Eleanor's father gave her a huge hug as he whispered in her ear, "Darling, I have never seen you so happy in my life, and you are the most beautiful bride I have ever seen. Continue to be as happy as you are now and life will bless you."

"Father, thank you, and Mother for making my wedding possible and letting me choose the one I truly love, for without love you have nothing," spoke Eleanor.

Joseph's Birth

Eleanor arose with a special feeling on the 6th of January, 1807. A mother sometimes feels it is time for the birth of her child. In her case, she seemed to have an extra-ordinary feeling of joy. It was a brisk, winter day outside the cozy home, a place you did not want to leave, especially on a dreary day.

John awoke early to enjoy a hardy breakfast before the long trip to Hardinsburg to serve as Commonwealth's Attorney. Eleanor instructed the cook to prepare food for the road knowing John would be gone for several days. She thought time was close for her to deliver, but said nothing. Eleanor's experience of labor and childbirth prepared her for the second birthing to come. A nearby midwife gave Eleanor additional confidence until John returned home to his family. Now as he prepared to leave, Eleanor tiptoed to reach John's lips. The pregnancy was difficult because of weight gain. This time Eleanor exceeded her normal weight by twenty-five extra pounds.

She kissed John and held him close to her. Eleanor often wished John's occupation was farming like her father, but she knew it would not be fair to compare the two because each person must do what they truly love in life to be happy. She knew the importance of supportive wives to a man's success in society. Being married to John at first proved challenging. As the daughter of the wealthiest land owner in the county, she had been used to the good life and to being waited on by servants. Now being a wife meant she planned for family functions and dealt with problems on a daily basis.

John loved to spoil Eleanor with presents on her birthday, anniversary, and especially at Christmas, her most favorite time of the year. The celebrated events brought joy to their young lives.

Eleanor dreaded John's absence and missed hearing his laughter ring in the halls. But most of all she yearned to be with him. "Here is the food prepared for you John," said Eleanor. "I wish you did not have to go," as she forced a smile for John. The food placed in the hand woven basket would be welcomed in a few hours. Eleanor handed John his wool hat and traveling coat. The team of horses scampered to the main house. Inside the buggy extra food for the horses filled the floor.

Winter storms struck suddenly without warning. It was hard to tell what could happen in a brief time out in the open. Absence from the comforts of home and without protection from the elements could cause hardships.

"I will house the livestock at the Liberty Stable once I reach Hardinsburg," said John. "Twenty miles is a dangerous journey in January through that rugged road. You know how it becomes impassible in the long, cold winter," cautioned Eleanor.

"I have traveled the passage since a small lad. I know every bend, stretch, hill, and creek. You know I will be careful, Eleanor. Give me a kiss and keep a smile for me until I get home," he responded.

With goodbyes said, John left. He told Eleanor to expect to see him in two days and nights but to her it seemed like eternity. No sooner had John driven out of sight, Eleanor wailed the first towing of pain. She thought to herself, "I should have told him."

The cook and housekeeper, Maria, would go for the midwife. She franticly ran to the barn and saddled a horse and rode to Stephensport six miles up the edge of the river. When she arrived she found the midwife missing. A neighbor shouted and explained the midwife took off to deliver a baby, fifteen miles away, just a few minutes before Maria arrived. With this information Maria knew she must hurry in haste because Eleanor was alone. Suddenly the weather deteriorated rapidly.

Waiting alone at home, Eleanor watched from her window. The snow suddenly ascended on the freshly frozen earth. Each snow flake made its début as original and others joined to pick up speed, changing the scene before her. Intrigued by the winter storm Eleanor decided to write in her journal.

"To keep my mind off of the pain I am enjoying the scenery. One tree positioned alone nuzzles against a woven fence keeps guard as a settling hushness provides comfort and serenity for me as I am safely sheltered in my favorite chair resting against the window.

"Hearing the fire burning behind me gives warmth reaching to welcome the evening while snow continues to paint the pastures a painter's white. The sky is overcast completely with pale gray giving the top composition the perfect palette to smoothly blend for a work of art only created by the divine. Two crows now answer back and forth to each other. The black crow flies forming a small curve about the ground as distant sounds echo along the landscape. Abruptly the snow pauses, takes notice, only gradually beginning as if one snow flake at a time joins a crusade of participants uniting to complete the parade on mother earth."

While traveling to Hardinsburg, John kept thinking of Eleanor's quietness. Her happy spirits probably concealed her true feelings. He kept remembering her smile and felt the need to return after traveling over ten miles. John commanded the team, "gee," making a complete turn for home. The horses twisted between trees, large holes, and rough edges and traveled through a mud lane barely resembling a country road.

The wind started blowing and snow falling made it impossible to see the road ahead. Steadying the team became impossible. The animals soon frightened and the wind changed into the most powerful sound, causing huge trees to bend down as if touching their roots. The path became an obstacle of twisted trees. John fiercely tried to remove the trees but could not without first unhitching the team from the wagon. One of the horses spooked and ran into the woods. The only sensible thing to do now was to capture the runaway horse and head for home. After searching frantically, the horse disappeared. Darkness approaching made it more practical to get to the house in a blizzard!

Eleanor, feeling alone but being no ordinary woman, realized a storm had developed. Maria was probably going to be late with the midwife. As her contractions from labor got closer she understood that protecting her child was the most important thing. She must be brave and calm. Eleanor's experience of working with midwives enabled her to process the knowledge necessary to deliver her child. Now the moment arrived she had looked forward to, and feared. No loved ones were close by her side to comfort her. Eleanor, all alone and time running out, gathered her thoughts and planned what to do next, put more logs in the fireplace, gather sheets, and bring warm water close to the bed side. The unbelievable pain numbed Eleanor's back causing her to barely move. How was she going to pick up even a small log? She had to do it no matter how, even if it meant crawling. Eleanor located more oil for the lamps to have good light.

The pain, almost unbearable, and contractions came closer together. In between the pains Eleanor took relief from labor as she thought critically, "Be calm. This is not complicated. I can do this." But how could I be calm not knowing if I will deliver my child never seeing my beloved husband again? How could he possible survive the elements? How could he lead the horses home? How would anyone find him? I must do this alone for John," thought Eleanor with tears streaming down her cheeks.

She pulled a quilt her grandmother made as a wedding gift from the turtle back trunk and placed it on the bedside. It would not be long now. Alone, Eleanor pushed as hard as possible, and delivered the child. Eleanor recalled how Indian woman had done that for generations out in the snow. She thought, "I can surely do this in a warm, comfortable home protected from the harsh wind and blowing pellets of snow." She cleaned the child with water and wrapped him safely in sheets and held him closely to her breast and fell asleep exhausted from the ordeal.

As John approached the distant house things seemed normal. A soft light reflecting from the large windows cast long shadows on the fallen snow. Snow started to drift along the banks of the ditches down the long avenue of Oak trees.

He rode the horse to the barn rushing to the house to find no one. The door was difficult to open. John shoved the door and screamed, "Eleanor, Eleanor," his beloved by name. No answer. He frantically searched from room to room and surprisingly saw an unbelievable sight. A glowing fire, a lighted room, warm and safe away from the cold, blustery snow blizzard outside the window pane, housed the young mother and her newborn child. Both Eleanor and the baby were fine. John, cold and dripping wet, acted wisely and removed his frozen clothes immediately. He took his place beside his beautiful, brave wife and newborn baby and did not leave their side until he heard someone calling his name a few hours later. "John, John, wake up John, this moment!" said Eleanor in a weak voice.

Finally, Maria managed to get through the snow drifts with the help of neighbors. The unbearable journey home proved Maria to be a pure heroin walking all the way. She picked one foot up at a time making a path through the snow drifts. Maria knew that she had to make it back to the house, for Eleanor's life depended on her. The inner voice gave Maria the strong endurance she had to have to return to help the Holts.

The blinding snow and cold took a person's breath away making it more difficult to walk while keeping your balance.

Blinded by the bright light Maria entered the foyer. It took her eyes several minutes to adjust from the poor conditions of the outer elements. Warming herself briefly, changing to dryer clothes, and moving her numb hands and feet, Maria energized her strength. She forgot about her own condition and remained faithful as the caretaker to Mrs. Holt, the child, and John.

Mr. Holt chilled, and with an awful cough, needed attention. Maria tended to the family's needs and withstood the temptations of sleep. She prepared hot soup, and when Eleanor awoke gave her nourishment, and said, "Mrs. Holt you are doing great and I am so very proud of you." Maria finally got John to wrap up in a thick wool blanket and set in a gentleman's chair beside Eleanor's bedside, for he would not leave his wife on this night.

The wind howled and trees blew and snow continued through the extended night. Finally, as daylight approached things seems to be better. The snow stopped, and the sight was amazing. Outside looked like a frozen wonderland as icicles hung from the roof top. Mother Nature's powerful snowfall of seventeen inches had decorated the woods, with snow attached to sides of trees making limbs droop. Fluffy, snow surprised human eyes. However, below freezing temperatures made life on the farm harder, taking hours to feed the beef cattle.

The livestock would not be able to find food because of the heavy accumulation of snow. Wilier, the hired hand, treaded the storm to help John with the animals. The cattle's fresh water came from chopping ice at the river's edge. The men labored hard coming to the house once to warm and eat briefly. Extended time outside was hazardous because of the reality of frostbite. Last year several people in the community lost toes and fingers.

Eleanor enjoyed her newborn for the first time since delivery. "I want to check on the men folks and make sure they are fine," said Eleanor. I'm afraid John will become chilled and catch pneumonia. He came through the storm and had to be frozen returning home. He should not be out in this weather. I don't want to loose him. Please take care of John for me. I will be indebted to you, Maria," spoke Eleanor in a whisper.

"Do not fret yourself, over the men folks Mrs. Eleanor," Maria answered. "You have more important tasks right now, taking care of the little one and you." The raging winter storm postponed the naming of the infant.

A weakened Eleanor had awoke a few times during the night and smiled briefly at John next to her side. She remembered John kissing her on the forehead and telling her he loved her and was proud of her.

For the most part, John stayed at home for the long, cold month of January. He felt his family needed him. People only traveled if they needed supplies, medicine, or because of an emergency. February brought better weather and by this time Eleanor was up and moving around the busy household. After a lot of thought, John and Eleanor decided on the name Joseph for their second child. The good baby gave Eleanor needed rest. Joseph brought attention and closeness from friends and family alike because he was adorable with beautiful blue eyes.

Eleanor took time to enjoy nature's calmness, and enjoyed her feathered friends, searchingly without a care in the world. A crow made his call as he passed over the damp earth. Fog hung over the landscape. Drizzle softly bounced touching the ground, while stillness owned the mid morning.

Eleanor's face lightened, "Wait," she said, and hurried to the side of the house as if the feathered friends understood. Once again Eleanor wrote in her journal: "A family of birds sitting high a top a tree is waiting patiently for the next flight to search for food."

"For three days since, pass gloom has settled in, except for the few moments of stolen sunshine casting rays, enlightening the soul. The soft rain falls on the already saturated fields just melted from last week's heavy ice storm with measurable snow and frigid temperatures making life on the farm more difficult."

"Eleanor, Eleanor."

"Yes," said a faint voice barely above a whisper.

"Here she is!" John shouted again.

"I was enjoying the view from the front entrance, and thinking about more pleasant days where sunshine will be a common feature and the children will be running and playing together under this beautiful old tree."

"Every day is pleasant, it is what you make it to be Eleanor," John said.

Parents read to little Joseph, played with him, and made him the center of attention as in most homes when a new baby has arrived. It was no different in the Holt's home. The responsibility of the mother was to train and rear the children and prepare them to attend college if possible. There were no schools close by and all the formal training to prepare a child for college came from what the mother had studied and read. Eleanor, a well read and an educated lady, prepared her children for a good and prosperous life. Her family promoted an education to prepare the children for their future.

Eleanor read classics to Joseph and trained him with every possible means available. Eventually her children mastered courses of instruction offered at universities. The Holt children were permitted to attend schools for short periods of time. Joseph, like any ordinary boy of the period, fished, hunted, and rode horses. His brilliant mind and extensive vocabulary made him noticed by all of his teachers. His maternal grandfather was persistent in wanting something better for Joseph than himself. Several times grandfather Stephens provided for Joseph when his parents needed assistance.

With the aid of grandfather Stephens, Joseph enrolled at St. Joseph's College in Bardstown in May of 1822. He was soon writing powerful themes in rhetoric and composition. These collections showed genius and imagination.

Eleanor once said, "Childhood is sometimes hard to exchange for adult life but with the guidance and patience of a grandfather who loves you dearly it is easier." Joseph's memories of his maternal grandfather would last his entire lifetime. The advice given to him to make something of his life instilled deeply in his heart of hearts.

The Light House

The light house on Summer Seat provided a comforting place for Joseph to collect his thoughts and remember past deeds. His grandfather, owner of the land, conceived the idea of erecting a lighthouse upon its summit; the friendly light would illuminate the streets in Hardinsburg, twelve miles east of the location. He wanted the lighthouse to guide the wayfaring man on his journey, and envisioned seeing the tower in the night sky from his home in Bardstown, Kentucky. He situated the building on a quite peculiar hill on the verge of a level plane rising gradually and with great irregularity on all sides to an altitude of perhaps a hundred feet above the general level of the county.

Joseph's first memory of going to the tower went back to when he was seven years old. Under construction the structure had progressed, but many of the workers feared the huge mass of stone. They frightened easily as the dangerous sandstones kept collapsing. Grandfather Stephens and little Joseph went to inspect the work one fall afternoon. After reaching the high peak they looked around to see if the structure was sound and strong enough to serve as a lighthouse. In the distance Joseph witnessed cattails standing tall at the edge of a large pond. "Look grandfather, look at those long sticks covered with brown, shiny ends." He spoke fast, excited in capturing his grandfather's attention.

Stopping for a few minutes, Grandfather Stephens and Joseph enjoyed all the sights surrounding them. The Monarch butterflies gathered nectar from the last of the fall clover. A black bird sat high atop the walnut tree overseeing other birds at work. The breeze refreshed the man and the boy, warming their faces on a hot afternoon. A squirrel skipped through the edge of woods, scampered up the tree, and climbed majestically, finally reaching the hidden entrance of its nest. A red-headed woodpecker drummed in the neighboring tree, and in the distance, sounds could be heard of travelers. This was enough to captivate any youngster. Grandfather Stephens commented, "Yes, Joseph, the world is wide awake today, and it is good to have you out of that big, stuffy house. A young boy needs more fresh air and a break from studying too much."

A trio of doves glided gracefully by, two doves flew in front and one lagged behind as not to be in a hurry. Grandfather said, "For the journey is an adventure into the moment of the next minute bringing peace and happiness to those seeking to find it."

Finally, Grandfather Stephens and Joseph looked at the base of the structure and inspected the circumference of the tower. Joseph's grandfather, a determined man, pursued the idea until it became reality. He wanted to establish as many projects as time permitted, leaving his family a destiny. The work on the tower continued with one mishap after another. More sandstone rocks were anchored making a larger base to support the structure. The beauteous tower delighted the eye.

Each week the workers talked among themselves. A few concerned workers discussed their fears causing panic among the stone layers, as well as with the men hauling sandstone up the dangerous point with mules. The leaning tower made the workers refuse to work in fear the tower would tumble down upon them.

Young Joseph later recalled that golden day, "My grandfather, being a persistent person, talked to the crew and told them he would not hold it against them if they left." As soon as the laborers departed, he made a short trip to the Elizabethtown area searching for workers with more experience working on high structures. Within a couple of weeks the work resumed on the lighthouse.

Joseph's Grandfather and Grandmother Stephens made a trip by boat to Louisville to order windows for the lighthouse. It was important to have the right type of windows for the light to transcend upon the countryside of Breckinridge County. Special ordered windows allowed a powerful and intense beacon of light to emit from the lighthouse. The windows took several months to make and were shipped by barge to Holt. Two months passed and finally the windows arrived.

Travel from the river banks of the Ohio was difficult, especially if the loads were heavy. Slaves diligently drained the swamps by the river by dragging huge logs to help release the water. A team of oxen waited in between pulls. Often when heavy fall rains came, the fields became soggier, hanging up the teams pulling supplies.

Young Joseph, intrigued by his grandfather, proudly shared information with all of the boys of his neighborhood. Joseph would boast, "The lighthouse is going to be the highest structure for miles. The outside of the tower is chalky white, built on top of an isolated rock. The foundation sinks deep into the huge bed of stones making it stronger to survive a massive storm."

The community felt very fortunate having such a remarkable and visible landmark. Community pride brought family and friends to see the lighthouse. The huge beams would shine to lighten the dark sky, making night travel safer.

The lighthouse was the talk of Hardinsburg. No one before had attempted such an undertaking this far west. The mothers of the community packed picnic lunches on Sunday afternoons and took their families to enjoy. More skeptical fathers considered it a waste of time. A few people imagined traveling in the night only in the event of a dire emergency and considered the tower to be a foolish waste of money.

One year passed with the tower only one-third finished because of delays. Joseph's Grandfather Stephens brought Grandmother Stephens to the sight to see what she thought about the project, and her first reaction was, "It is just too plain. Richard, you have spent a fortune on this tower. Lighthouses should be catchy to the eye, making the traveler feel relaxed and soothed by the grand beauty; not just a tall object stuck up in the sky. Why not add color with a huge, red stripe in the middle of the tower? Red always excites people making them feel warm and comfortable."

A small argument developed between Joseph's Grandmother Elizabeth and Grandfather Richard. His grandmother stated very firmly, "Lighthouses should be beautiful and send out bright rays of light to the passing patrons."

Joseph's grandfather then hired an architect from Louisville. The architect agreed that a nice, red stripe would add beauty to the tower. He also suggested an extended seating area at the base as well as the top of the tower. The still uncompleted lighthouse already served as a unique meeting place, for young couples to talk and take walks up the stairs, and to star gaze on splendid nights. To add to their comfort, the architect designed a circular stairs widening at the top with comfortable seats. Windows made up the top layer of the lighthouse giving spectacular sighting. A wonderful night's showing of the constellations, planets, and dusting of stars thrilled astrologers.

Finally, plans finalized and the lighthouse became reality. The tower became known as "Summer Seat."

Standing there, time seemed to stand still at Summer Seat. Young Joseph admired the work behind it, "The foundation of sandstone rock is twenty-four inches thick, and four feet wide. The lighthouse's diameter is sixty feet. There is a feeling of comfort snuggled against a woods close by. You can see for miles in every direction," He commented.

Joseph loved visiting Summer Seat in the winter with his Grandfather Stephens. While Grandfather prepared the tower for winter, young Joseph, a natural writer, began writing in his journal:

"I remember the terrific task of hauling these sandstone rocks up the steep elevation. What determination to develop a lighthouse such as this! The day is cloudy with a solid overcast of medium blue. The atmosphere is as if you know someone knows you have come to visit but not to stay." Interrupting Joseph's writing, came the call "Joseph, Joseph," from Grandfather.

"Yes, Grandfather, I was writing in my journal."

"Well, come here my boy, I want to show you something," said Grandfather patiently.

"What is it?"responded young Joseph.

"It is my wish little man that I want to be buried at the base of the tower. As a Revolutionary War Soldier it is my wish to be buried here along side your Grandmother. Things are changing and I want the peace I have always known. I want to be among the distant sounds of the hawk, and the leaves can wave to visitors as if welcoming them to a breath taking view of the gorgeous landscape I love."

"But why are you telling me Grandfather?" Spoke Joseph quite concerned with a sad look on his face.

"Because I know you will make my wishes known. And when it is time for me to die, I want to sleep my final sleep waiting for the Judgment Day upon this summit away from noise on this place of peacefulness!"

"But Grandfather," said Joseph, "I don't understand why you want to be so far away from us."

"I will always be with you Joseph. When you feel the breezes touching your cheeks, and the deer making a path, I will be along side every step you take. In the future the moss will cover the rocks and the ground will sink with fallen sandstones. Small limbs will have fallen and the sandstone rocks will shift in great strives, but I suppose the circle of rocks will still show a great deal of hard and energetic work went into this project of several centuries past when we are all gone. In the future to visit the summit will put you in touch with reality to realize a war hero of the Revolutionary is buried here along side his wife. This is the most peaceful place I have ever known. It reminds me of the early years when I was young, for surrounding me will be rocks, all tossed in every direction, dry leaves covering the spot which makes it hard to visualize and it is snug along the hillside blending into the environment," replied Grandfather.

"That will be years from now," said Joseph.

The years passed rapidly and Joseph would make his final trip back to the top of the summit to bury his Grandfather in 1831. In his eulogy he concluded, "Peace be still and have a blessed sleep. You deserve to be blessed where no one will bother you and you can be as free as the wind blowing upon your gravesite. The trees of the forest will be as still as stones and breezes will blow so quietly as if whispering a soft prayer to those present. This is the heavenly spot on earth where your spirit is enthroned with serenity existing with peace. Here you can be as you were in the days of early explorers when things were pure, clean, and true in nature." Joseph looked sadly at the last earthly home of a great man, his grandfather.

Joseph remembered all the times when he had heard whispers of people over his grandfather being foolish to spend money on such a dream project. But Joseph knew from his grandfather that he had a dream, a vision that he pursued. Joseph also learned that it was good to follow those dreams. Grandfather's vision of building a lighthouse was one Joseph would not forget.

As he left the site at the end of the service, small pellets of snow were falling as if to cover the tracks of all who saw the lighthouse and grandfather's grave. The afternoon turned to cold with tiny sparkles falling from the sky as if angels' halos had dropped to cover the trail leading to Summer Seat.

The Long Walk Home

Soon more education beaconed for young Joseph. But could the family afford it? With the aid of Eleanor's brother Daniel, and father, Richard Stephens, who shipped steers to pay his tuition, that became reality.

The young boy enrolled at St. Joseph's College in Bardstown, Kentucky in May of 1822: the school was only a few years old. He started writing powerful themes in rhetoric and composition.

In one case, a professor named Father Elder brought Holt's theme into the classroom, and without permission, read it out loud. The class liked the composition and considered it humorous. But Holt, having tender feelings, thought the reading of the composition made him look ridiculous, even though Father Elder meant it as a compliment to the young writer.

Joseph had a quick temper and his temper would cost him much sadness beyond belief. Outraged by the professor and the class laughing at him Joseph stated, "Professor Elder will hear from me through the medium of the press." Joseph began a seventy-five mile walk home. It would be a long, difficult journey, but Joseph was determined to walk every step of the way back to Holt's Bottom by the riverside next to the Ohio River.

It was November 11, 1823. As he walked, Joseph thought about what he wanted to do. "Why am I so sensitive? Why do I take everything to heart?" With each step taken his shoes grew heavier, with the dust flying. The road abounded with fine dust particles had been blown as if a cloud opened and started spitting tiny pieces of matter.

The warm sun shone on Joseph's face as the wind blew his blond hair into his eyes. Joseph started tiring. The seventy-five miles had not seemed far when Joseph started, but now his stomach growled. He only had a light breakfast before going to class. Joseph thought about his mother's tasty chicken and dumplings.

He hoped to find a farmer driving a team of work horses to get supplies at Elizabethtown, but he only saw people working in the fields harvesting the corn and putting the crop into the wagon. Joseph was too proud to stop by a farm house and tell the folks he was traveling alone and was hungry. People being inquisitive, questions would be asked. He was not in any mood to explain why he was traveling alone without food, horse, and only a bag with a few clothes.

Joseph was seventeen, young, tall and strong. He could reach home in three days provided cooperation from the weather. This being Monday country folks would be working harvesting the fall crops.

As night grew nearer Joseph decided to camp under the stars. A small stream provided a tranquil, peaceful site to rest. Maybe he would catch a fish or two and relieve his hunger pains. Joseph located a reed by the stream and found a string in his belongings. Seeking a hook, he turned rocks over and searched underbrush by the banks of the stream but nothing turned up not even a nail to make a hook for fishing. Distressed, Joseph took one of his shirts and used it to wash. He decided to try and locate some berries for supper. The fall sounds of crickets chirping and coolness of the evening after sunset was all around him. Rustling of leaves among the scenic golden colors caught Joseph's attention.

Hickory nuts were falling like small drums, pounding in unison with a steady beat recurring. A little before sunset from behind a large red bank, the sun broke through with a grand view. Gray, shadowy, puffy clouds extended the rays touching tops of tall grasses as echoes of crickets called to each other.

Joseph prepared to doze and get relief from the exhausting trip, but suddenly heard the strangest scream imaginable. It sounded like a woman's scream, but eerie. He jumped quickly to his feet and it started again.

"What could this sound be?" Joseph thought. He knew survival techniques his father had taught him. He was not a backwoods boy, even though he lived in a rural area far from town. He had spent his time relying on his studies, learning as much as possible in the quickest time. Education was prized as the largest single time investment Joseph's family had given him. Since the early time as a toddler he knew his family refused the ordinary life for him. Joseph wanted to be a well studied, trained lawyer with high goals to go far in life.

John W. Holt, Joseph's father, had been concerned about his son's health and wanted him to have more recreation in his life. At this moment Joseph seemed to agree with him. He wondered if his legs would carry him as fast as he might need to run for safety in case of a wild animal attack.

Joseph sat silently as his thoughts focused on staying awake. Perhaps the scream Joseph heard was from a panther who had wandered from the great Appalachian Mountains to hunt in a more plentiful region of the bluegrass? Joseph had let himself get into this predicament of being alone without shelter, or food, and the wild animals of the night all around him.

Grandfather Stephens once said, "Sometimes a person's pride costs them grave defeats." Joseph now knew he should have not taken this venture so lightly without concern. Being young, what could possibly happen to him? Joseph struggled to stay awake. Clouds in the dark sky covered most of the stars, making the night even darker. A few hours passed and now the moon seemed to send light helping Joseph to watch in the distance when small bushes moved.

Joseph became aware of his environment, the sounds, smells, and the sights. Footsteps were putting weight on the soft earth. Small twigs were breaking as well as leaves being torn apart by a force not seeming to hesitate to notice what might be in its path. He rose slowly to see what he was up against. Before Joseph could spring to his feet a daring open-mouth panther, showing a wide range of sharp teeth took flight on a large boulder and continued to growl with a dangerous disposition. The panther seemed to enjoy his own roar and moved at a fast pace shaking his huge paw as he stood on the extended ground.

Not having any cover or place to seek shelter from the wild animal, Joseph decided the best move would be to run. Too afraid to look and see if the big cat was close behind, he mingled in and around trees trying desperately to distract him. At one moment Joseph paused briefly and listened to see if he could hear the running of large paws. The sounds he heard were like a hopping of some sort. Joseph supposed the animal in the clearing did a lot of leaping. The only thing that saved him was he was lighter on his feet and the huge panther wore down from the fast pace of the chase.

Joseph would long remember that night. There was no use to try and sleep now. After an experience like this it would not be wise or safe to stay in the area. The panther could return and the next time he could be hungrier and Joseph might be less lucky.

As each new day is a beginning, the morning could not be welcomed enough by Joseph. The problems he thought he had earlier seemed only minor. The blisters on his feet that caused his feet to bleed would soon heal. His sunburned face would be soothed with a cool bath. Fresh ironed clothes would make him feel new. Joseph's head was aching from no food, but he was thankful to God for sparing his life when he encountered the panther in the middle of the night.

The saying "there is no place like home" is carved deeply in his subconscious mind. Joseph said out loud, "Family is so important, it helps me gain strength to pursue when my body tells me I am tired and weary but I must continue to my beloved home to those who cherish me dearly."

After walking several hours, Joseph met a peddler in a black wagon. The peddler stopped the wagon and asked Joseph where he was traveling and Joseph replied, "I am traveling to Holt, down by the Ohio River." The peddler responded, "I am going in the direction to Joesville and you could ride part of the way and rest." Joseph decided to let a stranger help him and climbed aboard the tacky little wagon that had a hard board for a seat. But at least he was riding instead of walking. The stranger was traveling through the country with ointments to help ailments for people and animals. Joseph asked, "Do you really sell any of this and does it work?" The stranger introduced himself as Spence and told Joseph that his best seller was called Black Diamond Ligament. He said it was good to use on horses for healing.

Joseph introduced himself as a son of John W. Holt of Holt, Kentucky. He explained to Spence that his brother Robert was a medical doctor in the community. The time passed quickly and the team finally approached the long, narrow trail to Stephensport. Joe climbed down from the small over-stuffed wagon with his light bag of clothes, and said, "Thank you very much for the ride, I appreciate it greatly." Spence committed, "It was a treat to talk to a young gentleman like you. Good luck to you, and I hope you reach home before dark."

Joseph walked faster for with each step he could feel closer with comfort of home. The sun's golden tones colored the sky with a light, lavender canopy, looking like a curtain pulled for a performance. Cattle grazed without noticing the day drawing to a close. The sounds of persistent crickets told you autumn is passing rapidly, as many trees had already shed their leaves. Dogs could be heard in the distance. Joseph could see smoke coming from the little slave shacks setting in a row behind the big house and realized the mothers of the slave houses were now cooking the evening meal for their own families.

The fields of dark green were bright as the freshness of the new wheat, thriving over the scattered patches where tobacco had been grown. As Joseph crossed the narrow Sinking Creek, he saw the mighty Ohio looming out to him to welcome him back once again from his studies.

Joseph's pace widened again as he began running down the dusty, dirt road. He had taken the challenge and had withstood the pain and now at last he could see his three-story home with beautiful iron works in front. His mother, Eleanor, opened the front door and extended her long, slender arms to embrace her son at last. She hugged him and said, "I am so surprised to see you Joseph," and they walked hand in hand inside.

Joseph dreaded the moment when he would have to tell the reason for leaving St. Joseph's College, especially after the hardships the family had experienced for him to enroll. Father entered the setting room with a startled look to see Joseph. "Son, I am glad to see you but what on this earth brings you home just weeks before the term ends?"

Gathering his courage, Joseph replied, "Father, since a little boy you and grandfather Stephens explained to me honor is one of the most important traits for a southern gentleman to posses. My honor was insulted as one of my teachers, Father Elder, brought my writing in class and read it aloud without my permission. It made me look ridiculous in front of my classmates. The entire body of students laughed at my work. I did what I have been taught to defend my honor. Father, I told Father Elder he would hear from me through the medium of the press."

"Joseph, you need to reconsider and think about the issue before doing something you might regret later," his father replied. "Since you are at home, I am a little short of help maintaining the plantation. We will see about making up the work missed in the spring when college resumes."

Joseph enjoyed life back home. Everyone sparkled with delight to see Joseph home once again. He and his brother assisted their father when possible to give him a needed break from stressful business encounters. Robert and Joseph packed several years of living into several months, knowing they would soon be separated again by schooling and their profession.

After a cold winter and a busy, rainy spring the Holt brothers wanted adventure before going their separate ways once again. Joseph told Robert, "Let's talk mother into fixing us a picnic basket. I'll explain to her all the details so she will not give us a problem," smiled Joseph.

"You know she is not going to go for the idea, and she has a good hold on Dad's decisions," Robert said.

"I'll speak to her this afternoon. Just leave it to me, I can handle mother," Joseph said reassured.

"Mother, Mother," called Joseph across the extended yard.

"Yes, what Joseph?"

"Wait a minute, Mother," spoke Joseph politely. "Robert and I want to take a row down the Ohio, but only with your permission. Dad always says I need more fresh air and wants me to be more adventurous like Robert. We would be gone for a couple of days enjoying the scenery, fishing and having time for just the two of us before hitting the books again," expressed Joseph.

"You promise to stay close to the shore and be safe," cautioned mother.

"Mother, Robert is older and will make sure we take safety precautions," promised Joseph.

"What did your Father say about this trip Joseph," questioned Mother.

"Father said, 'If your mother favors the trip then it is fine with me.'"

"Then I guess I had better prepare a hearty supply for you two boys," she replied.

Both brothers prepared the small rowboat with a blanket for a cool or wet day, packed extra clothes, and gathered fishing poles. Excited, the boys went to bed early to get started by daybreak. Rising before sunrise, Robert and Joseph gave their mother Eleanor a big hug and told their father they would be extremely careful. Eleanor placed the weighted basket of goodies in Joseph's hands. "Thanks Mother. Robert and I will eat divinely while away," Joseph said.

"Don't worry we will be fine, I will look after Joseph like always," Robert promised.

Rose

While attending college at Centre in Danville, Joseph most enjoyed debating. Of slavery he once said in one of his talks, "While we tolerate slavery, we are only feeding and nourishing our own destroyer, like the hen on the serpent's eggs. From the nature of man when he is appropriated and held in slavery he must be an enemy of the government which thus suffers him to be appropriated and it is but just to conclude, that the slaves of the United States are enemies to our government."

As a young man Joseph witnessed slavery, learning the mistakes of his father and grandfather. Joseph believed it unfortunate to keep slaves in human bondage. Owning another human being as your said property had grim consequences.

Joseph prepared for a life of law, writing, public speaking, and newspaper editing. Being absent from his beloved family in Holt's Bottom, Joseph stayed in close correspondence by writing faithfully, receiving letters concerning events there.

Preparing for a career in law, Joseph studied under Robert Wickliffe, one of the most noted lawyers in the state of Kentucky, and visited home on occasion, corresponding weekly by mail.

But an episode soon changed not only the family's life, but would have an impact upon Joseph until the day he died. Rose, a faithful and trusted servant, told of all that in her first-person. She arrived at Holt Bottoms Plantation in 1826 and became part of the Holt family.

"Heaviness hung in the newness of the daylight hours. Long anticipation of weeks kept deep in the dark, musky cellar of a prison under a cruel man's home, I barely had enough food to eat to stay alive. Being a woman, penned up like an animal was more than a person could stand, not knowing if you would live or die or ever experience daylight again.

Last week, confined more in a crowded, vermin-infested slave jail, I tolerated tongue-lashes with the common run of Negroes."

The sad, slave girl felt pain for the unborn child in her womb. Her ill-fated heart beyond repair now, not having privacy, being caged with men from day to day, weeks on end. "One month had passed since the other slaves and I had tasted a satisfying meal. Praying daily to God to please hear my cry, I begged for help."

Sounds of banging and forceful footsteps approached the cellar door. The heavy, chained doors were unlocked as brilliant sunlight poured in, hurting the eyes of those bound in chains below the house.

"Behind Stone, the slaver, several house servants carried trays of the best food the other slaves and I had witnessed in weeks. Fried chicken, potatoes, green beans, and heavy loaves of baked bread with large stone jars of steaming, hot tea greeted me."

Edward Stone spoke with a rough, growling voice, "Now you niggers eat all you can, because some of you need a little fattening up before the big sale down South." The food vanished like dew before sunshine, and some men ate so much they became sick.

"I ate slowly at first, enjoying every bite." Rose whispered under her breath. "As I chewed, I thought of mother's cooking and home in Lexington. Even though born into slavery, I up until now lived a fairly decent life being a daughter of a house servant. The master's wife had taught me to read and write. I knew this was a privilege only few enjoyed.

"The torment of living under The Grange, in an iron barred cellar, required unlimited courage. Continuously, the slaver bought slaves, all over Kentucky, confining them in unhealthy conditions. When the cellar became too cramped, Mr. Stone planned the long walk from his home to the river at Maysville. The slaves bound together by chains walked the long distance. On reaching the flatboat, the captives were transported by craft down the Ohio to sell at auction in the Deep South."

Resin spoke out to the group, "You know it is no good keeping us down here in pens. We will die if we do not get out soon."

A big guy named Wesley told stories passed down from his grand pappy. "My grand pappy told me many times it is death to be sold to the plantations of the South. The overseers have no mercy, their only interest is in cotton pickin'."

The slaves stayed yet another month in the cellar until finally Mr.

Stone secured enough merchandise to fill his flatboat. He expected to make an enormous profit. At the sight of Mr. Stone, I reminiscenced, "Being sold to a kind, gentle master would not be so bad."

Rose remembered her mother saying, "All that the overseers in the South cared about was picking cotton day after day until young men soon became broken down with bad backs, with hands swelled like prunes from the sun beating down on them, and taking only a short lunch time of thirty minutes, barely enough time to grab a cold biscuit, a piece or two of jaw meat and take care of body functions in a private manner.

"I dreaded the crowed slave pens, and imagined being placed on the auction block as Stone's said property. The slave coops were eight foot square, seven feet tall, erected on damp brick floors with small barred windows near the roof and with heavy iron grated doors. All of Stone's slaves were taught to act out a part during the auction to bring more money."

"The time is approaching when Mr. Stone will gather us like dogs in chains leading us to Maysville to the flatboat headed south." Stephen said.

"Well, Stephen, that is why we ate good food, last week, so everyone got fattened up for a better price with more muscle and strength," Jo said.

"I wondered how God allowed these slave traders to use humans for their own personal benefits. It was inhuman, if you lasted from hard labor in the fields, happening to be blessed with a pretty face, it turned into a curse, because the master might use you for sexual desires, not caring if your insides were torn apart during child birth or maybe even death."

The crew of four men, consisting of Howard Stone, David Cobb, Humphrey David and James M. Gray, talked to each other discussing the trouble with slaves. "It will be good to get rid of those trouble makers anyway," Howard said.

"This will be a lesson for other darkies in Kentucky, seeing what happens when they become unruly giving their master's embarrassment," laughed James Gray.

"I wept silently, thinking sadly to myself, I was sold and shipped away because of the embarrassment to my master Ringer's wife. What about my embarrassment to be taken during the night from the little dwelling where my mother, sister and I had always shared and felt secure?"

Rose, seven months pregnant, a thin, tall girl of maybe seventeen lived with a sadden torture, fearing her destiny. Her yellow skin, her deep-set eyes, her straight, black hair and her quite attractive rich olive complexion made her noticeable. Being the only female, she remained speechless unless the men slaves asked her a question.

Edward Stone, a Kentuckian, made profitable living trading slaves in the South. Noted for buying both men and woman, Stone caged them together in the huge cellar of his home.

"Stone done bought five more darkies three days ago and they are too weak to put down here in the dungeon with the rest of us," Wesley commented. Still and heavy, the air smelled of body odor from wounds of bleeding men, who had taken violent blows to the head. Urine ran in a small stream through the cellar. The confined spaces made it impossible to take care of human waste. Flies swarmed, while rats roamed the premises as if they ruled. Slaves endured the pain of heavy irons bound on the hands of men, and woman handcuffed and chained together by shackles.

After a week of nourishing food, the prisoners appreciated the few stolen moments of bathing in an enormous tub. All slaves received new clothes to wear. Workers disguised old slaves as younger ones by putting blacking polish on their matted, curly hair. Rubbing oil on faces caused the slaves to appear healthier, with a glow to their skin. Everyone had to learn a trick to perform during the auction to make the price higher for the bidders.

Seventy-seven slaves reached the boat at Maysville, Kentucky, beginning the long trip down the Ohio, with fear in their hearts of only negative things to come in their lives as they experienced more hell.

"I listened as the flatboat traveled the path many others before had trod of similar hardships," Rose witnessed. "Maybe if I had been born ugly the master would have left me alone and I would still be on the plantation in Lexington with my mother and my younger sister, Anna," Weeping, Rose wondered once again about her younger sister Anna going through what she had, except Anna was only twelve now. Thus, there were things in life worse than death Rose realized.

Word passed among the slaves that this was the last business trip of trading in Negroes for Stone. He publicly announced as the flat boat pulled away from the dock at Maysville, "This is the last time you will see me trading Negroes, when I return, I will be returning as a planter only."

"On the morning of September 17, 1826, unguarded troubles below the deck began. Feeling the uneasiness of the cargo of human bondage, I heard whispers of the planning troubles. All seventy-six Negroes planned to attack completely surprising the crew of four men including the slaver, Mr. Stone," Rose recalled later.

The slaves gathered axes, wood, and knives to fight a fierce battle of hand-to-hand combat, planning to overtake the crew and Stone. Rose worried, "What will be my part in this revolt? Will I get killed? How will I fight being pregnant and a woman?" The four crewmembers had hazardous experience dealing with slaves. The young girl feared that, if the plan failed, she would be punished with the group.

Armed and dangerous, the slaves planned their escape when the flatboat reached the town of Stephensport in Breckinridge County, about ninety miles south of Louisville. The thought of seeking freedom gave them unexpected, emotional strength, to fight a battle for their lives. They killed all four crewmembers along with the slaver, Edward Stone of Bourbon County.

The dead men were weighted with objects and thrown in the river. The leaders of the revolt grabbed over $2,000 dollars of valuable property, then sunk the vessel. Seventy-six slaves fled on to the Indiana side of the river. "In the mass confusion, I carefully slipped quietly through the bushes, along the banks of the Ohio, while the fighting occurred. I decided, 'If I respond calmly while the killing and screaming is occurring, maybe no one will notice me.'"

Being tall, Rose crawled slowly down the banks, continuing to travel by the river's edge. "I must have walked, crawled and scouted seven or eight miles now because I am completely out of breath," Rose sighed. "I must rest or I will not survive."

Hair dripping wet, knees bleeding from crawling over the river gravel, hot sand sticking to the dried blood, and flies buzzing around her, Rose felt like a wounded deer someone had shot. Her once neat, new dress now lay in tatters with rips down the front. Rose's hair, stringy with tangles made by the river breezes, gave an unpleasant appearance. Her dry, swollen lips burst from long exposure of hot, melting sun. "Being chained in the cellar for too many weeks made my skin tender," Rose thought.

Feeling helpless with no hope, Rose prayed, "Dear God in Heaven, I have tried to be a good girl but first I was raped and then laughed at by other slaves on my home plantation in Lexington, next sold by my master as an embarrassment for his selfish pleasures of the flesh. I am now carrying his baby. Mutiny erupted on the slaves' boat of Mr. Stone, killing all the crew including him. The planners of the tragic event took the majority of the group setting out to Indiana for freedom. Please save me, and my child. I promise to help others to freedom, Dear God in Jesus name I pray." Moments later, Rose envisioned a white dove. Was it real? Could it be a sign from the almighty or was she so weak she hallucinated?

Being of faint condition, because of dehydration and extensive heat, Rose fainted by a small cover of trees with zigzag vines attracted. She fell asleep, awakening in a short while to a soft, wispy voice saying,

"Who are you? Where did you come from? How did you get here girl? How am I going to get you to the big house without being seen?"

Rose awoke and opened her eyes. The exhausting trip down the river had taken all of her strength. The slave woman, Mammy Bell, dragged her back in deeper, to the huge bank, under the cliffs, looking around making sure no one saw her. Nearby, field hands labored, cutting tobacco. Mammy Bell hurried to the big house a quarter of a mile up the steep cliff from the riverbanks, murmuring, "What am I going to tell the misses? If I tell her, she may give her to the authorities. Should I let her rest and take her food? No, that would not work because she is too weak to travel farther in her condition."

Mammy Bell finally said, "Misses, misses we have trouble in our hands."

"Mammy Bell," said Eleanor, "what are you talking about trouble in our hands?"

"Well, Miss Eleanor, I went down to the river, just like always, to catch some of those fresh fish like you so love when I heard a faint noise in the bushes. At first I thought it was a scared animal but it did not run away like animals do, in fact it could not even move."

Out of breath, Mammy told excitedly, "There is a young Negro girl of about sixteen, heavy with child in a bad condition. I pulled her up under the larger bank by the steep cliff, extending outward over the bank so she will not be noticed."

Eleanor panicking, "What is the meaning of this, you know we could be jailed for hiding or giving assistance to a runaway."

Mammy explained, "I did not know what to do, she was so helpless. I just could not force myself to leave her in the hot sun alone."

Eleanor told Mammy Bell, "As soon as we finish the evening meal, help me to leave unnoticed. When the night grows dark, we will bring the young girl to the house, but John must not know because we are taking a grave chance sheltering this female."

"I have always known you to be a good Christian woman of kindness, Miss Eleanor," Mammy Bell said.

The day dragged slower than normal, with persistent interpretations of unannounced visitors from the neighborhood. One of the slaves from the field named Jed ran breathless to the big house to share the news barely speaking. "Slow down, Jed, so we can understand what you are trying to tell us," Eleanor scorned.

He told of the mutiny and the escape of seventy-seven slaves, and their killing the crew and the slaver in bound for the Deep South. Miss Eleanor told Jed not to spread this information until things calmed down. This could be trouble for all if it was not handled correctly.

The color left the cheeks of Eleanor, for what if this run-away had grimly assisted with the mutiny and the killings of five white men. Eleanor daydreamed at supper. John said, "That was a terrible incidence up the river just a few miles from home. You never know the danger you face with slaves."

"But John, we treat our slaves as family, they are safe and we care for them," Eleanor stated.

John told Eleanor she seemed to be somewhere else this evening. Eleanor said, "I need some time to relax on the terrace and enjoy some hot tea," Eleanor could not stand the suspense any longer. The table was cleared as John spoke softly, "I believe I'll have a smoke and read in the smoking room, dear. I'll be upstairs later, by then maybe you will feel better getting fresh air on the terrace."

Eleanor, not knowing how to kindly decline smiled and replied, "John, I really need to rest for a short spell and then I will be fine."

Mammy Bell awaited for Eleanor in the shadows of the large Gingko tree. Together they pilgrimaged, down the steep banks, trying to save a young life they did not know. But it was their duty to help a soul in need.

On arrival by the riverbanks, the young girl moaned in a paralyzed status. Eleanor, with the assistance of Mammy Bell, carried the Negro girl to the cellar of the house. Here Eleanor gave specific instructions to the trusted house servant, Bell. She told her to keep the runaway quiet while nursing her back to health. "We must be careful, Bell, our lives are at stake. Nursing this injured girl after everyone is settled for the night will be tricky. While the field hands work in the tobacco patches, you be careful caring for the pitiful creature God has sent to us."

"It will be difficult for me because I normally let you run the errands, gathering canned fruit to prepare our meals," Eleanor said. The quietness of the night challenged the two women to care for the girl.

"Merciful heavens!" Eleanor explained with a sigh. "These clothes have to be cut with scissors so as not to cause pain to the girl." Working side by side, assisting one another, Mammy Bell and Eleanor bathed the rescued girl with cool water, clothing her with a cotton nightgown. They tugged, pulling it gently over her plump belly. The unfortunate, young, slave girl remarkably retained youthful features of slimness, except for her mid-section.

"Well, this girl surely was a house servant, treated well, and cared for because she seems to be fairly healthy, considering the cuts, bruises, and scratches from today. Something very dramatic occurred for her to travel at an unexplainable speed the little framed body could not tolerate," Eleanor said.

Rose's eyes suddenly opened. Responding now, "What makes you two kind women help the likes of me when you do not even know me?"

"I guess we are out of our heads," Eleanor stated.

Rose felt it only right to speak to Eleanor and Mammy Bell as if she had taken truth serum. "My life has been good except for the last year. Things were good until master slipped into our slave shack one night last February saying, 'Come on girl, and take a walk with me.' My poor mother pleaded, begging him to take her, but he only laughed, dragging me in one of the vacant slave houses, laid with me, and now I am caring his child. I was sold because of the embarrassment to his wife when she found out her husband's unfaithfulness."

Weeping now, Rose explained how she had being penned up in a chained cellar with all men. The memories, being too frightening, caused Rose to tremble with flashbacks of inarticulate sounds of grief and pain, remembering the filth and the chains so unbearably tight they caused massive burses, cuts, and bleeding. Rose lived with terrible headaches, being so sick she vomited seventeen times in one day. Finally, she slept once more.

Meanwhile, news of the tragedy at Stephensport caused Joseph Holt to make an unannounced trip home from Lexington where he was studying law, to make sure his family was safe.

Rescue

Rose lay resting as Mammy Bell and Eleanor entered the secluded cellar. "Only the good Lord knows what this little gal went through last year," Eleanor said, covering her mouth with a weak sob.

The memory, not a pleasant one, appeared in Eleanor's subconscious of the dangerous route and actions Mammy Bell and she had lived for the past few weeks at Holt Plantation. It simply was a miracle they had kept the secret from John. Eleanor's heart ripped apart by holding the secret from the man who trusted her with every breath she took.

"Rose, wake up. We must discuss our plan." Yawning and awakening from a peaceful sleep, Rose listened. Eleanor drew a long breath. "We are all right," she said, "but covering our tracks is essential. We must seal the secret in our hearts forever, never telling a soul. If we can do this, our reactions of calm, patient, and brave will cause attention to be elsewhere."

"Maybe so," spoke Rose faintly.

Eleanor continued, "We will nurse Rose until she is well, revisiting the idea of her arrival as a niece of yours, Mammy Bell. Rose will be sent here by her dying mother's last wish, to set her daughter free upon her death.

"By the high heavens, that is perfect!" said Eleanor. "No one will question me. I am only involved with socials, not causing stirs or gossip about what I do. The community knows I care for people who need special attention, like widows but not publicly taking daring deeds of recklessness causing scandal in my conservative family."

The instant Mammy Bell and Eleanor left the cellar, sounds of a buggy lingered from around the bend of the main road. "Do not be frightened, Mammy Bell, it is only John returning home," said Eleanor. Their eyes focused as the buggy drew closer to the two women.

"What are you all up to today?" John said in a fast rate.

"Why do you ask," replied Eleanor with a surprising look.

"Well, if I did not know better I would say you two are up to something mysterious, because your faces are a ghost-like white."

"Miss Eleanor, I am going to finish picking those flowers you wanted in the garden." Hurrying away to give Eleanor and John private time, Mammy Bell went about her way, singing as she picked fall roses in heavy bloom.

Ascending from the carriage with sounds of leaves crunching between his feet, John asked Eleanor to join him on a short ride to enjoy the beautiful fall foliage. Remembering the past weeks, Eleanor decided it wise to invest time with her beloved husband. They drove away with heads as close as if it were their first carriage ride together.

The wind calmly whistled soft tones as tuning nature's orchestra. The stream shouted gurgling flips of sounds, crashing on the colored rocks of unusual hues of blue, extending shadows reflecting light on them as they drove.

John wondered how to bring the taboo subject up to Eleanor, knowing the only thing possible was straight talk to his love. "Eleanor, I need to speak to you about something troubling me for some time."

"Yes, John what is it? What is bothering you dear?"

"Well, you have a different personality lately. There is a distance between us. I know you better than anyone," John spoke softly and tenderly. "I see you portraying your character, but your heart has something missing. Your inner strength is one reason I fell in love with you. The evening you proudly made the graceful entrance down the stairs at your parent's home, you captured my heart. Something is troubling you deeply. Your smiles are shallow and you are not as talkative as normal."

The breeze cooled the afternoon, as the wind tossed Eleanor's hat. A red headed woodpecker made his mark on new territory above the carriage's top. Pausing for a moment, Eleanor spoke tenderly, "Why John W. Holt, you never told me your feelings about my zest for living life to the fullest," smiled Eleanor.

John stopped the carriage helping Eleanor dismount. He pushed Eleanor's arm gently so she was close enough to feel his breath. "Eleanor, your smile is deep beyond the surface of your intriguing face. The magic of those hazel eyes always draw me to you," John sang out his words with his southern draw.

"After seeing you, no other girls interested me and my thoughts were only on making you the best part of my future," said John with a flirty wink.

"True love is one of the strongest empowerments of happiness. Many search for it, some pass it for other treasures of worldly goods, but only a few captivate the chance to make love reality and treasure it for what it is worth," said Eleanor.

"While we are on the subject of love, tell me Eleanor what you have done," John demanded.

"Uh," said Eleanor, "I do not know where to begin." For a while John stood and looked straight into Eleanor's eyes.

"Well," said John, "the best place to start is at the beginning." Finally, Eleanor let the tears cloud her eyes. They fell as if a river had overflown its banks. They flowed down her porcelain face stinging, burning, and dripping off her chin. Her insides ached from the pain making it difficult for her to swallow.

"Oh John, I love you more than anything, so please forgive me, for I have taken a grave chance on our family's reputation. You know how I have a strong will to help others," said Eleanor, speaking in between sobs. "Remember the sad episode at Stephensport two weeks ago with the killing of the slaver, and crew and the slaves who escaped? Well, Mammy Bell found a young girl bruised and battered lying in a crunched position under the high cliffs by the river's edge. John, she is the same age as our boys and pregnant. It was not humane to turn her over to the sheriff with his hostile men to hunt her down like a wild animal."

John surprised Eleanor by speaking calmly, not yelling. But why should that surprise her? Eleanor was never afraid of John, knowing he was a pure man of proper breeding. He would study the situation, giving it much thought, conceiving a plan to rescue the young slave girl. John appreciated the spirit Eleanor possessed.

Most ladies would not have considered the possibility of saving another human life at the risk of the consequences of jail time or surely a high fine and possibly both. But Eleanor was more than the common wife of the early 1800's.

"It is a waste of time to talk about what has happened now," said John. "We must develop a careful plan to save this girl."

Dark approached, making the time fly rapidly. It is amazing how speaking the truth empowers the heart. Eleanor had been taught to invite the blind or poor to a feast and not always invite your rich friends, acquaintances, and family. God's word says you will be blessed if you help others in need. This runaway needed more aid than anyone Eleanor had encountered.

On the trail home Eleanor sat close to John. The wheels turned, grabbing the dust, while the horse picked up his trot to make the ride smoother. Startled doves flew in front as if clearing the way for travelers on this eve of a September evening.

After carefully placing John's prized horse, Shattegay, in the stable, Eleanor and John walked, relieved from a heavy burden, to the main house. Candlelight flickered from the windows, lightening a path for the couple. Walking to the house, John quietly explained to Eleanor the plan of Rose's arrival to the plantation.

In the night before traveling to town, Rose would be placed in the bottom of Eleanor's carriage, hid away with baskets. The next week John would meet Eleanor and Mammy Bell three miles from the home place. Carefully observing the surroundings, the three would discreetly move Rose over to John's carriage. To allay suspicions, Rose would dress in traveling clothes with luggage. They would say that Rose was coming to live with her Aunt Mammy Bell. The last request of her dearly departed mother from Lexington, they would claim, had been to send her oldest child to live with family in Breckinridge County.

Rose would never surrender hope, for her pain being so deep had touched her soul. "I will be safe and loved with this family," Rose knew.

Finally, after an exhausting ride from Lexington, Joseph Holt arrived at the Holt plantation. It felt good to return home, South. The river bottoms were beautifully graced with golden hues of leaf color. Upon arrival, Joseph was greeted at the twin entrance of the front of the mansion by a new servant.

"Good day Master Joseph, so glad to have you home," said Rose.

"How do you know I am Joseph?"

"Well, that is not so hard sir. Your portrait is in the main hallway," replied Rose.

Brushing the conversation short, Joseph moved faster upon entrance to the home. Eleanor rushing down the winding stairs hurried to Joseph. "Mother, who is this new servant girl, and where did she come from?" spoke Joseph softly.

"It is a long story, but I will share it now, son," said Eleanor. After explaining to Joseph how Rose came to them she said, “Everything is all right, for your father has taken care of all the details.

“But mother, what do the neighbors think?” Spoke Joseph out of concern. “Don’t they think it strange that a young, pregnant slave appears out of nowhere?”

“Your Dad is very convincing, and a good, honest servant for the community. They have said nothing. The whole crew was killed and Rose, being the only female, was not even missed,” Eleanor replied calmly.

“But I am sure one of those slaves probably saw her escape,” said Joseph.

“It has been over two weeks and things are back to normal Joseph,” spoke his Mother.

“Well, you know how I feel about slavery. No good will come from this mother,” Joseph spoke with authority. “This could be detrimental for our family if word ever gets out or if one of the slaves tells the truth. I do not like lying,” said Joseph.

“Rose will be faithful and will serve us for many years, ” spoke Eleanor.

“I hope you are right mother, for as an attorney, I consider this is a serious matter. I understand you are a strong-willed lady, but you must promise me now you will never do anything like this again.” She did not. But her example of courageous action Joseph remembered.

The Baltimore Convention

Relieved that his family had escaped harm, Joseph returned to Lexington to work under Robert Wickliffe. Riding back gave him moments of silence to reflect on his college career, and note that the unfortunate incident at St. Joseph's College in Bardstown had not ended his formal education after all. He painfully remembered, as well, how the county had suffered and survived a dramatic depression. Yet, despite that, the Holt's family situation had permitted him to enter Centre College at Danville.

Joseph had succeeded at college because of his familiarity with French, history, and philosophy, and his knowledge of the basic classics, as guided by his mother. Daydreaming as he drove the carriage, Joseph recalled fondly his favorite subject, debating. He remembered his happiest times on the debating team at Centre.

Of slavery, Joseph once stated in one of his talks, "Another incalculable disadvantage resulting from slavery is that it affords a continual course of contention between the states in favor of slavery and those opposed to it. We can see the coolness between this state [Kentucky] and Indiana. The animosity through weak will grow and it will have a tendency, a mighty tendency, to sever the Union. But the Union is the very life of our government and without it, we could not exist as an independent nation. Thus, it must be a disadvantage to the United States to encourage slavery, since it has a powerful tendency to destroy this government, to destroy that Union which has been formed for our preservation.

"Slavery is contrary to every principle of justice, every precept of morality, every feeling of humanity, every sentiment of honor. But here color determines whether a man shall be a freeman or slave. In vain may you plead justification? You may convince the sordid followers of wealth, but not the free of America."

Joseph also delivered talks emphasizing his strong, independent beliefs condemning laws for imprisoning people for debt. He also stressed the need for Kentucky to develop free schools throughout the state, and

Young Joseph Holt. Courtesy of Library of Congress Manuscript Divison.

Joseph Holt in Paris. Courtesy of Library of Congress Manuscript Division.

Mary Harrison Holt, first wife, daughter of the distinguished Dr. Burr Harrison. Courtesy of Library of Congress Manuscript Division.

A slave included in the collection of Joseph Holt's pictures.

A slave included in the collection of Joseph Holt's pictures.

Margaret Wickliffe Holt, second wife, daughter of Kentucky Governor Charles Anderson Wickliffe. Courtesy of Library of Congress Manuscript Division.

Governor Charles A. Wickliffe, Kentucky's governor from 1839-40, of Washington and Nelson counties. Courtesy of the Kentucky Historical Society.

Took leave of my beloved parents
& home on the 4th of April 1850. After
a happy sojourn of a few days with
my sister from whom I had been
so long separated journeyed to New York
where I spent the most — week of
my life. On the 24th we sailed
on the American Eagle & after a
voyage of thirty four days were
landed on british soil - London. the 28th May
Oh! the awful sea-sickness! Let he
who has never been sea-sick write
of a life on the Ocean wave, the
gorgeous sun rise & sun set -
neither of which were seen by
me) bounding billows, &c &c.
But here we are in this greatest city
of the world & on one of its most
beautiful streets - Regent - unsurpassed
in the elegance & richness of its shops.
the throng of people and the thousands
of vehicles of every description which

1850 diary of Joseph Holt, page 1. Courtesy of Library of Congress Manuscript Division.

pass continually from eleven in the
morning until twelve at night.
It is impossible for me to become
reconciled to the abominable habits
of these English people who convert
the day into night. You may as well
ask for the Queen's crown as for a cup
of coffee before nine o'clock. And would
be considered quite [illegible] to dine
before six — at which time the nobility
are taking their morning drives.
May 30th. Visited today the Tower of
London the most celebrated fortress
of the world. Here numerous illustri-
ous personages were imprisoned and
beheaded. Anne Boleyn, Katherine
Howard, Sir Thomas More, Archbishop
Cranmer, Lady Jane Grey & others. Sir
Walter Raleigh wrote here his history
of the world. The cell where he was
confined is still exhibited.
The Horse Armoury is most interesting.
The centre is occupied by a line

of equestrian figures, clothed in
the armour of various reigns. Those
assigned to Henry eighth, Henry, prince
of Wales, & Charles 1st are known to have been worn
by them. That of Charles 1st is the most
magnificent, it is richly gilt and
ornamented with arabesque work.
The regalia contains the jewels of
the sovereigns, the richest of which
is that worn by Victoria. This cap
of purple velvet is enclosed by silver
hoops, covered with diamonds; surmount-
ing these hoops is a ball, covered with
small diamonds, bearing a cross
formed of brilliants, in the centre of
which is a splendid sapphire. In
the front of this crown is the heart-
formed ruby said to have been worn
by Edward the Black Prince. This
crown is estimated one million
of pounds sterling.
May 31st Took a steamboat [illegible]

1850 diary of Joseph Holt, pages 2-3. Courtesy of Library of Congress Manuscript Division.

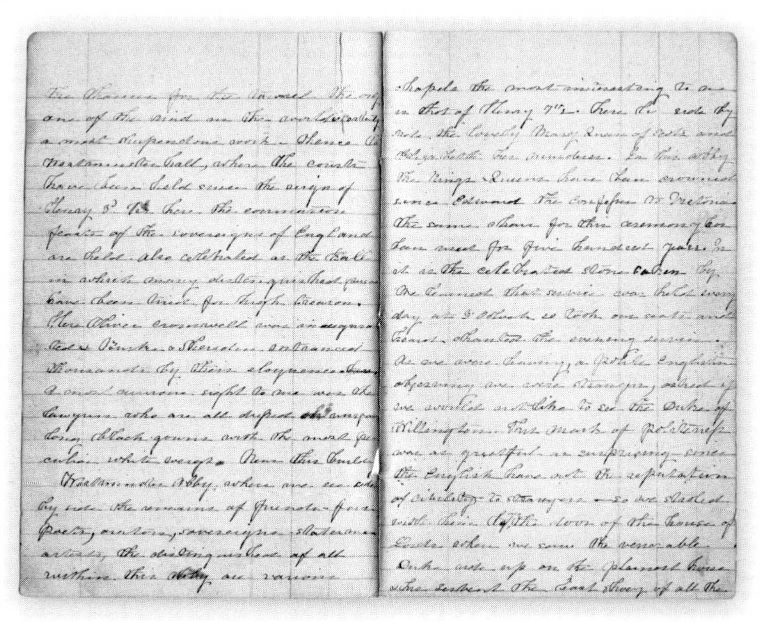

the Thames for the tunnel. The only
one of the kind in the world & certainly
a most stupendous work. Thence to
Westminster Hall, where the courts
have been held since the reign of
Henry 3rd. Here the coronation
feasts of the sovereigns of England
are held. Also celebrated as the hall
in which many distinguished persons
have been tried for high treason.
Here Oliver Cromwell was inaugurated & Burke & Sheridan entranced
thousands by their eloquence. [illegible]
A most curious sight to me was the
lawyers who are all dressed in ample
long black gowns with the most peculiar white wigs. Near this building
Westminster Abbey, where are side
by side the remains of [illegible]
poets, orators, sovereigns, statesmen,
artists, the distinguished of all
nations. This Abbey is [illegible]

chapels the most interesting to me
is that of Henry 7th. Here lie side by
side the lovely Mary Queen of Scots and
Elizabeth her murderess. In this abbey
the Kings & Queens have been crowned
since Edward the Confessor to Victoria.
The same chair for this ceremony has
been used for five hundred years. In
it is the celebrated stone taken by
[illegible] that service was held every
day at 3 o'clock so took our seats and
heard chanted the evening service.
As we were leaving, a polite Englishman observing we were strangers, asked if
we would not like to see the Duke of
Wellington. This mark of politeness
was as grateful as surprising since
the English have not the reputation
of civility to strangers — so we started
with him. At the door of the House of
Lords where we saw the venerable
Duke [illegible]
[illegible] of all the

1850 diary of Joseph Holt, pages 4-5. Courtesy of Library of Congress Manuscript Division.

Abraham Lincoln. Courtesy of Library of Congress.

Battle of Antietam, lithograph by Prang & Co., 1887, after Thulstrup. Courtesy of Library of Congress.

Major Allan Pinkerton, President Lincoln and Major General John A. McClernand on the Antietam battlefield. Photographed by Alexander Gardner, Oct. 1862. Courtesy of Library of Congress.

Members of the Military Commission for the trial of Lincoln Conspirators. Left to right: Judge Joseph Holt, Gen. Robert S. Foster, Col. H.L. Burnett, Col. D.R. Clendenin. Courtesy of Library of Congress.

Military Commission for the trial of Lincoln Conspirators. Portrait includes, standing left to right: Brig. Gen. Thomas M. Harris, Maj. Gen. Lew Wallace, Maj. Gen. August V. Kautz, and Henry L. Burnett. Seated left to right: Lt. Col. David R. Clendenin, Col. C.H. Tompkins, Brig. Gen. Albion P. Howe, Brig. Gen. James Ekin, Maj. Gen. David Hunter, Brig. Gen. Robert S. Foster, John A. Bingham, and Brig. Gen. Joseph Holt. Courtesy of Library of Congress.

Conspirators on trial, taken June 5, 1855 by special permission of Maj. Gens. Hunter and Hartranft. In the foreground may be seen Judges Holt and Bigelow, Maj. Gens. Hunter and Hartranft, and other members of the Military Commission. Courtesy of Library of Congress.

Seated, left to right: Hon. John A. Bingham, Judge Joseph Holt, and Holt's Assistant, Col. H.L. Burnett. Courtesy of Library of Congress.

Taken a few minutes after the arrival, the execution party carries umbrellas for shielding from the sun. The condemned, left to right: Mary Surratt, Lewis Powell, David Herold, George Atzerodt. Courtesy of Library of Congress.

All is done. Hanging hooded bodies of the four conspirators. Courtesy of Library of Congress.

Judge Joseph Holt, Judge Advocate General, U.S.A. Courtesy of Library of Congress.

Judge Joseph Holt, Judge Advocate General, U.S.A. Courtesy of Library of Congress.

hoped that citizens would understand the advantages of establishing free public education for all.

Joseph told no one why he left Centre College in January 1825. However, he soon made an agreement with "The Old Duke," Robert Wickliffe, to tutor his sons, while studying law under Wickliffe's supervision.

In June 1828, Judge Paul I. Booker dispensed the oath to Joseph allowing him to practice as a counselor and attorney-at-law. Joseph worked in a partnership for two years with the famous Ben Hardin, and two years later dissolved the partnership.

Soon after, Joseph started his own practice, becoming very successful in Elizabethtown. He traveled widely and gave an influential speech at Hardinsburg, preceding the 1828 presidential election. Mr. Holt's speech indicated his strong support for the New Court and the party of Andrew Jackson. Barbecues drew crowds in Hardinsburg, Elizabethtown, Louisville, and many cities in the state, and speakers gathered there as well.

Being successful with his law practice, Joseph turned to the more inviting, intriguing and faster-paced city of Louisville. Moving to Louisville in 1831, Joseph proudly hung his shingle on Jefferson between 5th and 6th Streets. The move helped him enjoy being popular with the powers in Frankfort.

Appointed Commonwealth Attorney by Governor Breathitt in 1833, Joseph held the office until his friend died in 1835. Not being reappointed and or having few political ties, Joseph wound up his private practice, setting off to the Democratic Convention at Baltimore on May 21, 1835.

Smells of cherry blossom and leaves springing from a long winter's sleep filled the nostrils of everyone stirring on the glorious day in May. Well-groomed delegates from surrounding states arrived in the bustling, overcrowded streets anticipating the unexpected. Carriages with soft leather cushions made it comfortable to arrive in style. Drivers alert with watchful eyes spied for the arriving carriages so as not to have the buggy wheels tangled. Sightseers witnessed reporters carrying pencil and paper to find a story to fill the headlines of the day.

Upon entry to the Fourth Presbyterian Church, those attending enjoyed the noise associated with crowds, and the excitement ringing in the air. Gentlemen in trimmed beards and mustaches arrived in their suits of fine cloth, covered by dust as they dismounted. Important people attending the Democratic Convention stomped their boots to remove loose dirt trapped from the journey. It was indeed a welcome matter to arrive in the fair city without an incident of a stage turnover. Many stage drivers drank to excess, making such trips more dangerous.

Joseph Holt planned an early arrival at the convention by coming one day prior to registration and organization. This gave him needed rest from the bumpy, rough ride by stage, and allowed time to refresh with a bath and a good night's sleep.

Conversations took place all over as delegates politely introduced themselves and prepared for the long schedule of events. Hallways and entryways crowed suddenly while handshaking soared. Smells of food lingered from the streets gradually entered the premises. A clock striking the hour reminded those in attendance to find their place in the Presbyterian Church to begin the Baltimore Convention.

President Jackson decided to have the Democratic Convention a year early in order to ensure the nomination of his chosen successor, Vice President Martin Van Buren. Delegations from twenty-two states and two territories arrived.

At work several men organized the lectern, and started setting the scene in the sanctuary of the church. A welcoming committee soon tapped the podium calling the Baltimore Convention to order. A congressman from New York asked all to take their seats, as the shuffling of papers, and personal items quieted as history was in the making.

Joseph Holt, a delegate from the Jackson Wing of the Democratic Party, carried with him letters of introduction to Martin Van Buren, the choice of this branch of the party. However, the party did not agree on the nomination for vice-president. Richard M. Johnson of Kentucky, promised the nomination by Jackson, found strong opposition in the Virginia delegation. The southern men opposed Johnson for vice-president for having a slave mistress and mulatto daughters. They wanted W. C. Rives as their candidate.

Johnson's name was placed in nomination, but some delegates blocked the move to make it unanimous. Several others attempted to talk, but the chair refused them. At this moment and critical point, Holt was recognized from the floor and began speaking.

Stillness filled the room as Joseph Holt satisfied their attention with well-chosen words. His speech touched the audience's deepest emotions, as he offered a heart-felt message in Holt's dramatic style. His words caused the delegates to recollect the values and ethics of their great nation.

Joseph began stating the principals for which the party stood. He presented the western idea of democracy. Joseph continued, "If, Mr. President, you at this moment transport yourself to the far west, you would find upon one of her green and sunny fields a person who had sprung from the people, he was still one of them, and his heart in all its recollections, its hope and its sympathies was blended with the fortunes of the toiling millions....

"When this nation was agonizing and bleeding at every pore, when war had desolated with fire and sword your northern frontier.... He rallied about him the chivalry of his state and dashed with his gallant volunteers to the scene of hostilities resolved to perish or retrieve the national honor." Holt had described the War of 1812.

Joseph shared the account of the Battle of Thames, in which Chief Tecumseh had been killed, following an account that individual Johnson of Kentucky had been responsible. Joseph's voice echoed through the church ringing, intensively, as if he were present to give vivid account, for the auditorium was spellbound with his grand speaking voice. Joseph closed with, "There is a voice from the great valley of the West, from the North, and the South calling for this war worn soldier, such, sir, is Richard M. Johnson of Kentucky." He devoted, the final moments to patriotic appeals and friendly compromises to the nomination. The crowd enthusiastically backed Holt with a standing ovation. Joseph paused momentarily, for the loud clapping, striking up force again, spoke earnestly about what it meant being an American, "We must think of the future, making Americans stronger. Sacrifices will begin with honest works from the Democratic Party, attaching its policies to the hopes of its people." The roars lingered beyond the windows with sounds penetrating into the streets. Large crowds now gathered closely to the huge entrance of the church.

With the affective speech of Joseph Holt, nomination was secured for Richard M. Johnson. Two Kentuckians linked together, Indian fighter of the War of 1812, and orator, successfully helping compromise hurt feelings brought the Democratic Convention of 1835 to a successful end. After Holt's brilliant delivery, the delegates wanted to meet the man. The crowd moved closer together, trying to speak personally to Holt.

Reporters standing in arm's reach, were shouting, "Mr. Holt, what do you plan to do now, after promoting the delegates to support Johnson?" Smiling at the crowd, Joseph replied, "My plans are to support the Democratic Party by my presence, speaking engagements, and endorsing candidates to successfully win the contest of 1836."

The results of the Democratic Convention in Baltimore, Maryland, May 20-22, 1835, resulted in the nomination of Martin Van Buren of New York, for president, and Richard M. Johnson of Kentucky, for vice president. Twenty-nine year old Joseph Holt's words would soon grace the headlines of all the important papers of the day.

As the convention closed, the excitement continued into the streets, on the crowded sidewalks, with newspaper reporters flagging available coaches to speed away with the story.

Afterwards, when the crowd thinned, Richard Johnson approached Holt personally, with an extended handshake. "Joseph, your words were the most important ever spoken about me. You not only rallied this convention, but rallied my commitment to serve this country, rousing my patriotic feelings. I owe you for saving my political life."

"I not only spoke for you, but for hope of the nation," stated Mr. Holt. "Congratulations, on your nomination. We must rally together to win the election." Joseph left the premises with good cheer, realizing the empowerment of his words. It felt good to see the party united. The excitement created would be taken home, with the delegates giving reports to their individual states telling of Joseph Holt. The story would spread across newspapers about the 1835 Democratic Convention's success in building strong principles for the nation to support in the upcoming election of 1836.

Meeting Mary

In 1835, Joseph, now twenty-nine, decided to move south, seeking a fortune. Arriving in late fall at Port Gibson, Mississippi, Joseph resided there two years. Moving to Vicksburg, he enjoying the competition of the southern bar there.

Over the next several years Holt's law practice thrived. His reputation magnetized observers, entertained by his unique, masterly, courtroom style. Holt seemed a driving force, delivering powerful talks to his audience. His performances left juries spellbound. Well-equipped for his clients, he presented heavy evidence bearing on his cases. One of his most prized, noted cases involved Vick Newitt vs the Mayor and Alderman of Vicksburg. The case involved land Newitt had suggested dedicating to the public as Front Street and Commons. The case carried into the highest courts with Holt, the winning lawyer, representing the city, and the losing side represented by the noted orator Sergeant S. Prentiss. This case helped build Joseph a highly respected law practice, completing his dream of becoming wealthy in four or five years, and retiring.

But such hard work caused dull living, and a strict, routine life. Joseph longed for social company to share his success. The long and lonely evenings passed slowly. Joseph, now thirty-two, wanted a spark in his life. Holt searched the faces of young women. On voyages of river traveling from Vicksburg to Kentucky he always noticed the faces of any pretty girl on board the steamer. It was a weakness he could not deny himself. At night Joseph dreamed of a suitable lady, his perfect woman being beautiful, loving, caring, sophisticated, youthful, and zestful.

Desiring commitment and love, Joseph longed for someone with a warm heart, someone who would cherish loving him, not his wealth. One such woman might be a young girl named Mary, whom he had met earlier in Bardstown.

November 18, 1836
Dear Mary,

I am truly grateful for the lugged letter. Answering your last one has been long delayed, not because my dreams upon you have been fewer or the memories that cluster about your bright face less hallow I cherish, but because from week to week, I have been nursing the fond expectations of meeting you pouring into your ear, thoughts of love, which my letters have so fully uttered. At least I had believed I should have been able to name the time at which I could certainly visit Kentucky, but the divinity that shapes has willed it otherwise. I am still tugging at the oar, not knowing when fallest of this bondage. These vague thoughts of you in which my heart has for nearly two years been reserved, are proving but the glumpies, the saint has of heaven in his dreams and in the waking have cold reality. I find myself again struggling through a life, whose path is thorns, whose aliment is tears who can not control his fate?

The tone of your letters made a most painful impression, reading, "However fruitless my passion - however clouded its results, I had hoped to escape the sting of your reproach. I have not deserved it. - My own conscience tells me so. Every sentiment I have breathed to you should ward off so gulling an inflection. You ask why am I so mysterious? Why am I less frank than you have been? These are strange questions. I have bared my heart to - my fate is cast - I repeat, I will allow you to make for me no sacrifices, - I have already urged let not one tear fall or one tint of loveliness fade away from your summer in waiting upon hopes which may prove to me but dreams, never to be realized. Your visions that I had, the treasure I would throw them and myself at your feet.

"May I not still take to hear from you? Until someone more fortunate than myself, shall have warmed your heart and have I let us be apart - Nice interesting thought and feeling with you are the only source of happiness that left me.

"Aedreia - Be they anxious remembrance who never can forget -"

Upon receipt of this letter, Joseph received in return this correspondence from Mary.

January 9, 1837

Your letter of the eighteenth has been received and read over and over again. In search of something. I know not what? None the less this food for my weary spirits. A merry mood you were in when it was written. I envy your disposition.

You look with indifferences upon all things; meet disappointments as you should with fortitude. Sights and tears fall as powerless upon that callus heart of yours as dew drops upon the ocean.

What would I not now give possession of such a treasure? I would have escaped the anxiety my heart has been a prey to for the last twelve months. Your letters are not such as to convince me that I am not thought of with some indifference. Why not be as candid with me as I have been with you? I cannot accept much longer of this state of suspense and anxiety. My neighbors are unkind enough to believe Mr. H. quite luke warm in his love, for most of them have come to the conclusion that he does not intent to make his appearance here again. They say it is impossible for one who loves truly to remain long absent from the shrine of his devotions. It is indeed something of a mystery to me; almost two years have passed and with in a few days travel, answer me, "Do they speak the truth?" Enough of this.

Another year is gone and this day is a bright and beautiful beginning of a new one. I have partly promised to attend a party this evening. I would go but my little interesting lawyer student has crept into a secret which has put a stop to all my schemes against him. I have lingered any inducements to mix with the gay and the light-hearted. I will remain at home and read the Life of Monarch and dream of happier days.

The editor of the *Louisville Journal* says you have been nominated for the United States Senate. He also accuses you of being the assistant editor of the Advertiser. This little piece of sarcasm shows how acutely he feels the force some of pen's remarks. Mr. Prentiss has at least gone to Congress. You see I am not wholly ignorant of what is going on in your city.

I should like to know who this exquisite being is that you make mention of in your last letter. I have some fears that you steal the recollections of this dark eyed daughter yet be victorious. Keep a strict watch over yourself that should you find this little spark of admiration into something more ardent.

You have a kinsman living at Mrs. Ciezier's whom I fear is in some danger of Wife Earlham's. A few days since, as unfortunate as I always am, getting into one perhaps or another. Just as all things were arranged as they should be in accordance with your ideas of right and wrong, Mother and sisters, being kind, left them alone to the enjoyment that I should secure someone, to rescue me from the melancholy which might oppress me, should my Southerner friend desert me?

I rejoice to hear the widow is to be married. She has been the cause of many moments of sadness to me. Did she know of your kind wish, she would feel herself greatly indebted to you? As the letter I is a favorite of yours, I have filled my epistle with it. My letters have many faults but I hope you are generous enough to look over them.

Do write oftener; Why always wait and answer before you write again? You might at least write two for one. Were my tears left I might write more?

Farwell,

Mary

P. S. I would like to see your expression when you read the lines of sickly sentimentality at the commencement of my letter.

After receiving this letter Joseph did a lot of serious thinking, "Have I waited too long and worked too much?" More trips to Kentucky would be necessary or his future chances of winning Mary would be lost to someone else.

Joseph craved simple things; sharing, laughing, traveling, all without a price. Watching friends, he realized something in his life was missing. Could it be possible to awaken his spirit? Did he possess charm to attract beautiful woman? He once over heard Mr. J. O. Harrison give an account to one of his friends. "That young Mr. Joseph Holt definitely would be quite a catch with his good looks, brilliant mind, and proper upbringing, not to mention his estate."

Joseph trained with proper etiquette, understood the importance of being a gentleman, gaining respect from associates and friends. Being more mature now, Joseph sought after someone to trust his most inanimate thoughts.

Holt, tall at 6′ 2″, slim with a dark completion, brown hair, and captivating manner, drew attention upon entering a room, charming ladies at social events. Joseph had stated in the village of Bardstown that he was only interested in becoming a powerful lawyer, not falling in love. The young girls swarmed over Joseph like bees on a honeysuckle bush. Prominent families groomed their daughters hoping to intrigue the promising Mr. Holt.

One of Joseph's many acquaintances had been Mary L. Harrison. None of the other girls in Kentucky had caught his attention like her. She never tried to be silly impressing him, but Mary, intelligent and attractive, would not wait forever, not even for Joseph Holt. His wealth did not impress her as it did others. She had been patient, hoping he would make more trips to Bardstown to see her. Joseph realized he was not the only young man in Mary's life. He knew he must pursue this young woman if he was to have a chance in winning her for his own.

He received another letter from Mary on November 5, 1838.

> November 5, 1838
>
> Last night I received a letter, my eyes greeted the well-known handwriting making me happy, melancholy, and you talk of the gulf the fates have thrown between us. If you allude to my ambition only of your love, I can not for wealth, it does not intrude itself in my dreams of happiness, a home, competency, is all I ask. You say I am proud and ambitious, and desire the prompt and power of the world, and its noisy homage, I say you do not know my heart, no you do not, and you know your own still less. If you think it is not your proud haughty spirit that is unwilling to see others around you revealing in happiness which you do not possess.
>
> You ask me to write that you may know that I am not wedded; you must have a poor opinion of me, thinking me fickle indeed if you believe my heart so easily changed, perhaps you have seen the widow and her soft black eyes making you wish that such be the fact.
>
> I will not peep into my mirror for fearing I look most wretchedly. I have been indisposed for some weeks, but have improved rapidly within the last twenty-four hours.

You must not expect me to write again until I have seen you! Will you think me unreasonable if I request a visit from you this winter? Write soon and tell me. Adieu, ---

When you read this simple little note outcast it but throw it into the fire hoping the next may be more interesting. Farewell do not forget....

Mary

Joseph decided his best intentions would be to break from his busy law practice in Vicksburg. He would finish all his cases and prepare to travel to Kentucky. He sent word by letter informing his parents he would spend time on the plantation and would arrive in February.

Traveling up the river, Joseph had forgotten how beautiful the land by the river could be. With trees still bare he could eye the mansion as the boat neared the landing dock.

Joseph was happy as the steamer pulled into the docks at Holts Bottom. He enjoyed walking every step up the steep incline toward his childhood home. It felt good to breath fresh air, and Joseph's 4,400 acres his grandfather Stephens had given him, gave him strength seeing it once again.

Joseph realized money meant power, and provided a life of leisure, but he knew his money could not make his heart happy. In 1839, Joseph's life was about to change forever on his return to Kentucky.

Walking on the Holt Plantation, Joseph made notes in his diary, "The gray, blue canopy of clouds overcasts the sky, this day of February. Trees still bare from winter's long stay, show life existing with buds becoming aware of spring. The sun burns through fabric of cotton, warming legs of those caring to venture out, walking the fields, and absorbing sunshine.

"Cattle grouped together by the river bottoms, populate the land, as several mothers watch in the foreground, young calves cuddle safely protected from the outside world. A world wind living a short segment blows gushes of wind, scattering dust across the fields."

Quietness gave Joseph needed time to think. He dreamed of future times, wondering what this landscape would consist of in two hundred years. Would his childhood home be standing? Would the farmland be in crops of native grasslands? Would his home be a special place for people to visit? Joseph's thoughts returned, daydreaming about faith and existence.

Finding the special person to enjoy was as unique as the stars in the sky, sharing grace and presence of youth. Being connected with Mr. J. O. Harrison gave Joseph privileges in spending time with Mary, and he visited her uncle's office often.

Joseph needed a woman to love him, not his money. Yet her family must be acceptable for his career. Visiting and assisting Mr. Harrison, truly helped Joseph's self-confidence, and he grew closer to Mary.

Joseph remembered the echoes of his mother, Eleanor, telling about the love of his father, "Love can be a strange occurrence, a feeling like no other. Melodic echoes whisper passionate dreams reserved deep into your subconscious. Your heart is warmed with tender feelings, lifting your spirit to a most joyous occasion. Give yourself the opportunity to trust your feelings, take chances letting the person you admire, understand you. Be a genuine listener, voice conversation using your true personality."

Joseph's father, John, shared with Joseph a love for his mother, "Love strikes at an unexpected time in your life. The adventure will never be the same no matter what you do. Take advantage experiencing love because life is unpredictable and what you have today could be lost tomorrow."

Joseph thought about life with Mary. When stopping through Kentucky two years earlier he did not have intentions on making a connection with a young woman. That early morning, when she had stepped into her uncle's office, her presence had given warmth that caused Holt to admire her physical beauty.

As he said later, "The first glance of Mary portrayed her as a kind person. Her smile shone with radiance, lightening a path like no other. Her brown hair pulled back from her face let natural ringlets fall on her forehead giving an innocent look. Mary's features were striking with hazel eyes captivativing, pouty lips drawing attention, and an attractive nose completing her gorgeous face. At first, I noticed dangling earrings swinging back and forth as she walked. She definitely caught my attention, because I turned to get a second look, of the most beautiful girl in my world."

"The driving force of my personality has caused me to continue pushing myself to nothing but work, leaving little for formal engagements. I realize my presence at Bardstown should have been greater. Also, I know now I should not have been so frank as to spout at the mouth making a comment, I definitely did not seek any young girls to court."

Joseph thought how he could get more involved in Mary's life. He would rent a room in Bardstown, taking invitations to dine with the Harrisons, visit old friends, and become a regular in the community. The evening dinners might secure, for Joseph, the affection from the family. Closely observing Mary's father, Joseph noticed Dr. Burr Harrison had a kind and generous heart. The Harrisons, Burr and Elizabeth, were raising Dr. Harrison's orphaned niece, Lizzie, who had become a significant part of Mary's life. Joseph realized the closeness between Mary and Lizzie.

After arriving in Bardstown, Joseph learned that many doctors traveled to Bardstown to study under Dr. Harrison.

Dr. and Mrs. Harrison permitted Mary to date the honorable Mr. Holt, for he met their expectation as a trusted, southern gentleman. Joseph was easy to get to know, making the family feel comfortable around him.

It was agreed upon by Mary to attend church with Joseph in Bardstown. On a bright, February morning Joseph prepared for church. Mary surprised him by being ready and punctual. Holt slowly approached the front steps to Mary's traditional white, columned home, when suddenly, the wind rearranged Mary's hair, tossing her wide brim hat. Being a gentleman, Joseph chased the hat, retrieving it for his date.

"Why, thank you Joseph," said Mary. "I will have to hold my hat today."

"It looks like we might get a shower later on," said Joseph. The couple made more small talk, discussing spring on their way to church.

The carriage made nice tones of balanced rhythm with the turning of each wheel. As Mary reached for the support of Joseph's hand, he obliged, feeling her comfort. Mary thought how comfortable it was to be with someone wonderful. She had looked forward to seeing Joseph all week. Toward the end of the date, Mary dreaded the return home. She already missed Joseph's smile, hoping next week would bring another date.

His love existed, but it had not surfaced before in his person. Joseph now knew love, and excitement. He imagined hearing Mary's voice. Stored in his memory, her fragrance brought Joseph the memories he desired.

Joseph had difficulty concentrating on work, continuously thinking of Mary. During the week, Mary felt sadness creep in her heart, missing the company, laughter, and dazzling smile of Joseph Holt. To ease the lovesick pain, Mary wrote in her journal. "My subconscious mind imagines the next encounter, or touch. Exchanging smiles and eye contact with Joseph warms me. I definitely long to experience the moment when Joseph and I shall be together, cherishing each others company and kindness."

Joseph and Mary L. Harrison made a handsome couple. Mary, having been brought up in a well-respected family, fit nicely with Joseph's set of friends. Joseph adored Mary's southern glamour, her pretty face, small frame, and delicate features.

They enjoyed each other's company for two months. Finally, one Sunday afternoon Joseph found Dr. Harrison alone, working in his office by the house. Joseph asked if he could have a few minutes of his time. "Dr. Harrison, I am ready to settle down. I have acquired savings from my law practice and wish to make Mary my wife. My wishes are to live in Louisville, and continuing practicing law in Vicksburg for a few years. Mary will be well cared for and secure. I hope you will grant permission, for I truly cannot live without her love."

"Well Joseph, I was expecting this, but a father always dreads to hear those words. I realize you will provide my daughter with security, if she chooses you, then her mother and I fully agree."

"Dr. Harrison, you have made me the happiest I have ever been in my life," said Joseph.

"One restriction, Joseph, the wedding must be here, and promise me you will bring her home often." Both men shook hands walking toward the house to share the wonderful news.

Mary's father gave his blessing. The wedding day was set for April 24, 1839, at the home in Bardstown.

April 1839

The afternoon had overcast skies patched with shades of white and mediums of blue. Breezes blew on new spring leaves, caressing trees. Birds sang perched on limbs, investigating fields of deep, rich greens. Dandelions persisted in the fresh lawn of the new season. Darkened clouds approached, gathering forces for a thunderstorm. Rain brightened manicured tulips, still clinging two Sundays after Easter. Saturday's wedding in Bardstown approached.

Much fieldwork would be completed in the next few days. Teams of mules would plow flat fields, preparing for the beginning of new crops.

The wind, picking up speed, gained strength and caused rocking chairs to rock, side by side, on the front porch. Drooping lilies were beginning to fade, with leaves turning yellow.

A grandfather clock in the foyer struck 1:30, reminding that time does not stand still. The rush, to complete final packing, was evident. Next, house servants would be collecting trunks for the trip. The Holt family planned to depart early Wednesday morning arriving rested for the wedding day celebration. Lodging would be with Mary's family, as the Holts would be their guests.

A LETTER WRITTEN BY MARY HARRISON TO JOSEPH HOLT

April 22, 1839

Dear Joseph,

I can only speak to you from my heart. Your captivating spirit shows a gentle side others are not aware of, as I am.

It is difficult for me to leave my family, even though I am a grown woman and am self-supporting. New encounters have always been difficult for me. I realize change is often good, but yet my mind has hesitations about my immediate future.

Becoming a wife, adopting a new role, as well as the title of Mrs. Joseph Holt has cost me much thought. Spells of daydreaming have me wondering if there will be enough time as man and wife. I realize how vigorous your ambition has driven you to take challenges, pursuing your career as a statesman, realizing you will be away from me often.

I understand uniting our strengths, dissolving our differences, and compromising our wants will help us be happier, as husband and wife. I will do everything possible to make you happy, support you in your work, hopefully spending many years together. I definitely want a family to fill our home with love because love for me is forever.

Joseph, my life is yours, praying, always to keep you close to my heart. My genuine smile is open for you.

As we take our vows on Saturday, this will be on my heart:

May our marriage consist of serenades
Of loving sounds graced with
Natures painted portrait of a couple
Who will honor, cherish, and support
Each other as love is forever blessed
With our two hearts and divine bond
To guide us through the path
God gives us.

Love for you,
Mary L. Harrison

The rain pounded on Mary's windows. Each drop made varying notes as if playing a soft tune. This made traveling difficult for Joseph and his family. Mary wondered if the double buggy would stay atop the soft, dirt roads. Many times in the spring roads would get soft, causing wheels to sink deeply in shallow earth, causing delays traveling.

Mary hoped the journey would be pleasant, so the family could travel with ease and enjoyment. No use to fret over the issue though, because nothing could be done to change the weather.

In Mary's early morning devotion, she prayed for traveling mercies for Joseph and his parents, relatives, and friends on their way to the wedding Saturday. "Papa made a wise decision preparing the grounds a week in advance," she thought. When the rain ended, slaves could groom the vast lawn preparing it once again for the reception.

The First Presbyterian Church had been reserved in case of inclement weather, but Mary would not even consider the consequences of a dreary wedding day. In her heart she knew the sun was going to shine on Joseph and her on their wedding party at home in Bardstown.

If the weather cleared, Mary would make her final trip to the dressmaker in town for the last fitting. Her dress must fit as if she were a doll. Already Mary had practiced the hairstyle she would fix for her wedding day. She chose to let her hair be pulled away from her face, letting it hang in curettes, like Joseph liked, dropping, almost touching her bare shoulders. Mary kept busy the next two days helping her mother prepare the house, going over final details, making sure last minute items were in order.

With the last trunk placed in the carriage, the Holts, Joseph, Eleanor his mother, Elizabeth his sister, and John his father, climbed into the carriage. Joseph's brothers Richard and Thomas would leave later in the afternoon from the plantation.

As Joseph pulled the reins closer leaving the front entrance of the circular driveway, he glanced back, for one last look at his childhood home. After this day it would never be the same. The innocent days of boyhood would be gone. Would Joseph be as happy as he had been?

What a sight in front as the family traveled, driving down the avenue of primitive oak trees that had never been cut by a saw! What premonition and dignity they had! Standing so majestic looking over the family as if protecting, sending out warm welcomes to those arriving, and gentle goodbyes to those departing, linking a protective shield, and securing the feeling of love linked with home.

A few clouds gathered in the sky, but sunshine broke through making long rays reach the top of the clouds to the bottom of the earth. In a moment the brilliant sun shone so brightly that the intensity was too much for the human eye to endure, yet the sight was captivating.

Joseph's family waved with friendly gestures to the local people, traveling farther and farther toward Hardinsburg, and then to Elizabethtown. The family would be stopping ten miles from Elizabethtown for the night, at Cousin Lisa's house.

Rising early, enjoying a hardy breakfast, the family began another adventurous day back on the road. As Joseph drove the buggy, he noticed the road was becoming muddier as they approached Elizabethtown. The creeks were overflowing with debris washing on the banks. Logs and tree limbs flowed in fast- paced water. The ground, saturated from heavy rains of the past week, made it difficult for the double buggy to make good time.

With extreme effort of a trusted, dedicated team, the horses pulled with a strong force, not seeming to feel the extra burden of the muddy roads. Joseph's father began questioning whether the family would be able to cross the small bridge, now in sight. Joseph being young and persistent told his father they would find a way, even if it meant detouring, taking a route over higher ground. Elizabeth, Joseph's sister, said, "Joseph, I'm sure Mary understands. We will be just fine, but may arrive much later than we anticipated."

Just ahead before the family reached the small community of Boston, Joseph called out, "Whoa" to the team of horses. Another family traveling in a road wagon, tried to cross the Rolling Fork River, got caught in dangerous, rushing water, and the small wagon tossed in the swift current. This caused the children to be thrown out in the turning, swirling water. The children, a boy and a little girl, screamed for help, while their mother hung on to the wagon seat turned upside down. The father, torn between saving his wife and rescuing his children, panicked in a frozen trance.

Joseph, a good swimmer experienced with river current, told his dad they must save the children. John and Joseph dragged the children to the banks of the river. The father of the saved children was forever grateful, thanking the Holts. The mother of the children was still in shock after almost drowning.

The Holts helped the young family into their crowded buggy. It was only a few miles to a small community where the family could get shelter, and gain strength from the scary incident. With yet another delay, Joseph very patiently comforted the despaired couple, saying things could have been worse. Waiting several hours for the small river to go down, the Holts safely crossed, getting back on the road again. This trip would last as a memoir, forever reminding Joseph of the obstacles faced traveling to Bardstown for the most important event of his life.

Regardless of the troubles along the way, Joseph endured. His father told Joseph, "In life one must continue even though it is difficult, causing a person to have concerns about their destiny. Yet destiny is for believers who have faith, and confidence, believing in encounters, teaching many times the hardships, necessary to overcome life's obstacles, gaining wisdom and character."

So far, Joseph had been dealt a fair and nice life, and he dreamed about marrying Mary, whom he adored and loved. Joseph's family approved of this match securing the happiness of their second-born son.

Mary's grace, kindness, and goodness showed in her spirit. How sad it was for one to marry a female who was cold, uncaring, not welcoming her mate to their bed chamber. Joseph's friends were sometimes commenting about how often married wives would become distant after a child or two. They did not enjoy the company, the excitement of having great pleasure with their own spouse.

John said to Joseph, "Joseph are you really ready for this commitment?"

Joseph responded, "Dad, I have waited all my life for someone to love me for me. I am excited about beginning a new life with Mary and starting a family."

John sat very still finally responding, "Eleanor, I remember our wedding day. I became the happiest man in the world when I knew you were mine and mine alone. I still feel the same today, even though your mother and father had some hesitations about our marriage because you were so young and innocent."

"Sometimes young and innocent is the best wife because women marry often for wealth and security. They have little or no feelings at all for the groom, and end up being miserable for the rest of both of their lives," said Eleanor.

Eleanor asked Joseph to stop the buggy for a brief moment because she wanted to trade seating arrangements for the last few miles to the Harrison's. She did not want to be a bothersome mother, and sat quietly beside Joseph. Joseph noticed his mother's stillness as the horses picked up their hooves continuing. Eleanor commented, "Joseph it seems as though you were just born yesterday, and I remember the snow storm on the night you were born. It seems we have always had a close bond between each other. Joseph, I am very proud of your accomplishments. You are divinely gifted, having great talent in writing and speaking. I will never interfere with your happiness. We pray your life blooms with sunshine from heavens blessings."

Joseph took notes mentally as the scenes before him keyed in on Mary's street. Dazzled by a friendly atmosphere, arms wide open as if greeting visitors were a common pleasure, carriages lined the streets as we drew closer. Both sides of the Harrison's property were now overflowing with family members. Letters would be sent after the wedding by Mary to those unable to attend.

Mary's father had given as a dowry, linens, cooking wear, and three hundred acres (normally only given to sons), which made Mary quite a wealthy lady in her own right.

She was very fortunate remaining in control of her business, allowing her to be independent. Without restrictions, Mary's kindred spirit would mature nicely into an accomplished southern wife, one Joseph would be proud to call his own.

Thursday evening was soon approaching as the family reached Mary's home with only a couple of hours of daylight left. Joseph's tired and hungry family desired a hot, comfortable bath. However, these were the last items on Joseph's mind. He desired seeing Mary, and hugging her. It seemed an eternity had existed since they had spoken.

Mary had worried all day because of the rain delaying the arrival of his family. She knew Joseph would be there, even if he had to walk. Running across the lawn calling Joseph's name, Mary anxiously ran to her fiancé. Standing proud and tall, holding out his long, slender arms, Joseph received his promised bride with a welcoming kiss.

"What happened to you Joseph, your clothes are in shambles?" said Mary.

"It is a long story, I'll tell you later, but right now I just want to see your face," smiled Joseph.

"I was so worried about you crossing over the swollen streams. It has rained for most of the day. I did not think it would ever quit," said Mary.

"You knew no matter what, I would definitely be here," spoke Joseph calmly.

After a long embrace with family spying, Mary and Joseph strolled through the neighborhood. Joseph did not remember being exhausted from the tiring trip, and was not bothered by his attire. Mary, breathless, wanted to hear the entire story. Joseph promised to share every small detail after having time to be alone before the evening meal.

Dinner was truly enjoyed, as both families shared conversations and stories about the bride and groom. Afterwards, the women talked in the parlors while the men enjoyed a smoke in the smoking room. The servants cleaned, putting away what was left of the delicious food. All turned in for a peaceful night of needed rest.

Friday became a fast-paced working day for everyone, including the bride and groom. Popular morning weddings allowed an exuberant party following the reception, going into early evening. This allowed the newlyweds an early start on their honeymoon long before dusk.

It was not permissible for the bride to see the groom on the wedding day, because it might bring bad luck. Awakening to sounds of songbirds, namely a mocking bird, Mary opened the lace curtains adoring her room. She had looked out this window many times, but today was different. This was her wedding day. The day she dreamed about, but somehow it seemed dissimilar today. Even though she was happy, sadness was in her thoughts. It took courage to leave her home making a new home with her husband. How would he treat her? What would Joseph expect as a wife? She had never been with a man and her mother had only told her very few things about being a woman.

Mary prayed Joseph would be gentle.

Her ritual had begun with bathing, applying powder, and grooming and styling her hair. The wedding dress, secured in Mary's room, hung in the wardrobe.

As typical in 1839, the marriage would take place at the home of the bride. The wedding cake for the bride and groom occupied the grand foyer. Mary's home awaited all the expected guests.

This morning Mary wrote in beautiful penmanship, addressing three letters in fine script to her closest and dearest friends, unable to attend her wedding. Mary unfolded the last love letter Joseph had sent her two weeks ago. She reread the letter many times as Joseph spoke about the uniqueness of their love and trust for one another. Joseph had quoted Mary as saying, "You will soon be my very own Mr. Holt."

Mary, now ready to become a dedicated wife and companion, read the section of the letter where Joseph said he could not wait for her to be his wife, clinging only to him. Mary realized the importance of the convenant of marriage and the bond for life. She considered the letters from Joseph precious, tying them with a pretty silk ribbon.

Mary carefully took pains in preparing her porcelain face, sparing rouge and lip color. She gathered her bridal handkerchief to catch the tears of joy as she ascended down the spiral stairs, hearing the glorious sounds of violins playing the wedding march. The sounds were as if angels were striking harps of gold. Her fair face, beautiful to behold, glowed radiantly, lighting up the room filled with guest making this the most pleasant memory in her life as well as Joseph's.

Being nervous was expected of a young bride, but Mary had been more than nervous this morning from wedding jitters. Catching her thoughts while slipping on her bridal gown, she realized the moment was here.

An artist had arrived early, preparing to catch the narrative of this event, the melodrama of the wedding, a novel in paint of Mary saying her vows with Joseph. A heartfelt moment of truth would be captured for all time, as the painting would provide a glimpse of a blessed occasion.

Mary captivated those in attendance. All eyes of the home were upon her as she made her entrance. She appeared as an angel ascending upon the earth for a moment, keeping everyone, including Joseph, magnetized. When the Reverend Adkins said the words "Dearly beloved, we are gathered here today to join Joseph H. Holt and Mary L. Harrison," the young lovers met each other's eyes with smiles of golden warmth for each other.

The ceremony lasted thirty minutes with Mary being so nervous, she forgot her lines, as Joseph coached Mary three times. The minister would say the lines and Mary would begin, but forget, causing the minister to repeat them. The house was the stillest Mary could ever recall, with guests focusing on the soft-spoken vows. Joseph smiled winking at Mary, giving her confidence to continue. At the end of the ceremony all in attendance said the Lord's Prayer, giving the feeling of being in church.

Though the wedding was at noon, the meal was referred to as the wedding breakfast. An elaborate buffet was served with a heavy and rich menu. Several kinds of roasted meat, sandwiches with savvy fillings on crustless, buttered white bread, croquettes sweets such as cookies, cakes, and candies, along with savories of nuts, and olives delighted the appetites of the guest.

The groom's cake was cut into small pieces and placed into little boxes for the guests to take home as a favor. It was tradition for the unmarried girls to sleep with the small box of groom's cake under her pillow, dreaming about her true love.

The time approached when Joseph and Mary would lead with the first dance. Mary looked over to Joseph saying, "I sure have a handsome fellow. I am glad you chose the black morning suit with the pearl-gray tie and gray gloves."

Joseph responded, "I am not thinking about my attire now, only about traveling to our honeymoon having complete privacy for one month."

The wedding went as expected with Joseph and Mary becoming husband and wife. The couple enjoyed the wedding party, with the guests rapidly progressing to the next segment. Here, the bride and groom would change into traveling clothes, catch a coach headed for Louisville where reservations had been made at The Galt House located on Main Street, then catch the *Mississippi Queen* for their wedding trip starting their new life.

Mary's father, the distinguished Dr. Burr Harrison, kissed her goodbye, while mother Elizabeth gave a loving hug with tears in her eyes. Little Lizzie stood shyly beside Mary still holding her flowers from the wedding. Mary looking straight at Lizzie, "We will be home soon and I will bring you a beautiful present."

"Oh, I will miss you so Mary," said Lizzie.

"I will be back before you know it, please take care of Mother and Father for me," said Mary with a smile filled with tears.

Joseph lifted Mary upon the carriage. They left the grand celebration and departed to the Old Tavern to catch the coach. She smiled while tears streamed down cheeks of pink. Mary, overwhelmed with a new, exciting title, embarked on her exciting future as Mrs. Joseph H. Holt.

Mississippi Queen

Excitement filled the air as people boarded *Mississippi Queen*, riverboat in Louisville. As Joseph and Mary entered the steamer, a devastating sight shocked them. Mary felt queasy, quite uncomfortable causing her merry mood to be dampened suddenly with moments of unbearable truth. Straight ahead with chains attached, young men sat in rows of six chained together, barefoot as animals, looking lifeless and sick.

Most prominent families in the South owned slaves, but Joseph disliked human bondage, for it treated people worse than animals. Joseph did not realize slaves would be aboard the steamer. Nor did he realize slaves would be in steerage below, not seeing sunshine. Joseph overheard one of the young slaves was being sold down south because of his fondness of the master's wife.

Joseph thought how cruel life could be. "Imagine being sold for being fond of your master's wife. Being sent away from all known surroundings." Families of the South considered it radical not to own Negro slaves. Despite having a kind and gentle family, Joseph had observed the inner suffering slaves lived.

Sometimes going against moral principals of your parents was painful. Joseph Holt had witnessed cruel awakenings of slave life endured daily, and observed the shallow life slaves accepted, affording the privileged owners a grand and exceptional life style. His disapproval of slavery had already caused public speculation about the native Breckinridge Countian. It took special courage to write speeches about the downfalls of slavery.

Joseph felt he could reach the common population speaking the truth about slavery, even if it caused him to have greater ties with the North, preventing him from uniting with slave-owners of the South. Joseph recalled his grandfather Stephens speaking, "Joseph, you must be your own man, following your path, doing your best to help others, not always thinking about yourself."

Joseph told Mary, "I am sorry, sweetheart, you had to see this. I had no idea slaves would be on this voyage. Something must be done about the treatment of humans."

"Joseph, you are always trying to protect me. I am not as fragile as you think. I have seen slaves treated like this before, but I do not like it. I feel helpless that we cannot improve the treatment of these young boys," said Mary sadly.

"Let's go to our cabin and refresh," said Joseph. "We will come back on deck later maybe to enjoy the sunset," spoke Joseph.

"May we stay just a little while, Joseph?" spoke Mary sweetly.

The trees tossed leaves back and forth in the wind as if playing a melody of happier tunes. Stopping for a few moments, resting, the wind gaining forces making treetops sway. Corn tops popping up from late spring planting began to take form across the fields. Patches of clouds overhead guided the vessel. Humid air on the steamer made small splashes from the river a treat for those watching the paddle wheels turn downstream. An enjoyable afternoon occurred when the sun became blocked by afternoon clouds. The fresh, flowing breeze would make dinner more enjoyable.

Mary wondered if the slave boys would receive food, after being tied for a night and day without movement.

Joseph and she had many glances while boarding the steamship. The ownership of slaves was a way of life in the South, meaning massive plantations, and a lot of acreage. What was the difference between master and slave? The fortunate were able to gain property, and owning land gave people strength in the south.

Joseph's father, John, told him, "The land will take care of you if you take care of the land, owning slaves without skills is expensive, but they can be trained to do services promoting growth for the plantation."

"True in a sense," thought Joseph. "But what about not having freedom except what a master grants." Many slaves felt they belonged on the plantation because it was the only life they knew. If things went well, slaves in bondage might be permitted to "jump the broom," or marry. Their children, however, remained property of the master, and many times families were split and sold. At other times young slave girls were abused by the master and had mulatto children.

Joseph recalled how his mother and sister Elizabeth had taught house servants to read from the Bible. Joseph remembered his mother teaching from the Bible about being in bondage. The slaves must have felt similar to the bondage of Moses' people who begged to be set free. One thing was certain, the issue of slavery was taking its toll on America, ripping apart the very heart of families.

Joseph and Mary had heard stories about how the so-called Underground Railroad aided many slaves to freedom. People risked their lives, assisting runaways as the slaves traveled many hours without stopping for food or rest. Eventually, the strong survived, reaching hidden paradise of a free world.

Food and drink with a change of clothes and cover gave a few hours of needed rest. Many times runaways were captured, taken back in a harshly manner, beaten, whipped, branded or disfigured. The master would not want to damage his property too much for it cost them money. The last resort would be to trade or sell slaves to another plantation, separating families.

Mary conversed with Joseph about slave conditions. Once noting, "You know, Joseph, all individuals have different ways to relieve emotions, tribulations, and troubles. The enslaved people help relieve pain by singing about freedom."

As Mary and Joseph noticed the team of six men chained together, being dragged up on deck before sunset, that conversation came to mind, the middle slave asked the man in charge if they could sing. The man answered, "What good would it do, no one wants to hear you boys sing?" Mary looked at Joseph nodding her head.

Joseph said, simply, "Maybe they can sing." The slaves responded,

"You got a right, I got a right.
We all got a right to the tree of life.
Yes, you got a right, I got a right,
We all got a right to the tree of life
The very time I thought I was loss,
The dungeon shook an' the chain fell off."

The young slaves sang for a short while as Mary thought to herself, "Religion is a fortune, I really believe. If slaves judged Christianity by their masters, not many would become Christians." The music sung was from the heart and souls of the captives in chains. Mary believed these deep religious emotions had been touched by Christ.

After the performance of the spirituals, all on board applauded for the young boys, as everyone settled to enjoy the view. Joseph reminded Mary they would soon be approaching Stephensport. It seemed strange to Joseph passing his beloved boyhood home without family there to greet him. They were still in Bardstown and would not be home for another day.

Rounding the bend at Stephensport the Holt Plantation began.

"Look, Mary, there it is," voiced Joseph.

"I had no idea it would be so beautiful," exclaimed Mary.

"I have waited long for you to see my home Mary," said Joseph proudly.

"For as far as I can see, my eyes welcome the sight, of land bonding with a blend of wildflowers, blooming trees, just as mother nature has carved a unique pattern, for the ground to gracefully extend to the river banks. It is beautiful, more beautiful than words can describe," said Mary.

After traveling five miles Joseph stood from his chair. He extended his hand pointing out to the boundaries of his boyhood home. The *Mississippi Queen* would pass by the landing area at Holt. Joseph recognized in the distance Mammy Bell and Rose at the river's edge drawing water, probably for washing. Small slave children were running along the water's edge splashing in the waves touching the shore. The smallest must be Rose's daughter Millicent.

The scene painted a mural in Mary's mind as the vessel continued on route to New Orleans. It was difficult to see the rolling fields, for trees in bloom along with steep banks extending two hundred feet, hid the appearance of the house. However, Joseph knew there would be one last chance to see the layout of the plantation, as they moved to the next bend in the Ohio.

Joseph said smiling, "Mary this is my beginning. This land gives me strength. It seems only yesterday I was running down those fields, fishing by the river, and traveling to college down the small dirt road."

"Joseph it is a paradise, a place to which you can always cling. We must stop on our way home, when the family is back," stated Mary.

"Yes, Mother and Father would love that," said Joseph.

"I long to walk the fields you walked, to stroll in the gardens you have told me about and described in your letters. Why haven't you brought me here Joseph?" Mary sighed.

"I have always been committed to do work first before having pleasure, but maybe now you can help me take time to enjoy more," said Joseph reassuringly.

Only moments passed and the plantation seem to slip from view. This was a happy time for Mary and Joseph and they resumed sitting cozily together on the comfortable bench.

While waiting for dinner to be served, Mary pulled her journal from her bag and began writing as Joseph enjoyed the sunshine and company of his new bride. "Traveling the river one could freeze for a short while seeing the world different. Most people lacked feelings or listening to the earth, not experiencing reality such as Indians. My enjoyment presses deeply as my spirit delights gliding over tops of deep waters, witnessing mature native grasses, as waves on land blow across long bottoms and fields as if an ocean tide had ascend on the sandy shore.

"Clouds marching across the horizon make shadows appear and reappear as the wind blows tops of tall grasses. If trees could speak, people could learn from their longevity. Living with productive years, plentiful, barren, drought, flood, storms and pleasant seasons, like seasons of life faced by the human race."

The setting of the sun gave stillness to an evening filled with lots of laughter. Moments of candlelight flickered giving shadows distinctive figures. Joseph and Mary were finally alone, undressing, preparing for the wedding night bedchambers.

As Mary approached Joseph he touched her and said, "Mary, I have admired your beauty for the entirety of this day wanting to get you alone. Your skin is so soft, and the reflection of your body causes me to want your love more than you could ever imagine. What could be more exciting to be devoted to someone such as you? Mary, you light up a room when you enter, and cause heads to turn when walking down a street, or entering or exiting a public building. Just to imagine spending the rest of my life with you is going to take getting use to and awakening each morning with a beauty beside my pillow."

Mary replied blushing, "Joseph you are embarrassing me on our wedding night. I know I am naive, even though I am a grown woman. I may not understand what you think I should."

Joseph smiling, "Believe me, Mary, it will come natural." Mary did not know if she was ready to become a wife. Joseph undressed completely, walked over to the bed, set up with a pillow propped behind his head and just sat there smiling. Mary made her entrance from behind the dressing partition with a long white lacy gown.

Joseph hugged Mary kissing her the longest kiss yet. Mary tumbled at the thought of what was occurring. She would soon lose her virginity, remembering the vows she had spoken earlier. Mary would make Joseph happy being the wife he had anticipated, by waiting patiently two years with only a few letters to keep them together. But she was empowered with a strong heart, reserving her love with absence, trials and months of separation while Joseph pursued his career. Mary proved to be smart by waiting patiently for her little law student who had proved to be a southern gentleman.

Mary thought, "What could be greater than having a man love you this much." The night settled with darkness covering the skies. Birds made music as waves hit the steamship. In the grand stateroom Mary did not get much rest, because Joseph kept her awake most of the night, rubbing her hair, caressing her shoulders, touching her long, lean, gorgeous legs, and discussing their future, engaging in love making on their first night as man and wife.

Life as Mrs. Holt

"Matrimony changes lives," thought Mary. Thinking of her husband, Mary knew she wanted to be a good wife. After a month long wedding trip to New Orleans, Mary and Joseph had purchased a home on 233 East Walnut Street in Louisville. The inviting, quite neighborhood featured neatly arranged individual fencing, which separated joint properties. Joseph also secured five acres accompanying the home for the privacy he desired. Availability of the English styled home had surfaced two months prior to their wedding. Excited and intrigued by beauty and space of the home, Mary longed to decorate the wide halls, graced in hand-carved moldings.

Already Joseph had planned how he wanted to add details, with French paintings complimenting the foyer. He had suggested that Mary be painted by Mr. Conaria.

As it stood now, the stairs of solid oak displayed beautiful works. Floors shined as reflections lighted all corners of the Holt's home. Mary rapidly planned decorating their home. She dreamed of beautiful, patterned oriental rugs, a warm fire, and rooms filled with kersoline lighting, all completing a cozy atmosphere.

Lemule, the trusted servant, brightened the outside premises by adding coats of paint to the Victorian fence surrounding the home. The oversized yard provided Joseph space for collecting exotic plants and trees from his travels. Friends continuously brought saplings and seeds to the Holts. While at home, Joseph enjoyed trimming hedges, and helping maintain the vast formal garden. It provided a welcomed retreat from long, hot summers in Kentucky.

After settling in for a month, Joseph prepared to travel back to Vicksburg to his established law practice. Mary suddenly realized the realities and difficulties of long separations. She had endured them before, and would manage now, with help from her parents and servants. She had been accustomed to kind attention from Joseph, and when he left she felt she had parted with the dearest one on earth. Mary magnified everything, even having difficulty sharpening a dull pen to write letters.

For two years Mary endured long, trying separations from Joseph. Trying to keep her spirits uplifted, she wrote three or four letters a week. Writing seemed to relieve the pain and sadness she felt. It was hard not receiving but one letter, sometimes two letters, a week from Joseph.

Joseph's handwriting had become more difficult to read now. Even Mary had difficulty deciphering his script. She tried very hard to please Joseph by excelling in all things, particularly in composition, but Mary was afraid she would fall short of Joseph's expectations. Oh how she wished Joseph could be home to see the moon beams playing in the night. As Mary sat alone at her window thinking of Joseph, her thoughts led her to almost give up her existence, just for one sound of his voice. When she recalled his words they seemed like distant music.

Mary risked criticism from Joseph, even severe words, so she could profit by them. She knew her letters might fall far short of anything Joseph would expect or would wish to see from Mary's pen. She wished for Joseph to coach her to improve, so she could write beautiful letters.

From time to time Mary traveled from Louisville to Shepherdsville to Bardstown to stay with her parents for short times, and in writing from there she explained to Joseph, after his departures back to Vicksburg, how she would be as contented as one could be, after a separation from one whose presence to her was the very bread and wine of life. She had no idea that she should feel so lost, so desolate without Joseph. He was the very life spring of Mary's heart. She could even visualize his smile.

Miss Polly Ball, housekeeper for the Holts, kept the home tidy while Mary was away in Bardstown. She craved getting home to Louisville. Hard times had set in for Mary. She missed her beloved Josie as she called him. She wanted to see him, sought to do so on her own, an almost unheard of thing in this era. In her letters to Joseph she spoke about the clerk of the *Gray Eagle*, a regular U.S. Mail Steamer, not being an honest man, and for Joseph not to have much to do with him. Mary remembered Joseph telling her to have a Kentucky note changed, but the clerk from the *Gray Eagle* sent her a New Orleans note, and when she approached the clerk he told her he would change it upon the next arrival to Louisville.

What made her more unlikely to venture south on her own was on

May 17, for example, a mob surrounded a southern gentleman Judge Wilkson from Bardstown. On his way to be married to Miss Eliza Crozser, he was threatened by a gang of rough men seeking his money. Later, he returned to Bardstown and was united in marriage unharmed.

While Joseph practiced law in Vicksburg, Mary forwarded letters from brother Robert to Joseph. For her, she had to manage a loving relationship secured only by letter writing. Mary realized that telling her loneliness to Joseph would cause unhappiness for him, making his business more painful, and emphasizing the problems of living separated from her.

Happy times made separation periods bearable, such as when Mary and Joseph visited Cuba, bringing seeds back for their garden. Mary did visit some in Vicksburg. Boarding in hotels in Mississippi was not as grand as home, but still proved delightful for Mary. She enjoyed their private time together when Joseph sat in their favorite chair, and she sat in his lap.

Traveling in fall to Vicksburg became a tradition. Mary usually planned traveling south with trusted friends, feeling comfortable on the voyage. She booked a private stateroom, the best accommodations on the steamer. The voyage took three or four days, depending on weather, but one fall journey presented a huge problem. That year the summer months had been very dry with no rain. Was river travel even a choice? Only a few weeks earlier the mighty Ohio had been so dry in places that wild turkeys could walk across the river. Because of the absentness of normal rainfall, Mary decided to take the stage to Vicksburg, though she dreaded the bumpy ride and dust. She felt like an early pioneer in Kentucky fifty years earlier.

Still, Mary needed to see Joseph. Her father examined her before leaving, but Mary still had a bad cough and tender breast. Most women in the area had the same symptoms because of changing fall weather. The check Joseph had sent Mary earlier could not be cashed because it was on a New York bank that had failed recently, leaving Mary with only three dollars and ten cents, not enough for a trip.

Joseph wrote Mary in the next letter telling her to open the safe and remove the gold pieces he had left there for her use in traveling to Mississippi. Mary, surprised by the amount Joseph had left her, now felt secure for the voyage. She sent Aunt Sally money to pay for all their debts while away. One debt concerned a woman named Ceclia. She had been almost without clothes and shoes when Mary found her. Mary had made arrangements to hire her out, while she went to Mississippi to be with Joseph. Ceclia tidied the premises, while Willy and Lemule tended the house and grounds.

As Mary finished packing, she recalled again the strong picture of dear Josie, as she called him. She remembered his sad look, on his last departure, and the melancholy smile on his lips. Her mind wondered, "Oh what I would give now for one sweet, sweet embrace." She hurried, fastened everything, and ascended into the carriage with her horse "Pony" leading the way. Lemule attended her needs as she rushed to meet the stage. Mary dreaded the ride in the cramped seat. She was a private person who did not enjoy sharing her personal life with strangers. A lady could not be careful enough!

Mary hesitated to board the stage, because of wild horses, but finally put one foot at a time, bravely ascending into the cramped area.The stage then began its journey. All aboard were truly relieved to reach the first station to eat, stretch their legs and then to begin again.

To relieve the fearful ride, Mary tried to pass time away writing in-between dips in the road. "On this twentieth day of September the sky is at its brightest refreshing the scenes. On board are an old man and a young boy headed to college. Scattered clouds of white and gray decorate a most appealing blue shade of total background as the powerful sun warms the afternoon.

"Even though the day is cool with a chill in the air, the warmth from the sun seems to burn your face, as we rested earlier at the stage rest. In passing by woods, a deep green color is present, but the feel of autumn is in the air. The rustling of leaves stirs emotions from quiet to a sudden sound, as if the soothing sea gently touches the bank's edge."

"Like a whisper in the breeze changing from soft and slow to louder and faster as if a fiddle player were adjusting rhythm of a song. A big white dog roams the yard of a near by house, acting protective of the family as the stage passes."

"The main road is busy today, weather still warm, and people are enjoying carriage rides a little farther from town...." Stage travel could be long and tiring as well as dirty and dusty. Mary would be greatly relived to arrive in Vicksburg.

On the way Mary wondered if the duel that was to be fought in

Lexington had occurred yet. Cassius M. Clay had challenged young Robert Wickliffe. Many thought they would not fight. Just a few days before, however, young Wickliffe left Louisville with pistols for the purpose of having them ready at the time appointed and in good order.

Mary thought, "Why can't men talk out problems instead of protecting their honor and someone losing their life because of it?" She would think of more pleasant thoughts, having a good time once she reached Joseph.

Joseph had told Mary about the new St. Charles Theater in New Orleans, opened by James Caldwell, seating 4,000. It was decorated in neo-Renaissance, and the most extravagant theater of the South. This would be a memorable outing Mary longed to see. It was reaching mid-afternoon when the stage finally arrived in Vicksburg. Mary hated for Joseph to see her emerged covered with dust. Traveling had made Mary appear as being tanned by the sun. She hoped to see Joseph waiting for her, but instead his assistant, John, stood close by with a carriage.

"Miss Mary, Joseph regrets not being here to escort you to the Washington Hotel. He is tied up with a court case from early morning. His instructions were to take you directly to the hotel, helping with trunks and baskets. Fresh fruit has been placed in your room for your comfort, and Mr. Holt will join you as soon as possible. He also has made reservations for fine dinning at the Bellarillan Inn for 6:30. Your black evening dress has been aired and pressed."

"Thank you John. I believe you have taken care of everything. I dearly appreciate your patience. Goodbye and I'm sure I will see more of you on this visit."

"Goodbye Mrs. Holt, and have a restful afternoon," said John.

Mary was relieved to be alone finally. At the desk while registering, Mary had requested a hot bath. Very efficiently servants were at work carrying steaming water for her bath. Clean towels and fresh soaps were visible. Sometimes simple things felt the best. How relieved Mary felt to finally be alone! She would revive her body and rest to greet Joseph.

No sooner than Mary recovered from dust and dirt and refreshed her face, than Joseph knocked on the door putting the key in before Mary could answer. "I am so glad to see you Mary, I always dread the time you are traveling to see me, and am only relieved when you reach Mississippi. How was the trip this time, honey?"

"It was worse than ever Josie. In fact for a while I wondered if I would ever see you again. I have never ridden on a stage that had such wild horses. Two times we had trouble getting the horses hitched. And then it seemed as though they were in control instead of the driver. I am just glad to be here," spoke Mary.

"Well, rest assured that journey is behind you and I have finished all the cases for the most part for the fall season. That gives us time together for at least a month."

The next few days Mary recuperated from the journey, resting to enjoy sights and sounds of the city. It had been a scorching day except for the few breezes cascading over high cliffs coming into Vicksburg. Relief was needed, for the temperature had soared to become very uncomfortable. For two nights, tossing and turning occurred without comforts of sleep.

Joseph and Mary decided to take a carriage ride on the outskirts of town, ceasing out miserable weather. It was always exciting to be driving at dusk, seeing the beautiful countryside. Joseph wanted Mary to dazzle Vicksburg with her natural beauty.

The couple watched the alluring sunset, blazing the heated horizon, and entertained each other's thoughts. However, the overwhelming heat caused them to head back for town. Joseph winked at Mary and asked, "Are you ready to leave, and maybe we can find a little café open and get a late night snack?" Mary nodded politely as the couple held hands under stars covered by deep clouds.

As Joseph and Mary approached town, a heavy downpour began with flashes of dangerous lightning. The thunder roared, showering the earth. Mary and Joseph hoped they could reach the safety of their hotel room before the heavy rains came. Suddenly, without warning, a huge lightening bolt struck near them. Only moments later blazes rose and started burning intensely.

Screams arose from people in the streets as they witnessed a frightening fire across two streets. Someone from the crowd shouted, "It's the hotel, it's on fire!" With the fire department in the early makings, they would do their best battling the blazes, trying to save the Washington Hotel.

As the rain slowed, shouting people ventured into the city streets. With panic in the air, men attempted to rescue what could be saved. Very quickly, Joseph instructed Mary to stay inside the carriage because of the intense lightning.

"No, Joseph, please don't go, and don't leave me here," begged Mary.

"It's too dangerous for you to leave the carriage, and maybe I'll be able to help save something. I have to help, Mary," said Joseph.

Mary knew Joseph was right, but she feared the blazes had gotten too much out of control. The hotel might fall, injuring people, who sought to salvage items. Many men from town headed down the street, attempting to assist the few firemen. By the time the crowd reached the hotel, flames were blazing out windows.

Suddenly, another massive bolt of lightning hit the Washington Hotel. Onlookers saw fire explode in the lobby. Quickly citizens entered, rescuing what they could, resting for a moment recovering from black smoke then making their way back again, trying to save as much as possible. However, after the third trip Joseph realized he would jeopardize his life and others around him if they attempted recovering anything else. The air had become too heavy and dangerous to breathe.

As the firefighters and concerned citizens were about to give up, a rain ascended with hurricane strength, pouring buckets of water on the burning building, as if God had opened heaven sending his angels to extinguish the fire. Within a few minutes the fire lost its power under a gentle rain.

Though covered with black ashes and soot on their faces and clothes, no one was injured. Even though the hotel had experienced huge losses, it had been spared and rescued by caring individuals of Vicksburg who gallantly risked their lives in a wicked storm to save an important hotel.

As things calmed a bit, Mary and Joseph realized their room had been totally razed, completely destroying its contents. Tomorrow they would have to seek a place to stay. But tonight Joseph and Mary would spend the night in Joseph's law office, snuggled safely together in the oversized leather chair.

As the sun arose the next morning, Mary and Joseph laughed at each other when they saw all the soot and black on their faces from the grand fire.

"I must have a bath Joseph, for I cannot trot around town in this dismay," said Mary.

"I have an idea," spoke Joseph, coming to the rescue of his beloved Mary. "Why don't we pay Mrs. Taylor a visit? You enjoyed staying in her place when you visited me in October of 1838."

"It sounds delightful to me Josie. I had a dreadful thought staying in that despiteful Kansas Hotel. Remember how I use to have terrible horrors of having to stay in that place?" asked Mary, a little happier than before.

"How could I forget? You tell me about it often," Joseph laughed. "We'll take a carriage over to Mrs. Taylor's house and both have breakfast and hot baths. I'll have her send one of the girls down to the dress shop to select one dress for you, and you can return later to buy more outfits. After we are both dressed, I have a surprise for you."

"What is it Josie? How could you have a surprise with all of this mess and us not having a place to stay for the time I remain in town?" Mary questioned.

During breakfast all kind of thoughts ran through Mary's head. "Just what could this surprise be? Unless Joseph purchased a gift before I arrived, he did not have time to buy a present" thought Mary.

After breakfast Joseph thanked Mrs. Taylor for cooking an additional breakfast for them as well as fetching an outfit suitable for riding for Mrs. Holt. When Mrs. Taylor's daughter arrived with the riding attire, Mary was somewhat surprised when she took the outfit from the box. Since she did not have anything else suitable, she dressed and joined Joseph. Luckily, Joseph had some clothes in his office, and could manage a few days without buying new clothes.

As Mary entered the parlor Mrs. Taylor said, "You are so pretty dressed in blue." "Thank you," said Mary with a smile. Mrs. Taylor told the couple she was glad to help them and told them to return anytime if they need a place to stay. Joseph gave his regards as Mary and he boarded the carriage.

"And where are we going Joseph? You are always full of surprises," commented Mary.

"I wanted you to have a pleasant memory and I cannot afford you to linger with the disruption of last evening's fire to dampen your spirit, so I have decided to take you to look at some country estates. I have a friend who just recently wed. He and his youthful bride are honeymooning in Europe for one year, so it might be possible to stay while they are away. There is a small cottage near where he is building his bride a mansion. I thought we could possibly rent the cottage and have more privacy. That is if you like the estate."

Upon arriving at Cedar Grove Mary's face lighted as Joseph slowed the horses and helped Mary from the carriage.

"Oh Joseph, do you think we could stay here for a while away from the noise?" asked Mary in her proper southern accent.

"I am personally going to speak to Mr. John A. Klein's manager to see if it could be arranged. Being a banker and personal friend, I believe the manager will accommodate us," spoke Joseph confidently.

After a short while, Joseph returned wearing a huge smile. He explained to Mary how it would take a few days to have the servants remove some personal items from John Klein's cottage, getting things ready for them.

Meanwhile the couple would return to town, to buy new clothes and visit Mrs. Taylor's for a few nights boarding until final arrangements could be made to return to Cedar Grove. Finally, two days later, Joseph and Mary happily returned to the cottage. The manager of the plantation greeted Joseph and Mary.

"I only wish Mr. Klein were home and Cedar Grove was completed. I know how you both are such good friends and this is the best I can offer you and Mrs. Holt," said the manager.

After a while Mary refreshed and unpacked all their belongings. The couple decided to take a short nap, and Mary began dreaming....

She dreamed it was before her marriage and she was home at Bardstown writing Joseph a letter, around September 1838. She had just read a letter not long since written by a gentleman to his betrothed begging her to learn to spell and write letters. "The moon has risen cool and calm, and with it I must tell you in time you must not expect it to partake of the hue of brilliancy of the morning, in as much of my feelings are very unlike it in every respect.

"We have had a very long and dry Indian summer. The sunshine is apprehensive. I pray now as frequently for rain and thunderstorms as I once did on board the General Brown for calm and sunshine. I think a few clouds and storms would improve my spirits. There is no sound I should like to hear as well as the sound of pellets of rain hitting against my window, except music of your voice, which is sweeter to me than any earthly sound.

"Were you safe from that miserable country in the sweet little cottage of your own with Woodbine roses? I should be perfectly happy – if your love holds faithfully. I am sure I should want nothing else, but would you, like many others, fly from your home in search of pleasure? A palace in such a care would be to me worse than the most miserable of cells. Do not think if any misfortune over takes us, that I would love you any less than I do, under all circumstances and in all situations I am yours and will love you on to the last."

Her dream ended and Mary awoke to the sound of a sweet mocking bird. "It was a dream and nothing but a dream," realized Mary.

Mary and Joseph enjoyed their special month together with long walks, picnics, horseback rides out into the countryside, and parties with the best families in Vicksburg. The most enjoyable time seemed to be when they were alone doing nothing special, except being together, talking about plans, discussing Joseph's homecoming, and retirement from the law. They spoke about traveling abroad, seeing the sights of Europe, and enjoying the freedom of being able to do what pleased them day by day.

The time approached for Mary to return to their home in Louisville. Joseph had promised that it would not be long until he would finish all his cases and return finally to live in leisure in Kentucky. Mary only hoped he would keep his promise.

Returning Home

Spring finally arrived and Joseph Holt made his final début from Vicksburg. As he boarded the steamer, he reflected on his life at that point. He had delivered his life's ambition to become wealthy, retiring at an early age. Remembering his promise to his bride of three years, Joseph proudly walked aboard the steamer, hearing the whistle blow as the ship pulled out of port. Joseph had gained in thirty-five years more than most people do in a lifetime.

Life had been hard for Mary, spending time away from Joseph in Kentucky while he worked in Vicksburg securing their future. Joseph anticipated a grand homecoming, seeing Mary, and sharing their special closeness. Spring revived hope for Joseph, for Mary had been sick for a few months. He expected that his return would help Mary's illness.

Joseph and Mary tried to crowd as much living as possible in the next four years. They enjoyed family, outings, friends, traveling, and most of all the unrushed lifestyle Joseph offered after retiring. But after two years absence from the law, Joseph got restless and sought to ride the circuit again, in counties surrounding Louisville. He missed the action of the court, and needed to stay close because Mary was beginning to show depressing signs of consumption. Her symptoms worsened with fever and nausea. Joseph had worried for months over her lasting cough. Mary, already small, had also started to lose weight.

Joseph would travel two or three days, finish his work, and return home to Mary's side. He thought that working kept his mind alert, forcing him to read, while seeing people revived his self worth. Returning home one day after attending court in small communities, Joseph suddenly realized Mary's condition was rapidly deteriorating.

Evident changes had occurred. She gradually lost the glow in her cheeks and smiled less. She did not constantly talk, or plan for events, or entertain as she had once loved to do. She did less of her own work, declining invitations, trying to put up a good front for everyone. However, she did not fool her father, Burr Harrison, or Joseph.

Dr. Harrison secured a doctor's assistant to live at the Louisville residence with Mary and Joseph. At first Mary was not fond of the idea. She despised the privacy it cost having a stranger in her home. Joseph traveled the circuit less because of Mary's condition.

The lung-destroying disease took a dreadful toll throughout the century. Entire families sometimes passed the disease among themselves. Being confined much of the time, Mary preferred Joseph to be out of the house, in a fresh and healthy environment.

The difficulty of Mary's sickness could be seen in Joseph's eyes. Being happy proved a challenge every day. How could a person laugh and respond when the one they loved was hurting? There seemed nothing to comfort her, except provide medical assistance, compassion, and love. Having family around worried Mary, for she feared the disease would spread. Still loved ones took the chance, being cautious while in the Holt home.

Afraid that Joseph might catch her disease, Mary always kept her mouth covered. The doctors told the Holts that Mary could have developed consumption from contaminated food.

Together Joseph and Mary's father, Dr. Burr Harrison, provided Mary with the only known treatment to help consumption. She received bed rest, fresh air, and mild exercise. The family carefully kept Mary isolated to keep from infecting others. But how did a family stay away from the one they so dearly loved, one so young and full of life?

Joseph arrived home from his short circuit trip. He heard weeping upstairs. As he followed the sounds, the volume increased. A deep sobbing cry made Joseph hurt. He gently opened the bedroom door to Mary's room.

"Why are you crying, Mary? I'm here," Joseph tenderly asked.

"Joseph, I cannot stand the thought of leaving you, with no one to care for you and love you," Mary barely could speak above her sobs.

"No one is going anywhere Mary. You are getting better, and stronger. Why just last week you walked for over forty-minutes and gained two pounds," said Joseph.

"Joseph, I am not that little naive girl you married. You have taught me to be aware of what is around me. Do you think I cannot see, or hear, or notice doctors coming and going weekly? Everything is being cleaned meticulously daily. I realize what my life is and what it has become for us as man and wife. My dear Josie, I wanted to give you children, so you can pass on to them your great brilliance and watch them grow."

"I do not have to have children to have a good life. You are giving me love and enjoyment. I only wish you felt better. I will try to stay at home more," commented Joseph.

"No, I want you to do what you love, for that is truly living. Help people by representing them and using your brain. You would not last long in this house all shut away from the things that have made you great. Please promise me you will always be adventurous, living an exciting life we have dreamed of," smiled Mary.

"I promise to do what makes you happy; however, being with you makes me alive, Mary," nodded Joseph.

"Well, then it is settled, you will continue traveling through small towns helping common folks, and I will remain at home trying to recover, gaining strength, and maybe I will accompany you on these local trips later," smiled Mary.

The Circuit Rider/Judicial

Retiring from a fast paced office and demanding schedule gave Joseph needed rest to recuperate from signs of consumption. However, Mary was more fragile and not as lucky. The disease stayed with her, even though she had had the same rest and treatment as Joseph. Joseph now considered it more feasible to travel across several counties practicing law on a part-time basis. In that way he could be closer to Mary, with her health problems, while continuing to enjoy law. The refreshed pace provided the welcomed peace Joseph's spirit demanded.

Awakening to crisp fall mornings of noisy birds preparing for flight, surveying the movement of living beings, small and large, Joseph met each day with eager anticipation.

He carefully packed his satchel with the necessary legal paper, pen, and ink, as he prepared for the wide-open small towns and developing cities in the early 1840s.

Stopping at the blacksmith's shop for inspection of Gallant Gentleman's shoes, Joseph walked to make certain he would not be delayed so he could reach the small towns on time. Most towns would conduct a months worth of business when Joseph arrived. All legal matters would be resolved until he returned next month.

As the sun shone directly over Joseph's head, he realized lunchtime had long passed and he had developed a hearty appetite since leaving his Louisville home early in the morning. As the buggy bounced over the narrow, bumpy road Joseph could see on the horizon a homestead of some sort. With each turn of the buggy wheel, Gallant Gentleman brought Joseph closer to a pleasant sight.

Directly in Joseph's path was a plain and simple house, yet strong and elegant, and graced by the lady who cared for it. He knew somewhat of what life was like for her, sweeping dirt and dust, sewing, mending, hanging ruffled curtains, preparing meals from home canned foods, walking to the spring, retrieving fresh milk, calling the cow, milking on a stool, sharing milk with barn cats to reward them for their honorable duty of keeping the premises rat free. The mother would be teaching the children from the Bible, setting good examples for her children, putting out a wash, and providing white starched clothes for Sunday that she had washed by the creek side.

Lye soap made in an open kettle over hot colds represented just one of the simple life styles. Everyone in the family had a job. Children were seen as a pleasure, and taught to respect adults. Old and young alike enjoyed life, even though days were long and tiring. People took time to stop and say hello with good thoughts in mind. Everyone knew their neighbors, cherishing the land, and treating it as a gift instead of a duty or job.

His revelry interrupted, the lady waved a kerchief in hand as her three children lined up, as if placed on a staircase. The dust from the buggy met the country folks before Joseph halted his horse. As the wheels ceased their turning, Joseph commanded Gallant Gentleman to stop. The kind-faced young woman with auburn hair and piercing smile greeted him with a friendly welcome. She approached Joseph, asking if he was lost or needed help. Joseph replied, "No, I am traveling to West Point."

She responded by commenting, "Sir, you are about five miles from the main road."

Joseph answered, "Ma'am, I realize I am off the main road. I became bored with traveling the same path, deciding to travel the unpopulated trail."

She said, "These are rough roads, scarcely traveled by a road wagon." She introduced herself as Dulce Leonard, explaining that her husband was away on business, traveling the river, but she and her children would be delighted to share supper if time permitted.

Mrs. Leonard invited Joseph to the evening meal. After serving supper the friendly host continued being gracious as Joseph's taste buds opened to fresh apple pie served warm. Joseph, the children, and Mrs. Leonard then discussed the demanding job of farming, but also worthwhile living of peace and productivity. The small girls sang a song in unison after the meal.

Joseph thanked the gracious host, giving his parting words as the young boys retrieved the reins of Joseph's horse, as he mounted back into the comfortable leather buggy. Driving on in haste, Joseph noticed the dried leaves making sounds as though a person was standing at the edge of the sea. The constant humming set the tune for a softer medley. As the wind shifted, the tempo increased, and the sun's reflection changed the colors in mid air.

Beyond the trees and soft rolling fields, the familiar sight of the Ohio River appeared, as always an important part of his environment as he traveled south. The river, always important in Joseph's family's life, helped the day's journey to be pleasant and rewarding. The river had brought his mother and father together as soul mates. It also gave his grandfather Stephens a blessing of inheritance for serving in the military when the country fought to gain independence from Great Britain.

As Joseph approached the outskirts of the small settlement of West Point, he noticed several boys trimming small reeds by the river's edge. Joseph paused for a short while, recollecting his own childhood memories. His childhood had passed so rapidly with most of his time devoted for studying. Joseph could still remember echoes of his mind, with the ever-present voice of his father, John, trying to get him to do more outside activities. He had always felt Joseph needed more fresh air.

The young boys now with cane poles in hand as if to say, "fish beware. We are inviting ourselves to a delightful late evening fishing, by the shore to catch as many fish as our baskets will hold." Joseph watched with anticipation as the young men rolled up their britches legs, wading to the water's edge to get closer, and possibly pull in a big one. The youngsters probably had worked a long day, beginning at daybreak, and fishing offered a delightful treat before sunset.

Joseph's horse acted as though he thirsted for a cool drink of water. Being a caring master, Joseph dismounted the buggy slowly, leading Gallant Gentleman to the water's edge. The young men approached Joseph with curiosity. Full of questions, the young boys asked what he sought.

Joseph said, "I am just admiring the scenery and wondered what you all are fishing for here?"

A big red-faced young man by the name of Buck stated, "We are trying to catch enough fresh fish for a fish fry and pie supper raising money for a new town hall." They invited Joseph to fish along with them, and he took them up on the grateful offer. How long had it been since he had taken off, without worry of a client, or the health of Mary, or an appointment?

The evening started cooling as the wind began building. Leaves rustled on the trees as waves hit the shore. Sounds of mothers could be heard calling children in for the night. Dim lanterns, lights lined windows, with giant shadows falling on banks surrounded the fishing party. What had challenged a proper gentleman to do something definitely not a characteristic of him? Had Joseph needed a form of relaxation? Had he gotten so wrapped up with meeting deadlines he had forgotten to live, doing simple tasks, the things normal people did everyday? The young men seemed excited and happy with smiles on every cast made, trying for another fish.

Joseph realized simple, carefree things bring out a person's true personality, helping them live from their heart. Money had always been important to Joseph, but he also realized wealth could not make him happy or take away illness.

Perhaps it was meant for Joseph to have this fishing encounter. Maybe he would develop more patience with clients and small towns who needed his expertise on pending cases.

Many fish were caught as the night progressed. Joseph felt he had contributed to the large catch. As the sun was rising over the horizon, Joseph placed his cane pole by his side, watching the developing miracle people viewed daily. The sun bounced over tips of dark blue and lavender clouds springing through, giving rays, seeming to penetrate from the top to bottom of clouds extending outward, as reflections scattered over the top of the blue-green water of the still Ohio.

Joseph would remember this outing for days and years. Being tired and dusty from the ride, Joseph asked the young fishing team where he could locate a nice bath and a clean bed to rest for a short while. They instructed their new friend, Mr. Holt, to the hotel in the small town. The food was tasty and he would rest quietly, napping and bathing before beginning a new workday.

Sleep helped relieve Joseph's weary body from a tiring day. Being bounced around on unleveled roads caused backaches, and made a person feel beyond his years. Joseph soon felt relief with deep and comforting sleep. After a short nap he was refreshed making his appearance to the town hall.

Around eight in the morning, Joseph embarked, searched for the sheriff's office, getting the information he needed. "Good day, Sir. How may I help you?" asked the sheriff.

"Sheriff, my name is Joseph Holt, and I am filling in for a friend who is ill. I am the circuit lawyer from Louisville."

"Mr. Holt I am glad to be acquainted with you. I am Mr. Ron Hall, town sheriff. The town has not experienced any dangerous situations. However, there has been a dispute over boundaries of some properties in town which could probably be settled out of court."

"Mr. Hall, if you could send for the conflicting parties we will get started on this dispute." said Joseph. Since both arguing parties lived near the edge of town they were retrieved shortly, meeting with Mr. Holt, and both agreed to settle their differences, saving the time of a long and drawn-out case.

Having finished business ahead of his projected time Joseph would make the next town Brandenburg ahead of schedule.

Traveling alone produced feelings of isolation and in some places Joseph needed an adult's conversation. Since Mary had been ill, Joseph seldom noticed females, other than those in his closest circle of friends. He wondered why this subject was on his mind? He did realize he would only be young once. It had been difficult staying in instead of going out, circulating with his prestigious friends, who made him laugh, sometimes angering him, but always compromising with popular conversation and topics for discussions.

Joseph's mind wandered as Gallant Gentleman marched on, and he did not even realize he had traveled so far. Staying on the main roads, his horse followed the trail as if he knew it by heart. The horse remembered the training Joseph had given him, when to travel with a trot, and how to take a slow pace. He followed Joseph's instructions, "Run up the hill Gentleman, slow now boy, walk down the hill, that's good."

On the approaching hill Joseph faintly caught a glimpse of something that seemed to be overturned. Under a strong hold and calling, "gee," he commanded Gallant Gentleman who willingly made the small turn, passing safely by the overturned carriage.

As soon as Joseph dismounted his buggy, he carefully walked to the front of the overturned carriage and saw a beautiful young girl of about eighteen examining the front wheel of her buggy. With golden hair pulled back from her face, her eyes intrigued. Kindness, happiness, and a feeling of warmth reached out to those who talked with her.

Joseph introduced himself, "Hello, my name is Joseph Holt, lawyer, from Louisville."

"Glad to meet you sir, my name is Dmaris Collins. My family just moved here from Virginia, and I am still somewhat unfamiliar with the roads. I was returning home from a visit to my aunt, when something mysteriously scared my horse, causing him to rear straight up making the carriage overturn. With the reins broken, my horse ran off into that clearing. I just climbed out from the wreckage as you appeared sir," said Dmaris cautiously.

"Miss Collins, I am afraid you might have injuries, let me take a look at you. I have a brother who is a doctor."

"Why that would be very kind of you sir, but I don't know you," said the young girl frightfully.

"True enough, ma'am, but the next person passing might be hours from now, and you do have a scratch on your forehead, with a cut on your wrist." Joseph said. "I have watched my brother wrap cuts. Since this is small, it will be all right until you reach home."

Dmaris thanked Joseph, smiling with gratitude. He would long remember this young woman, even though he was married and loved Mary, something about her freshness of spirit attracted him. Joseph escorted Dmaris aboard his carriage saying,

"We will keep an eye out for the runaway horse." Down the road about three miles the bay horse was eating leaves off of a leaning tree. Very carefully, Joseph rescued the animal securely tying the reins to the back of the buggy, allowing the horse to follow as the pair made their way to town.

Dmaris asked, "Mr. Holt, where in Louisville do you live?"

Joseph remarked, "I live at 233 East Walnut with my wife Mary, who has been quite ill."

"I am sorry your wife is not feeling well," responded Dmaris. "I am sure it must be difficult traveling alone, realizing your wife is ill and home alone. I am surprised the women of the towns are not chasing you Mr. Holt, for it is not often I encounter a fine gentleman as yourself. Many of the men in my community work from daylight to dark."

Joseph commented, "I realize farming communities are always busy. My family has a history of farming. Once you start it is in your blood, and you can't get enough. You can't wait for the next day to continue what you started the day before. There is a lot of risk involved because the weather can made it difficult to survive, or the market varies too much. The demand of your product is important with the prices you receive. What you sell must out weigh what you owe."

"Why did you choose the profession as a lawyer Mr. Holt, if I may ask?"

"I became interested in law early in life, and I was on a debating team in college. I realized I had a natural gift for public speaking. I really enjoyed speaking in public and I realized people listened to what I had to say. I enjoy writing, and practicing law, but my true love is delivering a message before an audience, seeing their response and reaction to the subject."

Joseph was thinking to himself, "It is nice to know I am still considered handsome and could be captivating to a young lady who knew nothing about me or my family. The appearance of a person seems to have a hold on your memory. You recollect over and over in your mind the experience encountered. The glances, smiles, and mannerisms correlate with each touch, sending special messages to your nerve endings telling you, you are accepted by the person's grace."

"Morale puts your imagination into a state of creativity, causing your senses to live and relive special moments, granting great satisfactions. The moment will be a unique experience out of unexpected circumstances. You must be true to your calling. You must endure the feeling of your heart for passion in your life."

He thought further: "We can gain a life time of knowledge by listening to strangers and people we make acquaintances with, using the information daily, living to make each day worth more. Listening is the key to learning and understanding. Listening takes patience. It is giving equal time, permitting others to share stories. You must be observant, with eyes as well as ears. Nodding in observance of the tempo or rhyme used to keep the beat of the speaker."

"Listening shows interest or concern of a true friend or colleague. It makes the listener more knowledgeable, more worthy to give advice.

"Listening can be exciting, like an adventure, or uncovering a new aspect of life. Finding out for the first time what the spirit can behold in the real world of living for the enjoyment of giving pleasure to those who seek to find truth within them."

This day had taught Joseph many lessons he would long remember. He would trust his heart to sort reality from fiction, helping him have intelligence to use practical reasoning, to help him live life to the fullest, sharing blessings he had discovered from others, while traveling the roads and backwoods as a judicial circuit rider.

As night approached the sky had set the scene, applying a total light blue brush to the sky. The moon anointed clouds, shinning brightly, and drawing attention to the new moon. In the distance a whippoorwill called, signaling night. Across quite fields, the sounds of birds and distant barking of dogs started the night into existence. Fireflies lit up meadows with faint light as frogs called from a pond within view of the home.

Over Joseph's home another star shone jubilantly as Joseph opened the front door to his home on Walnut Street. Home at last, Joseph was thankful for the adventures of truly living a wonderful day in beautiful Kentucky.

Mary's Passing

As Mary lay dying, Joseph tried to put on paper his deepest of emotions: "Remembrance of Mary is as gracious as time, for love will not let her go. Life's journey is vast holding memories deep of a youthful, elegance of time spent together, with love holding the world."

Memories of sweet smells of late summer blooms, long days, majestic sunsets, walks over rock covered walks, and running swiftly across the yard surrounding home caused Joseph to realize his loss on May 16, 1846. "Mary's smile forever indents passion, causing me to be more observant of moon beams shining brightly in the world left behind."

"Sadness grasps my heart as if it were torn apart. Leaving behind yet another memory, feeling goodness, but crushed, knowing Mary's spirit has departed, as no longer my wife. Shadows follow the path God has sent me on for destiny. Life sometimes has huge vacancies for happiness."

"Blessed with a good mind, and a talent to speak, but heartache breaks many a man. How do you continue life when love has passed you by? Love lingers on with memories of past, filled with good cheer. Emptiness brings back vague remembrance of pass happiness."

Joseph had known for weeks that Mary's health was rapidly deteriorating. He felt helpless, not being able to get her well. In fact, Joseph had been quite ill himself and had almost died from consumption. It was sad enough for Mary's mother to live, seeing her daughter die young. Dr. Harrison had passed away the year before, relieving him the pain of losing a child.

The funeral would be quiet as Mary had requested, with burial in the Harrison Family Cemetery in Bardstown. Mary would rest close to her father, Dr. Burr Harrison.

It was a simple funeral with only close friends and family attending. The mood in the Harrison house was quiet, with heads bent low. Mary's mother, Elizabeth, could not raise her head to look her family in the eyes. For when she did, tears flooded causing her vision to be blurred. A few of the elders from the Presbyterian Church came to try to console the family. Normally, the community attended the funeral of neighbors.

As the funeral began and eulogy was read, Joseph remembered a few weeks earlier when he and Mary had their last day together as man and wife. Flashbacks of their short time entered his memory. He recalled the first time he had seen Mary's face. She had made an everlasting impression upon him. Another moment he could not erase from his memory was their wedding day when Mary had ascended the stairs of her white brick home. Such a memorable day, quite glorious, and happy with the sun shining brightly! Still yet, another moment he could not forget had been when Mary arrived in Mississippi to see her Josie, as she called him, covered with dirt as if tanned by the sun.

Reality aroused Joseph as conscience reminded him that Mary had passed. Joseph remembered Mary fragile and weak in bed, looking at him as she had many times before, asking, "Joseph promise me you will always take care of Lizzie, treating her as our own."

"Mary, you have my oath, for as long as I live, in all things I do, I promise to support and visit Lizzie frequently. When possible I will include Lizzie in my travels. She will be as our daughter."

As Joseph's mind wandered back to the service, he heard kind words being spoken, and Lizzie played two of Mary's favorite hymns. Lizzie could hardly see the notes because of streams of tears filling her eyes. Mary had requested her to play the piano for she had often enjoyed listening to her perform as a small child. As the tune rang through the home, Joseph smelled the fragrance of flowers tucked in every corner, surrounding the small casket draped as a farewell to the beautiful gardens Mary had often strolled through with Joseph by her side.

After the music stopped, everyone arose from their chairs. Joseph took hold of Mrs. Harrison and helped her exit the house's side entrance. The horses stood majestically, silent as if they understood the service for Mary. Carriages lined a semi-circle ready to follow the hearse to the Harrison Cemetery. It seemed all too soon, since the family had just had another funeral, once more they all dressed in black mourning now, for the life of their beloved Mary.

Ladies held their kerchiefs in hand, dabbing at the tears streaming their cheeks. Joseph held inside unbearable pain. It hurt to breathe, and his body felt numb. Pallbearers carried the small bronze coffin draped with in-season flowers, as neighbors sat silently, watching quietly, and showing respect for the young woman who had graced the little village of Bardstown.

The family boarded carriages to the short ride from the family home on the square to the gravesite. Joseph thought to himself as he and Lizzie rode toward the burial, "The cemetery is smaller than I recall. It seems unreal to be putting Mary into the warm earth for a deep sleep. I know Mary's faith is strong and she will be greeted at the gates of heaven." With tears filling her eyes, Lizzie broke his meditation and remarked,

"It seems as just yesterday Mary and you left for your wedding trip, as I cried with happiness for you both and sadness for myself for being separated from Mary who has helped raise me from a small child to a young lady."

After the preacher's final words the family returned back to the Harrison home for a meal that neighbors had prepared. Most found it too difficult to eat. Joseph seemed to choke on each bite. Nothing had any taste; his life was empty. He felt numb with a terrible sickness of loneliness and fear about his life. He had just buried his beautiful, young wife beside her father in the Harrison Cemetery.

Over the next few weeks Joseph took care of the additional burdens such as ordering a tombstone and choosing a verse to be engraved on Mary's headstone. The most difficult part would be to return once again after the stone was set and read the inscription. It was almost unbearable for him, and he had not been able to part with any of Mary's belongings. Joseph knew that it was not a good idea to keep Mary's possessions. But he could not part with even one item. It was tearing out his heart to see objects that Mary loved, but he still could not give them away.

For two years he grieved, then, finally, he tried to throw off his depression over losing his love, and traveled to Europe and see the world. Perhaps different cultures, foods, people, environments, and lands would help him let Mary go, for he knew she was in a better place than she had been, and now, felt no pain.

It took courage to get out of the bed each morning and for Joseph it took his entire strength to prepare for a trip across the Atlantic. He realized he could not run away or cover his sadness, but he felt if there was a distance from the home Mary and he shared maybe life would be somewhat less painful for him.

Facing one day at a time, perhaps he would regain lust for living, and enjoy life. For Joseph Holt did not know how to grieve, or how to continue on in the environment he was in with its constant reminders of Mary. Everywhere he looked he saw her face. Her image lay deep in his subconscious. It would take years for him to regain his potential of being good company in public. For in Kentucky wherever he traveled, people out of concern would ask, "How are you doing?" It seemed best to go to a place where he was not recognized. Life would be simpler. He could just be a tourist, finding his way through a foreign country, without questions.

Joseph realized he would be lonely not seeing his mother, brothers, sister, and relatives, but traveling to Europe seemed the best thing to do. He reserved passage on a steamer and prepared to tour Europe for seventeen months. Maybe, when he returned home he would have a new outlook on life.

But how would Mary's family feel? Would they feel he had betrayed her memory by running off to another country? Would they feel like Joseph had to escape, be alone to think about his life, his plans, and try to start again, but this time without Mary? It would not be easy to leave but Joseph knew he had to.

Margaret Wickliffe

In Bardstown, Kentucky, in the antebellum South, one of the daughters of Governor Charles Anderson Wickliffe lived in their beautiful home called Wickland. It had been given to Margaret's father and mother as a wedding present from her mother's uncle, world famous surgeon, Dr. Walter Brashear. Her father, a prosperous, thriving lawyer, also had a political career with fame and fortune. His children enjoyed a life filled with riches of various kinds. Into that world would soon be introduced a most gracious gentleman, Joseph Holt.

Charles Anderson Wickliffe grew up near Springfield, and married Margaret Crepps in 1813. Their home came as a wedding present from Uncle Walter Brashear, along with eight hundred acres of land.

There they welcomed daughter, Margaret, into their world. Margaret's father was a kind and understanding man whom she saw as a child growing up give not only to his family and prestige friends but also to people who were less fortunate. There was a "vagrant room" at Wickland, in the wing to where entrance could only be gained through a separate stairway. Anyone who sought shelter for the night was given a safe and comfortable place to rest in their home.

It had taken four years to complete Wickland. Young Margaret's home, the place she loved, would prove difficult to leave because of happy memories of her growing as a proper young lady of the South. A black slave, "Mammy" dedicated her life to serving the family, and helped raise Margaret. At night, though, Mammy traveled to her slave quarters in the basement of the Wickliffe home.

Charles Anderson Wickliffe sought to treat his slaves humanely. They lived in small cabins close to the big house. When the family lost a slave by death, the Wickliffe's conducted funeral services in the center hall upstairs, in the family's part of the house, just like one of the family members.

Having slaves allowed Margaret's father to spend much of his time away from the children in his roles as state Representative in the

Kentucky legislature, an officer at the Battle of the Thames, as congressman, as lieutenant governor, and as governor of Kentucky and later as Postmaster General in the cabinet of President John Tyler. Such absences meant Margaret's father's homecoming was a joyous time. Great haste would be made with the news of Mr. Wickliffe's homecoming. His favorite dishes would be prepared and bountiful supplies of logs were hauled closer to the house to keep the fourteen-room mansion warm.

The family knew father's passion for gambling was a great way for him to interact with friends and he loved the company and the enjoyment of playing poker with all of his dear friends. Being skilled as a poker player, he many times won money off of his friends but they always returned hoping to win a few games of their own. The family would share father with his friends after a week of being together.

Margaret's father enjoyed his time with his family. "As there is nothing father would rather do than load up the carriage with all of us and drive to the Presbyterian Church. We have spent many Sunday's listening to the Bible being taught and the rewards rendered if Christians would follow the straight and narrow path God allows us to follow if we do his will. Sometimes father said we try to convince God we are doing the right thing when we do it our way but our Minister always told us who are we convincing?"

After away for a while, Margaret's father returned home in a carriage driven by young Ben, house servant of the Wickliffe's. Ben swiftly advanced down the lane approaching the front view of their home. Master Wickliffe stepped down from the carriage as the family gathered around for hugs. Around them, leaves tumbled, falling to the ground. A few leaves holding, clinging to the tree. The twelve-foot doorway greets the master of the house as he brushes off the leaves and welcomes the entertained guests who chose to come to the warm, hospitable Georgian mansion.

In the dinning room cooks and servers had created a most elegant table setting for Master Wickliffe's return. The mahogany table was set with the best china and crystal glasses from England. All of the silver had been polished two days before. Fall roses had been properly trimmed and placed in a decorative arrangement in the center of the large dinning table with huge candelabras giving the necessary light to accompany the evening feast. Dinner was delightful. Margaret's mother was smiling and father was laughing, telling stories of Washington and about the people he had met on the stagecoach. Things could not have been happier for the Wickliffe family. But, as Joseph had found, tragedy can strike unexpectedly.

There had been so much confusion in the kitchen with all of the hustle of preparing the lavish dishes for father's arrival, Bea, the cook, had left the old crane in the massive stone fireplace unattended for a short period of time. The coals had become too hot. When the door was opened for the second course, a thick fog of heavy smoke filled the rooms.

The smoke extended into the dining room and began filling the interior. Margaret's father told everyone to crawl away from the kitchen area to a door. He and all the servants ran to the water pump, rapidly gathering buckets, pouring water on the hot colds in the hearth. After several minutes of continuously applying water the fire cooled leaving the house extremely smoky. No one was hurt or injured during the encounter with fire, smoke, and panic. It burned on the first level but all levels suffered smoke damage. All of the satin drapes had to be aired and the lace under the satin would have to be hand washed, dried and hung again after the pressing.

After the fire, and the smoke damage, Margaret's mother told her sisters and her that after the big snows, they could go on a shopping trip to Louisville to replace some of their soiled clothes. They could all choose dresses for the spring ball. Ben would accompany them to the station and make sure they were safely on their way before leaving. It had already been arranged for them to stay at their aunt's house in Louisville. The girls would spend several days shopping for dresses and matching bonnets with silk ribbons. They had to have the latest fashions from Paris and wear the new trends.

As they walked in the large city, they took in the views in the busy, buzzing downtown where everyone seemed to be in a hurry. Margaret and her sisters, Nannie and Julia, dressed in their walking dresses of fawn silk with collar and cuffs of Maltese lace, and rode in a carriage to the Galt House to enjoy breakfast served in a relaxing atmosphere. There they were off for an adventurous day of shopping. Visiting one shop after another the girls looked at countless dresses and bonnets. They must have tried on everything in most of the stores, but all the dresses seemed to look alike. Margaret and her sisters wanted unique outfits.

On Fourth Street the girls decided to take a break from shopping and went into a refined coffee shop and bookstore. Nannie and Margaret purchased "The Ladies Wreath," an illustrated annual leather-bound volume containing 432 pages of stories, essays, songs and poems, all of which offered insight into the 1850s. Julia, being the youngest, wondered how they could waste so much time looking at old books and magazines. "Can't we go now? This is so boring and I have not found one intriguing dress all day," Julia asked.

"I knew it was a big mistake bringing along our little sister," Margaret whispered to Nannie.

"We can't complain, Margaret. You know that is the only reason mother allowed us to go on this shopping pleasure, because she knew we would have to behave and not bring attention to ourselves with Julia in our presence," winked Nannie with an eye roll.

Nannie opened "The Ladies Wreath" and began to read a short story titled "Elsie Gray, the Wandering Child." As Margaret drank coffee they had ordered, a poem came to mind.

Fashion

At a glance you have a put together look
Fashion is cleverness
What comes to mind before
Tailors sew it, plan it and
Try and sell it.

Fashion is being comfortable
With what makes you feel your best
And enjoy movement with ease.

Summing up the total feel of a person is the key to
The genuine aspect of relating your personality to others.

Defining yourself as tasteful, elegant, simple yet sophisticated
Make up the true look
Portraying the person.

Nannie glanced at her and said, "Margaret, are you ready to move on and see if we can find something before we call it a day?"

Her thoughts interrupted, Margaret replied, "Let's walk down Broadway and see if we can find a shop we want." They soon saw a sign that read Millicent's Boutique. They both smiled, walking a faster pace, anticipating great finds.

"I knew our day would get better if we ever got out of that old, stuffy bookstore," Julia smiled. Just as they expected, they finally found the fashion center of Louisville. Millicent, the owner, happened to be in attendance. She had just received several collections from Paris and had one dress of each kind. Margaret knew she had found the collection she had been daydreaming about in the coffee shop.

Millicent's Boutique had dresses just like the Grand Duchess Olga had been wearing. It gave Nannie, Julia, and Margaret ideas. They wanted something similar, but still something different. After discussing what they liked, the owner showed the girls the entire collection, with the help of two attendants. All three girls purchased several outfits. After all, the proper Victorian Woman spent a large percent of her time trying on clothes and changing from one attire to another to be properly clothed at all times.

After the completion of the timely, enjoyable, yet exhausting, shopping outing, Nannie, Margaret, and their small sister decided it was wise to return home to Wickland. They purchased return coach tickets and gladly said their good-byes to Aunt Bea. It had been nice to be away having the satisfaction of the city with sisters doing the sort of things young girls enjoy, having conversations about young men, without their mother hearing and giving advice.

It seemed they heard advice all the time: "A young girl could not be too careful in these days," or "A proper Victorian lady should not give her views on politics, or what she considers important in government. You should be as well a good hostess, be well-read, well-mannered, and stand beside your future husband, not to be outspoken or have your opinion on the topics of the day."

As the Wickliffe girls settled back to an inviting and pampered coach ride, a young gentleman approached them slowly and asked if he could be seated with them. They were reluctant at first but he seemed harmless enough and had a powering mannerism that drew him to Margaret. As she wrote later that night in her diary, "I will have to admit I normally am not attracted to men in particulars but this young traveler was different. He introduced himself as Joseph Holt. We chatted for miles and the time passed rapidly. I dreaded the departure and hoped I had farther to travel." As Nannie helped Julia gather their belongings, Joseph shook Margaret's hand. As he held her hand she noticed a firm and caressing handshake as if he wanted something more. They all laughed as Nannie, Julia, and Margaret departed from the stagecoach.

Margaret told her sister Nannie, "I know it was just a touch, but I keep reliving it over and over in my head. Why did I not invite Joseph to one of our social events at Wickland? I am old enough to be able to invite some of my acquaintances."

"I am going to tell mother that you were holding hands with a complete stranger, Margaret," said Julia.

"You do, and it will be the last time you ever get out of the house with us you little bother," stated Margaret with a look that meant you better be quiet or else.

Margaret's private diary now included the feelings of how she wished again to see the man she had met on the stage with her sisters. Margaret kept to herself for the next several days, living and going about daily life in constant routine.

Connections with her father's work and his political career meant for his children, brilliant social gatherings with gracious and courtly formality, the natural expression of cultivated etiquette. Pre-Civil War life focused on the present and protecting the future.

Margaret's father had arranged a setting with a local artist to paint her portrait. She was not very excited about it because she felt it to be embarrassing to pose for a complete stranger, but to satisfy her father and to be respectful she agreed to the ordeal. Margaret wore one of the dresses purchased on the Louisville trip.

Her hair was demurely parted in the middle with pink roses adoring her black hair. Her dress, was one of the latest Paris fashions, had matching lace off the shoulder line at the top of the dress and the sleeves with a golden, silk bodice tapered to a narrow waistline and to a beribboned full skirt. That would be the portrait of her in her twenty-fifth year.

After the portrait was completed, it was hung in the large hallway near the front entrance. Margaret thought, "What an embarrassment this will gain me when we entertain guests in the future."

The time soon approached for the much-anticipated annual Spring Ball. In the evening the fiddlers would be located in the hall used as musician's gallery.

The hand carved, paneled portals between the double parlors would be open to form a spacious ballroom. The fine architectural details of the rooms would be appreciated by all the attending guests, and the cream of society would be attending.

The southern belles all captivated attending gallants in high-stocks, flowering waist coats, and long-tail-cutaway coats, all awaiting the entrance of the best of the South, as the prized women gently captivated those waiting below, making their grand entrance down the swirling stairway. The musicians played violins, repeating phases with a whispery soft melody of soft-spoken tunes, meant to tame the hearts of lovers and capture the love spoken by loving glances stored in hearts.

Margaret walked slowly as rows of gentleman callers approached to take her hand. Her friends envied her appearance and her beautiful figure. She was kind and polite, but encouraged no beau. She continued to think about the person she had met on the stage, and she had little interest in the attending guests. As she was strolling through her grand southern home, someone gently touched her on the shoulder. She turned to face Joseph standing in front of her.

He reached for her small hand to greet her and she reached for his. Joseph asked, "Would you like to take a walk in the garden?"

Margaret answered, "What is keeping us?" When the couple stepped into the garden Joseph said, "I had hoped I would see you again and when your father invited me to the ball I was hoping you would be home."

Violins could be heard in the distance and the lights were much dimmer outside. Joseph started slowly dancing in a dreamy stance. Margaret's hands were cold as they held each other caressing. Holt commented, "My grandmother once told me if your hands are cold you are in love. Could it be?" Joseph made direct eye contact and then gently held her waist with one hand. He touched her cheek and they briefly kissed, quickly, secretly. Margaret was very nervous, afraid someone might see them.

She found herself in a position she had never encountered. She felt nervous and a desire to get close to this individual, but why? Why had she let him kiss her? She had not even tried to stop him. She was risking her reputation. Gentlemen did not kiss in public.

Joseph told her he had to be alone with her away from all others. Margaret knew the ball would last for hours and she wanted to be alone with him but she would be missed if she disappeared for a very long time and besides she could not walk out into the night with a ball gown. They decided to take a brief walk down the lawn approaching the front of Wickland.

Margaret had fallen for this young man but she must stay reserved, even if she was attracted and helplessly in love. She had heard of love at first sight. She had dreamed about such a love, with a man who loved her, in an environment where passion would awaken, with the bride harmonizing songs of paradise for her lover to hold her nearest to his heart, sharing their own songs with the brightest score.

Her mother had once said that, "Love is leaving behind the past life and anticipating dreams, enduring the atmosphere of the present to build on the plans and dreams as combined for the love that is in the making." Margaret now realized she must wait, but wanted to be with this man who seemed to have a true heart, a good soul, and inner strength. Margaret would wait for social and acceptable courting with an engagement and marriage of her choosing.

Marriage Request

Not long after the ball, Joseph Holt became a household name. Her father had mentioned several times to Margaret that Mr. Holt was quite wealthy and distinguished, making him a suitable caller for her, but Margaret had always been rather independent and had not liked her father to give her advice, especially about men. She had been pursued by several beaus before, but had not been interested or attracted to them. They were too old, too ugly, too poor, or too dull.

Joseph was also older than Margaret by years, but Margaret was not getting any younger. Her new suitor was good-looking, tall, and distinguished, and few met him without being impressed by his intellectual ability. He seemed to adore Margaret, but Margaret did not like to be rushed into anything. She wanted to take her time, since he had already been married and lost one wife. Holt, however, was ready to find someone to grace his company.

Joseph wrote Margaret inquiring about attending a party at his Louisville home. The invitation spoke of a few close friends and several prestigious people from across the state. Joseph's invitation included a ticket for the stage.

Margaret wondered to herself, "What if I don't want to go?" The mail would barely have time to reach his home but she answered in a letter saying she would be glad to attend the party.

Margaret's staged pulled into Louisville on Saturday. Waiting by the stage office Joseph appeared with a shiny buggy and two beautiful bay horses. He was dressed handsomely, and she could not keep from looking at him. Margaret had been surprised that her father did not require a chaperone to accompany her on this affair.

Driving down the busy streets of Louisville toward his private residence Joseph asked, "Margaret, do you love music?"

"Well, of course I love music, why do you ask?"

"I have been wanting to have a singer at one of my parties and I had hoped you would like entertainment as well as I do," said Joseph.

"I would love that. Who did you have in mind?" spoke Margaret with a tinkle in her eyes.

"That is one of the surprises I have for you this evening."

"Please tell me, Joseph I cannot stand the suspense."

"I quess I can tell you so you can prepare yourself. Jenny Lind is going to be in Louisville and I have arranged for her to personally entertain everyone tonight," he said excitedly.

"Really? I am going to meet Jenny Lind, and hear her sing!"

"I have heard she sings like a nightingale, and I wanted this evening to be very special for you," smiled Joseph.

Margaret was very impressed with the idea of meeting Jenny Lind. Upon arrival at Joseph's home, she had pictured many scenes in her head, but what she was about to witness seemed quite overwhelming. Mr. Holt's estate filled several acres, with the most gorgeous gardens. A long lane of beautiful trees and yard manicured as neatly as a refined lady surrounded the home. Joseph pulled the team up at the front entrance, and helped Margaret descend from the carriage to the front door. Margaret thought, "Wickland was beautiful but this home was impressive." Entering the foyer, Margaret was greeted like royalty.

"Your room has been prepared and Lemure will handle your trunk. You will find what ever you need and when you have rested I'll be waiting for you on the grounds. Make yourself comfortable. If you need anything else, ask one of the servants."

When Margaret opened the door, her first thought was, "What a beautiful room!" Her eyes caught the enormous, dark walnut bed that extended to the ceiling, draped with beautiful netting, and soft quilts placed at the foot. A fainting couch stood at the foot of the bed. Water had been drawn in a huge tub with rose petals sprinkled in the water and fresh flowers filled crystal vases throughout the room. She walked over to touch the water thinking it was cold, but the water remained warm and had a sweet scent. She decided to wash off the dust from traveling and refresh herself.

No sooner had Margaret undressed and was enjoying her bath, then she heard a tap at the door. "Margaret, Margaret," the soft voice called. Margaret knew it was Joseph because no one would be calling on her now.

"Yes, Joseph, I hear you," said Margaret.

"I realize you are probably tired but I had hoped I could spend some time alone with you before the other guests arrive," said Joseph in whispered words.

"You must have read my mind Joseph because I was thinking the same thing," spoke Margaret quietly.

She added with a hint of excitement, "I just wanted to bathe and relax a few moments. It won't take me long."

"I'll be on the grounds. Please find me soon," said Joseph.

Relaxing in the tub, Margaret daydreamed, "Joseph really likes me. First he told me to take my time and then he came by my room and asked me to hurry up so we could be alone. It makes me nervous being in the same home with him. My feelings are so happy and my emotions are high. I have never felt like this before. Everything seems brighter and happier when I am with Joseph or just planning to be. Even small things are a wonder when you have someone to share your thoughts, and your day becomes an adventure." Focusing to the present, Margaret hurried back to reality.

Moments later she dressed and walked down the stairs. She realized Joseph's home had wonderful comforts. He had just returned from a short walk and met her in the parlor. "It will be several hours before the guests arrive. Would you like to set on the terrace or stroll through the gardens, Margaret?"

"Please call me Maggie, I prefer it," smiled Margaret. "I would love to see your gardens, for the smell of roses encircles your home." Joseph observed Margaret as they walked. Her windblown hair fell softly against her face. He realized, once again, Margaret's elegance. Songbirds called to each other as if answering the beckoning of another from yet a distant meadow. Leaves on the tree moved graciously as pale blue skies surrounded the distant fields. The sun's reflection enlightened Margaret's face. Joseph reached for her hand. "Maggie you're beautiful. May I have a kiss today or must I wait in torture for yet another time?"

"Normally I would say wait, but you have been such a gentleman, such a handsome entertainer, you may kiss me."

Joseph moved closer to Maggie gently kissing her lips. Could it be that his emotions had surfaced once again? Could love be as exciting the second time? Was it possible to love another woman as much as he had

Gravesite of Judge Advocate General Joseph Holt, Breckinridge County, Kentucky. Courtesy of Kentucky Heritage Council.

The tombstone of Mary Harrison Holt, Joseph Holt's first wife, located in Bardstown, Kentucky. The inscription reads death date May 17, 1846, however, the death certificate indicates May 16, 1846.

Above: Susan Dyer standing at the grave of Margaret Wickliffe Holt, Joseph Holt's second wife.

Grave of Gov. Charles Anderson Wickliffe, father of Margaret Wickliffe Holt and father-in-law of Joseph Holt.

Gravesite of Edward Stone, slaver Kentuckian who made a profit from trading slaves in the south. He was killed on his last trip to the south, when slaves overtook his flatboat at Stephensport, KY, six miles north of the Holt House.

Susan Dyer standing on the remains of the limestone tower, "Summer Seat," the highest point in Breckinridge County.

The Smith-Harrison House, home of Holt's first wife, Mary Harrison Holt, daughter of the distinguished Dr. Burr Harrison of Bardstown.

Wickland, home of Holt's second wife, Margaret Wickliffe Holt, daughter of Gov. Charles Anderson Wickliffe of Bardstown.

An accomplishment this year.

Communiqué

2006 KENTUCKY'S MOST ENDANGERED HISTORIC PLACES ANNOUNCED

Seven sites and two broad categories of historic resources were identified as Preservation Kentucky, Inc. announced its 2006 list of Kentucky's Most Endangered Historic Places today in Frankfort. The

Holt House is selected as one of the 2006 Most Endangered Historic Places in Kentucky.

historic architectural, cultural and archeological resources in Kentucky that are in imminent danger of being lost or demolished. "Endangered" places are often threatened by neglect, demolition or insensitive public policy and are in need of special attention and creative solutions for a return to viability in their communities. By creating public attention for these threads of the state's historic and cultural fabric, Preservation Kentucky hopes to propel existing efforts and encourage grass roots advocacy on behalf of these historic treasures.

The 2006 Kentucky's Most Endangered list includes a new feature of highlighting special "Preservation Opportunities." These sites are historic properties currently seeking a new owner or investor for which demolition is not eminent, but could happen if the buildings do not find new owners in the near future.

During a press conference in the Capitol Rotunda, Joanna Hinton, executive director of Preservation Kentucky, Inc. said, "Preservation Kentucky has attempted to highlight properties that are historically significant, endangered

New Castle (Henry County)

Masonic Temple
Paducah

Kentucky's Rural Cemeteries
Statewide

East End Neighborhood
Lexington

100 Block of West Main Street
Louisville

Owens Hotel
Horse Cave (Hart County)

Judge Joseph Holt House
Breckinridge County

Dickerson-Fennell Building
Newport

Historic Downtowns
Statewide

Properties identified as "Preser... Opportunities" include:

Patterson House
Henderson

Columbia and Arcade Theaters
Paducah

Oldham House
Lexington

The selection of the 2006 Kent... Most Endangered Historic Plac... fourth such listing by Preservat... Kentucky. Previous listings inc... former YWCA building in Louisv... Quonset Auditorium in Bowling... the Falls of Rough Mill in Breck... Tobacco Barns across... "Arena Block" also kno... Water Company Block in... been demolished ... after... matter the end result, each cir... caused a renewed focus and conversation on historic proper...

Nominations for the Kentucky's... Endangered... solicited fro... Preservation... Kentucky m... preservation... professional... preservation... organizations... individuals throughout the state...

More information about each s... additional photographs are ava... www.preservationkentucky.org.

Holt House

Preservation Kentucky *Magazine announcing the Holt House as One of the Most Endangered Historic Places In Kentucky. Courtesy of* Preservaton Kentucky.

Joseph Holt State Marker.

This is the quarter page Breckinrigde County ad for the Kentucky Travel Guide. *Courtesy of* The Herald-News.

The Holt House and the surrounding 19.5 acres is not officially owned by Breckinridge County Fiscal Court. The county, through two grants from the Kentucky Heritage Council and the state Lincoln Bicentennial Commission, paid $158,000 to the owners after two apprisals.

County acquires historic Holt House property

HOLT – County Judge/Executive Ray Powers announced on Friday that the ownership of the historic Holt House and the surrounding 19.5 acres of property now belong to the citizens of Breckinridge County.

This follows a three year effort by over 75 people led by retired school teacher, Susan Dyer, to purchase and restore the historic home which was built by the Holt family i 1811 which has been vacant for almost 50 years. (See Interesting Person story on page 3A)

The first move will be to stabilize the building by replacing windows and doors and then acquire grants to restore the exterior of the three story brick structure located on KY 144 about six miles north of the intersection with U.S. 60.

The county has partnered with the Preservation Office, Kentucky Historical Society, Kentucky Heritage Council and the Kentucky Lincoln Bicentennial Commission to work toward the restoration of the home.

Holt was born in Breckinridge County on January 6, 1811. His parents were John and Eleanor (Stephens) Holt and the house was the center of a large farming operation along the Ohio River.

His education consisted of St. Joseph's College at Bardstown and Centre College at Danville. Holt was a lawyer in Elizabethtown and later Louisville and there he became assistant editor of the Louisville Advertiser and also served as commonwealth's attorney.

Holt moved to Mississippi and was an attorney in Port Gibson and Vicksburg. His law practice was so lucrative that he was able to retire at age 35.

Returning to Louisville in 1842, Holt worked on behalf of the Democrat ticket of James Buchanan and John C. Breckinridge in 1856. Holt served as commissioner of patents, postmaster general and secretary of war in the Buchanan administration. As a staunch unionist, he worked to keep his home state from seceding during the Civil War.

President Abraham Lincoln promoted Holt to brigadier general and he became the head of the new Bureau of Military Justice. In that position, he served as the presiding judge during the trial of the Lincoln assassins. Holt died in Washington, D.C. on August 1, 1894 and his body was transported back to his native Kentucky for burial in the family cemetery adjacent to the Holt House.

The Herald-News
editorialthn@bbtel.com

Newspaper article titled: "County acaquires historic Holt House property." Courtesy of The Herald-News.

Kentucky Lincoln Heritage Trail Courtesy of the Kentucky Heritage Council and the Kentucky Abraham Lincoln Bicentennial Commission.

Susan Dyer working at the 2008 Kentucky State Fair as a volunteer, promoting the Kentucky Lincoln Heritage Trail and Holt House, listed on the trail as an official Lincoln Site.

Photos of Judge Joseph Holt's home in disrepair. All photos courtesy of Kentucky Heritage Council unless noted.

One of two spiral staircases. Courtesy of the Technical Educational Class of Cloverport Independent High School, Teacher Neil Tindel.

loved Mary? Did Maggie really love him or his wealth? Joseph always wondered if true love could surpass wealth.

The stolen kiss had made his spirit happy once again. Life was offering him many rewards, and he realized the opportunity for new happiness, but time was approaching for the party. Guests started arriving, and they were embraced with a feeling of being truly welcome in Mr. Holt's home.

As the socializing and conversations began among the guests, musicians began to organize their positions nestled under the stairs so guests could move about without interfering. Soft tunes of classical music, played on violins, gave the home a friendly and comfortable atmosphere. Servants brought out the best of foods and fine wines. Then Joseph Holt called for the guests' attention and introduced the performer: "It gives me great pleasure to introduce one of the most loved singers in the world today. I am deeply honored to introduce Miss Jenny Lind from Sweden." The double parlor rooms became silent and then a loud applause for the remarkable opera singer who delighted the guests with her warm and coloratura voice. Miss Lind performed three selections and the guests warmly received her. It was a memorable time Margaret would always remember. Joseph had been clever to book Miss Lind for a personal performance rarely heard of.

The violins played sweet music with happy melodies for the remainder of the evening. As most of the guests had left and things settled, Joseph and Margaret spent the next few hours alone, talking and enjoying each other's company. All too soon, it seemed, Margaret said a friendly good night.

A few other guests spent the night, and the next morning they awoke to a delightful breakfast. Margaret, dressed by a quarter to seven, was used to getting up early, and this morning the birds helped her awake to sounds of beautiful harmony.

Later that morning, Joseph asked, "Margaret, would you like to take a ride through Louisville and we can return for a lunch out on the terrace?"

"I would love that. It is not often I get to visit the tenth largest city in the nation?"

Margaret thought, admiringly, "Joseph enjoys showing me the nice places, and he is so much fun to be around. I don't usually have this much fun on Sundays. It's nice to have a change, to get out and see summer springing up everywhere. I have so much to tell Nannie, Julia, Ma, and Pa about my trip."

Joseph and Margaret returned to his home and enjoyed a small lunch. Realizing she needed to catch the afternoon stage, Joseph said, "Maggie, I wish you didn't have to go. I could send your Pa a telegram and see if he would permit you to stay longer, but I feel like he would want you to return."

Margaret was surprised that she had a sad feeling about leaving. It seemed like she had just arrived. Saturday and Sunday had gone entirely too fast. Joseph escorted Margaret to the stage office and waited until she left. About twenty minutes out of the city Margaret noticed the fields of grasses growing tall. There seemed to be a haze and light blue clouds were beginning to gather. In the center were sections of white with pink tones. Margaret joined in the conversation about how humid the day had been for this time of year. "Yes, I surely hope we don't have an afternoon thunderstorm."

A heavy breeze blowing through the stage window didn't seem to help much in cooling the stage. Margaret remarked, "There seems to be more dust coming in than fresh air." She noticed a robin setting on top of a dinner bell as the stage passed a small house snuggled close to the open road.

Margaret observed the patterned treetops with formations of unusual shapes and her thoughts wandered. The city had been busy and noisy. She looked forward to the comforts of home. Turning back to the scenery outside the stage, Margaret spied a herd of cattle following each other in single file, probably moving to a shady area with good water. Pa always complained about cattle following the same trail each day, causing paths in the fields.

Pa would be full of questions and Margaret knew she would feel as if she were on the witness stand. This spelling trip had given her the most freedom she had ever experienced. Just then her reflections ended, for the team of horses seem to pick up pace, and the passengers on the stage noticed that perhaps the stage driver was trying to gain time hoping to beat a looming thunderstorm. The skies darkened, as the trees began swaying, and the wind's sudden blowing made it difficult to keep the horses steady.

Conditions worsened as the driver pulled the team to the side of the roadway. Speaking loudly because of the wind, the stage driver spoke with caution, "Ladies and gentlemen, this storm is making it too dangerous to drive. I am afraid the stage might tip over so I am requesting that we all get off of the stage and I will unhitch the teams and try to find a suitable place to tie them." Margaret spoke with fear, "Sir, you don't mean that you are asking us to dismount the stage and step out in the open. We do not have any shelter or any place to seek refuge."

The stage driver shouted, "Ma'am, we don't have a choice. The wind is getting out of control. We are safer on the ground than aboard this stage." At that moment a gust of wind almost tipped the stage and the passengers began rushing off. An older gentleman on the stage told the passengers this wind was more than a gust. He said he feared a tornado. Everyone ran for the nearest ditch to lie low trying to prevent being blown away.

The stage driver was having a hard time holding on to the horses. The reins had become as tangled as a young child's uncombed hair. The horses were rearing and were now spooked and out of control. One of the horses jerked away and Margaret, a good horsewoman, managed to grab the reins. Chaos abounded. One of the women from the stage was screaming and trying to make it to a ditch. The wind howled louder, making sounds like the sea tossing massive waves on huge rocks. A young man from the stage spied a barn about a quarter of a mile away and hollered, "We can make it to the barn if everyone moves fast."

The passengers from the stage ran with fear. The force from the wind made it difficult just to balance as they ran. A mother held her child with all of her strength, but as they wind increased, it pulled the child out of the mother's arms and sucked her away. The screaming mother had to be dragged to the barn by the older man.

Something told Margaret not to follow the others, and she instead jumped on the horse and rode as fast as she could. A powerful force tugged to pull her off the horse. However, she fought with all of her might and held on to the saddle horn of the horse. The horse was running against the wind, and Margaret feared she would be blown away also. A tornado began forming a small distance from her. Its power picked up the horse and lifted Margaret about ten or fifteen feet above the ground. With the darkened sky, blowing wind, and sound of thousands of oceans, Margaret realized her life could end any moment.

Still cloudy amid the confusion, she remembered her grandfather who once told how as a boy, he survived a tornado. It was as if it was yesterday and Margaret was a small child. She began to pray for help, "Dear God, please forgive me of my sins and please spare me, in Jesus name I pray." Margaret continued to hear the whirling wind above her head and was afraid to look.

Remembering her grandfather's story, Margaret could hear him saying, "If ever out in a tornado and without shelter, find the smallest bush or tree you can and hang on to it." Margaret raised her head just enough to try and see, but the thick dust made everything pitch black. She heard the increasingly deadly roar and began crawling, extending her arms feeling for a bush. Finally, Margaret grasped a small tree and hugged it with all of her strength. She hoped the mighty wind would blow over the small tree and spare her.

In the distance Margaret could hear a horse crying out. And then the winds began to weaken and Margaret tried opening her eyes to see the dreadful sight before her. But when things seemed quieter, then the noise started again. This time sounds of cattle bawling, and heavy metal twisting and turning through the air frightened Margaret even more. The raging storm now dropped heavy hail, beating down on Margaret's skin as if rocks were being tossed like seeds from a tree. When her environment finally became visible, Margaret was shocked. Ten huge trees filled the ditch in which everyone had first thought to hide. What was in front of her? She tried to figure out her suddenly changed surroundings. Could that be the barn? Did the others make it there? It was a building of some kind, without a roof, and only one side remained. As the dust settled, she could see some type of an image. Was it a person? Did anyone else survive? Slowly, one at a time, some of the passengers stood in front of what seemed to be the remains of the barn. A woman was weeping but seemed to be all right. The older man had a large gash on his forehead. The driver had vanished.

Margaret rushed as fast as she could to help the others. The horse's cry became louder, piercing Margaret's heart, for she could not stand to see or hear an animal suffer. She remembered Pa and how he would shoot a horse that had broken a leg or could not get well, to put the animal out of his misery. But where was the horse and who had a gun? After checking the survivors and realizing everyone was accounted for except the stage driver and a small child, Margaret spoke with courage to the older gentleman, "Sir, do you have a pistol on you? We must find that pitiful creature and relieve it. It is in dreadful pain, and it may be the horse that saved my life."

"Ma'am, I never carry a weapon and it may be too dangerous to get close to the horse we hear."

Margaret yelled, "We have to search and find that horse. We can't leave it to die alone in pain."

"Do what you think you must, but I need to tend to this lady," said the older man.

"She will be fine, but you stay with her and I will try to locate the horse." The horrible sound of a horse fighting for its life could be heard for at least a half of a mile. Fearful, Margaret followed the lingering noise that sounded like something was tearing its heart.

To her surprise when she finally reached the sound, the horse was lodged between two huge trees with its harnesses tangled in a mass of briers. The horse was fighting fiercely but could not free itself. Margaret realized she could not handle this horse herself. As she ran breathlessly for help, she finally reached a small farm where, safely sheltered together, a large family, stood out in the yard.

The farmer called out to Margaret, "Are you all right young lady?"

"Yes sir, just frightened somewhat. I need help, can you help me?"

"What kind of help do you need?" asked the farmer.

"There is a horse trapped and tangled, and if we don't get it loose it is going to injure itself, maybe even break its leg," called Margaret.

"Give me a minute. I will take my gun just in case we are too late." The farmer yelled to the oldest son, "Get the horse from the barn and saddle it." The farmer and Margaret rode together and reached the horse. The horse had gotten into terrible tangles with its head low and its feet in the air. "I do not see any way to rescue this animal ma'am," said the farmer.

"We can't just shoot the horse. We have to try," screamed Margaret.

"I don't see any help here ma'am, and it is too dangerous for me to try alone."

"But, you have to. You can't kill the horse just because you are frightened. I was frightened today, too, but we must save this animal."

"Ma'am, I told you before there is no choice but to put this animal out of its misery," said the farmer again.

"I won't let you do it. You are not going to shoot an innocent horse because he is tangled. You know the storm did this, and we are going to save him," said Margaret bravely.

"You are the most stubborn woman I have ever seen," the farmer replied. "What do you suppose we can do then?"

"First, we must think quickly on how we can loosen the reins. Then we must carefully and slowly help the horse pull itself up away from the trees." After six attempts and no success, the farmer and Margaret agreed there was nothing else they could do. The farmer took his shotgun off of his horse and walked close to the horse, aiming at the head. Margaret covered her eyes waiting for the dreadful shot to ring out, when a voice shouted, "I think I can help."

Margaret uncovered her eyes and gasped, coming over the ridge was the stage driver, leading three of the horses. With the efforts of both men, and after a lot of work, they saved the horse. The passengers gathered and rode to Shelbyville for shelter for the night while others in the neighborhood tried to find the missing child blown out of her mother's arms during the tornado.

The stage had been turned upside down, but with help of all it was up righted. The horse that had been freed was hitched to the back of the stage. It was only a few miles to town and the boarding house put up all of the travelers for the night.

Throughout the night the search continued. Men in the small community explored every rock, every bush, and every creek bed but could not find a trace of the child. Tired from no sleep, and nearly ready to give up, the group decided to return to the spot where the travelers first had taken shelter from the storm. To their surprise and relief the small girl was setting in the top of a tree with scratches and bruises, but seemed to be fine. One of the young men climbed the tree and helped lower the child with the help of the other men. Crying and frightened, with dirt covered from flying debris, the child reunited with its relieved mother.

This day would be unforgettable, a memory etched into Margaret's heart for the rest of her life. The news reached Wickland about the fierce storm, and Margaret's family set out to find her when the stage did not reach Bardstown. In her heart Margaret knew Pa would soon be there. She would have many stories to tell about this adventure, and would write soon to tell Joseph about surviving the tornado.

The next morning Pa arrived in a carriage to take Margaret home. She was quite untidy with her hair rearranged. Her blue dress resembled that of a battlefield nurse who had been in a line of danger. Pa gave her a huge hug and helped her into the carriage.

"Pa, I wondered at one time yesterday if I would ever see my family again," said Margaret.

"We knew something was wrong when the stage didn't show up at all. At first we thought it was late but then without any appearance we began to worry" echoed her father with his strong, deep voice.

"Thanks to Grandpa Crepps I am still alive by remembering one of his many stories," Margaret said as she smiled.

"And which one would that be?" asked Pa.

"You remember the one he has told a hundred times about him holding on to a little bush and the tornado blowing the horse away. Well, that story saved my life yesterday. I did exactly like he said and it saved my life," said Margaret.

"Well, that is over and we are glad you are safe. We'll be home soon."

The rest of the way seemed like eternity. The bumpy road jarred Margaret from one side of the seat to the other. Pa seemed in a hurry to get home. She rested and seemed glad her father was taking care of her. The muddy road caused the carriage to become a dreadful sight. As they came to a creek higher than normal because of the rain, Pa and Margaret waited for the water to fall, so they would make a safe crossing. She wanted to be at home so much. They were only one mile from the lane. Finally Pa said, "I think we can get across the creek now. We will go very slowly." The horses pulled the buggy through the high water, but the flooded creek caused the buggy to rise forward. Would another disaster occur on this trip? But with a final lunge, the horses brought them through.

Margaret couldn't remember a more welcomed sight than Wickland. Home at last. She did not want to leave for a long time, but after a few days of rest, Margaret was herself once more and decided to enjoy the outside to help relieve the stress she had suffered.

"Margaret, where are you?" called her sister Nannie from the house.

"I'm outside enjoying this beautiful day," said Margaret. "How can you stay inside when it is so gorgeous out here? Want to go for a walk?" asked Margaret.

"Sure," said Nannie. "Let me first run and tell Ma. I won't be long."

Near the house, on a small, distant path, a pond delivered ripples as the wind skated over the water tops. Bright sparkles of silver illuminated the water's surface as if playing a melody of many notes with the reversal of wind changing the melody of the song. It was good to wander and collect personal thoughts instilled within your heart.

"Nannie, I am having a hard time deciding on what to do."

"What do you mean, Margaret?"

"Decisions are difficult to make. How can I be certain about how my heart feels?"

"You must trust your feelings," said Nannie.

"Pa always told me to follow my heart, use my mind, and be true to my feelings."

Margaret realized Joseph wanted her to set a wedding date and he sought her response. She could decide on her own, or wait and let Pa get involved with the commitment.

Joseph wanted a reply to be sent to his summer home at Stephensport, where he resided beside the beautiful Ohio River. Margaret knew the wait would be painful for Joseph, awaiting her answer, yea or nay. Both girls went into the house, and Margaret made her way up the stairs. Ma was standing at the top of the curving stairs of oak close to Margaret's bedroom when she quietly strolled over to the side chair next to the bed and smiled at Margaret. "You know how much Mr. Holt adores you and he dearly appreciates you. Your Pa is impressed with his wisdom and he comes from a prominent family. You would never want for any luxury and he is such a gentleman of etiquette and up-bringing."

"Yes Ma, I truly understand and I am impressed with everything about Joseph. My heart feels weak when I get near him. He is tall, slim, and very attractive. But I am not sure I am ready to be the wife he would expect me to be. He is a statesman and into politics and there would be times of traveling where I would be alone while he would be off working on bills for the country," stated Margaret.

"Sweetheart, you know your Pa and I would never pressure you to rush into something you were not comfortable handling. I think it is only natural to have second thoughts about marriage. You will always be welcome here and when you do marry you could always come home to stay while Joseph travels for important government business," said Ma, reassuring Margaret.

Later that night Margaret fell fast asleep to dream. She realized Joseph had been aching from her departure. Dear Joseph was a patient and loving man who had told her in his last letter he would be perfectly content with her determination whatever it might be. She realized men can't wait forever, and it would be unladylike to lead him on in regard of the arrangement of an engagement. Margaret knew Joseph was ready to take a wife or go on. Was she ready to be a wife to fulfill his desires and passion? Margaret could imagine seeing Joseph standing at the front Iron Gate of his childhood home in Breckinridge County as if he were waiting for her to appear. Margaret suddenly awoke.

Then and there Margaret decided to respond to Joseph at that moment. Finally Margaret put on paper what truly came from her heart.

> Saturday, March 1, 1850
>
> My Beloved Joseph,
>
> I find more with each day that I cannot stay content at Wickland, the home I so love, without you. As the song birds serenade one another my longing for you grows with each word I write.
>
> With the disappointment which I could not help feeling from your letter received Friday past has rendered me almost unfit for writing. I somehow feel pressure even though you said you would wait patiently for my reply. I feel I must make a decision in haste. I do not wish you to come for me dear Joseph if it is not entirely convenient and agreeable, though I did hope in three weeks for you would find it so and enjoy at least one week at Wickland. However, you say different. Ma insists I ought not to go to parties with you until you are free to visit us all at Wickland and let us know each other more.
>
> I find my growing anxiety to see you has put a stop to all of the improvements, if ended any was begun, and I am therefore resolved to quit Wickland just to be with you. As soon as you receive this line from me, be assured I do want you to return to spend reserved time with me at Wickland and hopefully we can sit down loving together and name early a day for consuming our happiness agreeable to us.
>
> I feel I have not wounded your pride but so in exploring our love I will become only yours and yours alone on the night we

wed. I am delighted that I bring you pleasure and I will surely again permit you to present yourself in my presence as together we will decide without the open subject to be controlled by Pa's return home.

You are my most devoted and I will give my heart and being to you when you return and restore my confidence as your loving wife to be.

Maggie

After writing the love letter Margaret fell asleep and had to be awakened the next morning by her mother. The following day went by too fast as Margaret had let the morning slip away by oversleeping. The afternoon passed, as fast as the breezes blew.

As the day drew near to sunset, the wind's force could be felt as well as seen in the movement of the tall field grasses. Cedar trees lined the main road from town in a mixture of tall, short, thick, and bare.

Uncle Crepps returned with the day's mail he had picked up at the store. Running to the front of the house, Julia, always wanting to accept responsibility and to act older than she was, begged for the mail. With the last sunshine of the day making reflections on the leaded glass with rolls of prisms surrounding the entrance, she called out, "Margaret, Margaret."

"I'm upstairs Julia. What do you want now?" said Margaret impatiently.

"Well, it is certainly fine with me if you don't read the letter from your Mr. Holt that Crepps brought," snarled Julia. "Do you want it really bad? Then you will have to catch me!" screamed Julia.

Margaret yelling, "Bring my letter now or I will never take you with me again as long as I live."

The yelling and noise of running up and down the stairs caught the attention of Louise, the house servant. "Now you two stop this now before your Ma finds out about this chasing and wrecking the household," warned Louise with a firm tone.

Finally, at last, Julia handed Margaret the letter as she made her escape to her room on the second floor.

With trembling hands Margaret opened the sealed letter from Joseph. What would he say? Would he make an extensive trip all the way from

Breckinridge County to Bardstown and stay for a week at Wickland with more than enough chaperones to play out his every move. The letter began...

March 7, 1850

My most adorable Maggie,

Upon receipt of your letter I am willing to accommodate your wishes and will therefore be a true and tried guest of you and yours at Wickland. I have all faith in your letter dreams and want most to accept your undivided attention granting me graduations for pursuing more time, with less stress, when my heart of hearts can intertwine with your passion granting me wisdom of uniting our love for the happiness of our kindred spirits to be bound for eternity. Upon receipt of this letter I will surely be approaching Wickland as if carried on wings by the angels to reunite with my dear Maggie.

Your Most Devoted

J. Holt

Wedding Bells

The serenity of peace is a blessed feeling. Taking a few moments from her daily schedule, Margaret sat on the steps of the big house. On lazy afternoons she enjoyed being alone.

What carefree lives eagles have, she thought, as three flew over the edge of the yard! Trees were as still as dried-out stalks in the cornfield. Mother Nature had painted a perfect scene of baby blue skies with sunrays as bright as ivory tusk.

Why had Margaret's life become so complex? Why did things have to change so rapidly? Why couldn't she just live at Wickland a few more years and enjoy all the other weddings held each year at her home? Did true love only come one time in life or would you believe you were in love only to find someone else you might have been happier with in destiny?

Ma and Pa seemed to be happy enough. It must be true love or Margaret's heart could not feel so depressed and down from the absentness of Joseph. Margaret could tell by the way Joseph looked at her he was truly devoted to her.

It was scary for Margaret. Joseph had been wed before and his life had been filled with much pain when he lost his first wife Mary Harrison to tuberculosis. Trying to ease the pain, he had traveled extensively to Paris, explored Europe, saw the Nile River, and desperately tried to bury his pain with his gallant travels as he was trying to bring the passion for living, restoring his life once again with laughter and happiness.

The fragrance lingered on in the aftermath of the morning. "Oh my heart overflows, can I not make the moment last longer, sending out life's daily changes of fulfilling the dreams of my ancestor's great inspirations of living life the way it was planned to be lived?" wrote Margaret in her diary.

Around her, the plow digs deep into the soil giving the remembrance of spring. Clouds gather, forming new unions of magnificent growth, and the possibility of an afternoon shower. The landscape is transforming as if by the brush of a Paris painter.

The gardener is steadfast working pulling out stubborn weeds, trying to hide the natural beauty of the radiant queen of the flowers. Bumblebees fly by carefully as if trying new fragrances atop the old apple tree in heavily, white bloom. The mocking bird is busy once again trying desperately to imitate the tune of other feathered friends.

The warmth of the day has caused all to migrate to the welcomed outdoors of happy and lingering days with pure, sweet air-lavender with crab apple and sweet briers restoring the complaining young folks of Bardstown.

Joseph would soon be on his way and it would take several days journey to reach Wickland. Hopefully, Joseph would travel by buggy because the dampness of the river normally caused him to get colds.

"Am I ready for a life change?" Margaret asked herself. It was almost as if her family was marrying Joseph. Margaret knew Joseph would be well received by the Wickliffe family, for he certainly met father's expectations of a suitable husband for her. But the doubts of a bride-to-be still filled her thoughts.

Margaret anticipated the arrival of Joseph. The family would have a few days to prepare for his visit. Mother put the cooks to work preparing the best foods. The guest room was aired, cleaned, and supplied with soaps and towels. The servants prepared Wickland for the welcome of Joseph Holt.

It was late in the day and Margaret wanted to get fresh air. She wrapped up in warm clothes to prepare for the March winds, and escaped to the outdoors. Standing at the end of the brick walk Margaret could see dust flying and hoped it would bring Joseph. A party of blackbirds amidst the treetops made a noise almost relating to music. Margaret heard horses snickering as they raced down the lane from the main road.

Joseph reached Wickland at dusk, just as things were settling down. Margaret felt faint just at the sight of him. Her captivating smile charmed him at first glance.

She warmly welcomed Joseph, as a servant took hold of the reins of his horses.

Stepping from his carriage, he picked her up by the waist and swirled her around. "Joseph what has gotten in to you? Ma will see," said Margaret blushing.

The young boy led the two horses to the horse barn nearest the house.

"I believe it's permissible to embrace the young lady I plan to make my own," said Joseph with blue eyes cutting a welcome glance.

"Maggie, I missed you so!

The evening lacked the sun's presence. Bright reflections from the covered sun made a perfect silhouette against mountains of clouds moving as if stacked mountain upon mountain. Most of the sky extended with a mixture of medium blue with traces of pink scattered. A frog croaking at the distant pond gave a loud welcome.

Walking, Joseph reached for Margaret's hand, "Look darling, a sign from heaven." Enormous rays of sunshine shone through thick cloud coverage, sending sparkles of pure white colors dazzling the back drop of the decorated scene. "It's beautiful, Joseph. Just like your letter said. The angels carried you here on their wings."

The couple walked up the sandstone entrance as the young servant boy took the team, cooled them down, and unharnesed them from their long journey from Breckinridge County.

Mr. Holt was received well by the Wickliffe family. After dinner the family retired to the double parlor and talked for several hours. Margaret's family rejoiced with Joseph's company. The next day, a wonderful southern breakfast was served, and on the second day after Joseph's arrival, Pa returned home. The two discussed politics and their views on the news in Washington.

On Sunday the family attended church. A barbeque was held on Wednesday, allowing friends to converse and the opportunity to meet Joseph. Two afternoons Joseph and Margaret took carriage rides into town, to get away from the hover. At the end of the week he approached Margaret at the front door. "Are you ready, Margaret, to walk through that door and into a new life as my wife?" spoke Joseph without any hesitation.

"Joseph, the thought has entered my mind for many days. Your goodness, patience, dashing smile, that first introduction at the ball invited me into your heart. I am torn between two worlds, the only world I have known, my family, Wickland and now you. I realize I must choose,

Joseph." As the couple opened the door, Margaret pointed to the formation of two sets of clouds, one of bright white and one of dark lavender with gray background. She declared, "I feel as our lives compare to the existence of the clouds. We will unite and these clouds will be as a promise of rainbows as our union of a happy life."

The wedding date was set for April 24, 1850. Margaret had little time to plan for the wedding.

Wickland had been the scene for many weddings, usually in early spring and late fall because of the humid summer temperatures in Kentucky. Ex-Governor Charles Anderson Wickliffe knew how to entertain, and this event would bring many distinguished guests from across the commonwealth as well as Washington City.

Margaret had always dreamed of taking her vows on the lawn under the gorgeous magnolia trees at Wickland. Since spring's early arrival, Mother Nature would have scenic decorations and arrays of sweet fragrance from lilac bushes and lilies.

With only one month to plan the wedding, everyone had a job. Mother had invited Judge Rowan's wife over to discuss the big day. "I will be glad to help with the guests and offer Federal Hill for late arrivals, or if you need additional rooms," offered Mrs. Rowan.

"That certainly is very kind of you my dear friend, to open your home for my family," said Mrs. Wickliffe.

"I could never repay you for giving my children, house servants, and me a safe haven just a few years ago, on that day when Mr. Rowan frightened us all with his intoxication and had that gun loaded. I had to protect my family and did not have another friend I could call upon," noted Mrs. Rowan, with wet eyes.

"It was my pleasure as a friend, and I know you don't want to talk about it, but I remember it as only yesterday. Margaret, Julia, Fannie, and I had just arrived home and barely removed the dust from traveling on the stage. You were terrified and the children were frightened. Judge Rowan was a good man but his drinking sometimes got out of hand."

"I know when we sent Crepps to town to find the sheriff to go and talk to him, Judge Rowan explained that he had the gun out because he was preparing for a hunting trip. No one believed that, and we were glad to have you and the children for our guest for two weeks," sighed Mrs. Wickliffe.

"All families have issues to deal with, some are open and some are kept in secret. I am glad we have a true friendship," winked Mrs. Wickliffe, and plans were laid.

Margaret's wedding gown was designed as a ballroom style made of satin with a chiffon overlay. The dress, embroidered with orange blossoms, had a floral trim stitched onto the dress. The chiffon hemline was embroidered with a scallop edging. The style had seven layers giving the skirt a ballroom gown shape. Orange blossoms and floral trim accented the wedding dress with a matching veil. An additional spray of flowers were placed in the bridal bouquet and would be worn in Margaret's hair.

Sister Julia composed hand-colored invitations announcing the marriage, and designed the ceremony bulletins. The bridesmaid's dresses had similar open-cut style dresses with less lace, similar to the bridal gown. All segments seemed completed for the wedding, the food, the home, and the minister. One week remained!

On Friday before the wedding, Joseph surprised Margaret with a most beautiful silver ring carved with dainty lace cuttings, and a rectangle-shaped diamond. Margaret would wear the beautiful gift on the most special day in her life.

But weddings affect not just the bride and groom. Margaret's father and mother had breakfast alone five days before the big event.

"Things are going to be different around here. Our Margaret has had such an active part in everything involving Wickland. She has assisted and coordinated most of the events of Wickland. I am happy for her, in one way, but I hate to give her up to a stranger," said Pa.

"Stranger? Charles, Joseph is no stranger. In fact it was you who invited Joseph to the spring ball."

"I have invited many young men to our home, but somehow I did not feel this would be the one."

"It's destiny, Charles. You raise daughters to grow up, and get married. It's part of life," Ma said.

"I know, but I have a reserved feeling."

Julia appeared, "What do you mean about having a reserved feeling Pa?"

"Oh, nothing I guess your Ma and I realize that it is Margaret's time to be happy and we will accept her happiness." And the discussion ended.

The wedding day arrived as the scene became reality. Distinguished guests bustled in carriages with the lane flooded with buggies. The lawn flowed with violin music, as Wickland came alive with spirit. A pale blue sky and a warm, gentle breeze graced the atmosphere.

Margaret's dream became reality as she made her entrance from the front doors of her home to the south lawn under the magnolia trees. The family pastor from the Presbyterian Church performed the ceremony. Selections from the brand new New Bridal Chorus from Wagner's Llohengrin and the Wedding March by Mendelssohn accompanied the wedding party as they marched away from the arch in the yard. A daguerreotype of Margaret was made on the steps of Wickland. A feast followed with many guests staying at Wickland. Joseph and Margaret departed on the evening stage to travel to Louisville, caught a steamer, and then to New York to board *The American Eagle* for a voyage to London for a two-year wedding trip.

Not long into the voyage Joseph began writing in his diary.

> Took leave of my beloved parent's home on the 2nd of April 1850. After a happy adjourn of a few days with my sister from whom I had been so long separated, journeyed to New York where I spent the most gloriest week of my life!
>
> On the first day of May Maggie and I sailed on the *American Eagle* and after a voyage of twenty-seven days we landed on British soil this 28th day of May in London. Oh! The awful seasickness! Let he who has never been seasick wish of a life on ocean's wave, the gorgeous sun and sunsets (neither of which were seen by me) boundary billows. But here we are in the greatest city of the world and in one of its most beautiful streets, Regent, with its elegant shops, and oh the tyrant of people and the thousands of articles of every description which pop continually from eleven in the morning until twelve and one at night. It is impossible for me to become accustomed to the abominable habits of these English people who convert the day into night. You might as well ask for the Queen's crown as for a cup of coffee before nine-o'clock and to dine before six at which hour the nobility are taking their morning naps.
>
> May 30, Visited today (the Tower of London) the most celebrated perhaps of the world. Many were imprisoned and beheaded here

such as Anna Boleyn, Diathermia Howard, Sir Thomas More, Arch Bishop Cranner, Lady Jane Gray and others. Sir Walter Raleigh wrote here his history of the world. The cell where he was confined is still exhibited. The Horse Armory is most interesting. The center is acerrpried by a line of eyestrain fryness, clothed in the Arms of the various reigns. Those assigned to Henry the Eighth, Prince of Wales, and Charles the 1st, are known to have been worn by them. That of Charles the 1st is the most magnificent; its richly designed work makes it magnificent. The regular contains the jewels worn by Victoria. This cap of purple velvet is enclosed by seven hoops, covered with diamonds, surrounding these hoops is a ball, around with small diamonds, forming a brilliant, center of which is a splendid sapphire. On the front of the crown is the heart formed and is said to have been worn by Edward the Black Prince. This crown is estimated one million pounds of sterling.

May 31, Took a steam boat ride and this is the only one of this kind in the world. Hence to Westminster Hall, where the courts have been held since the reign of Henry the 3rd. Tis here the coronation feasts of the sovereigns of England are held. Also celebrated as the hall in which many distinguished persons have been tried for high treason. Here Oliver Cornwall was inaugurated as Buske a Sheradess entranced thousands by their eloquence. A most amazinging sight to me was the lawyers who are all draped with long black gowns with most peculiar white wigs. Near this building Westminster Abbey where we see side-by-side the remains of Scientists and poets, sovereign statesmen and artists, the distinguished of all within this abbey are various chapels, the most interesting to me is that of Henry the 7th. Here tis side by side the lovely Mary Queen of Scots and Elizabeth her mistress. In this abbey the kings and queens have been crowned since Edward. The same affair for this ceremony has been used for five hundred years. We learned that the service was held every day at 3 o'clock, so took our seats and heard the chanting of the evening service. As we were leaving, a polite Englishman observing we were strangers asked if we would like to see the Duke of Wellington. This mark of politeness was as grateful as surprising since the English have not these reputations.

On June the 4th we drove to Hampton's Court through the beautiful village of Cruchmin where Thompson lived, where is buried the lean of his seasons, and where he now lives and is the home of Pope. A lovely place it is. This cottage is very similar to the ones we see in our own country.

The drive from Thince to the Hamptons is surprisingly beautiful. The celebrated avenue of horse chestnuts is about a mile in length. This leads distinctly to the gate of flowerpots upon the entrance to the grandness Victoria has given use by throwing open for the public. And a glorious privilege it is to strole through.

The 14th of June, 1850 was the first day at Oxford. This celebrated seat of universities and a celebrated day it is in spite of rain. We drove first to Blenheim, the magnificent estate of the Duke Marlborough. There are about three thousand acres. The palace is grand. We strolled around this splendor where everything to gratify the eye is.

July 6, Saturday, from Cambridge to London = the happiest day of my life.

July 7, Sabbath, attended worship in the great Weblin Ohippel.

July 8, spent the morning arranging trunks.

July 9, spent a profitable morning in reading. Afternoon strolled through the St. James Parks.

September 24, churches, churches, churches, Leonardo da Vince's Last Supper.

October14, 15, In Rome

October 16, Letters from home.

October 18, In my room sewing.

October 19, Visited St. Peters.

October 20, A quiet Sabbath in our room, Strolled on the hills.

October 21, St. Peters.

October 22, Visited tombs.

October 26, Portraits. Portraits, portraits.

November 14, Left Rome for Naples.

November 18, Rain.

November 19, Tuesday, shopping in Naples.

November 20, Wednesday, visited the Castle Sant' Elm.

November 23, Mount Vesuvius.

November 24, Sabbath, reading.

November 29, To Resina.

November 30, To Salerno.

December 7, 8, 9, 10, 11, and 12, to Alexandria.

December 25, Reached the sight of the metropolitan of upper Egypt.

December 26, Only made five miles today, the delicious air, with gracious palms growing all so unlike any part of the world.

December 28, Today safraied several villages, like all of the towns in Egypt, a mile of mud houses, miserable raged men and woman without one future of comfort. The palms alone in groves.

December 31, This last day of 1850 has been spent most pleasantly & I trust profitably, only about 21 miles to Thermopolis.

January 1, 1851, filled with the saddest recollection!

January 6, after an early breakfast just strolled on shore for an hour. The romance of this river voyage is quickly dissipated by setting foot on shore where the soul becomes powered with emotions as we wade from village to village.

Joseph and Margaret Wickliffe Holt experienced so much on their wedding trip throughout Europe, exploring the Nile River, and had many adventurous travels on water and land. This experience would last a lifetime, as they saw grand things, as well as much poverty.

After traveling in Europe from 1850 through 1852, the couple returned home to Louisville, Kentucky, where they remained until the move to Washington, D.C. In April 1857, Joseph transferred his residence from Louisville to Washington City, receiving an appointment as Commissioner of Patents by President James Buchanan.

Postmaster General

In 1859, President James Buchanan commissioned Joseph Holt the Postmaster General of the United States. All across the country newspapers from Buffalo, St. Louis, Louisville, Washington, Memphis, Milwaukee, New York, New Orleans, and elsewhere praised the appointment. In general, they stated that Holt would be fair, honest, and dependable, that he would not be led astray, and that his high intelligence would allow him to head the United States Postal Service in a professional way.

Leading newspapers quoted his works, stating it would be impossible to induce him to swerve from the path of rectitude. His oratory, his rare endowments of mind, and his high moral attitudes made him one of the most singular exceptions to political preferment, they argued. The nation had reason to rejoice, the papers expressed, for Joseph Holt would fail in nothing that he undertook.

They noted that as an advocate before the courts, he had had no superior, and then as prosecuting attorney in Louisville he had been terror to all evildoers. Never a candidate before the people for offices, (although frequently pressed to become such), he had never asked for office at the hands of any administration.

Without solicitation upon his part, the stories emphasized he had been invited to accept the office of Commission of Patents, and through his faithfulness, efficiency, and devotion to the complicated duties of that position, he had impressed President James Buchanan.

Upon the death of the postmaster general, the chief executive had invited Holt to assume that most responsible and most arduous office. The new Postmaster General, they said, wanted to do justice, and to promote the national interest to all areas of the nation. High praise indeed, but would that translate into success?

Beginning in March, Postmaster General Joseph Holt addressed his employees in an appropriate and eloquent manner,

"Gentleman, standing upon the threshold of this difficult and,

> for me, wholly untried field of labor, I am most happy in the privilege of making the personal acquaintances of those who are to be associated with me in its duties. The lose of a faithful and illustrious public servant who was beloved of all has clothed this high office in mourning, and it is sad, inexpressibly sad, to enter upon it amid the shadows which hang alike upon it and upon the hearts of those charged with its administration. It is encouraging, however, to know that behind every cloud the sun still shineth, that if we are patient every cloud shall see its light again. I must earnestly invoke what I shall constantly need, and will no doubt, as constantly receive your zealous cooperation in meeting the heavy and perplexing responsibilities which lie before me. Be assured that it will be my unceasing endeavor to guard the feelings and reputation that rights and interest of all within and without, and at the same time, steadily inflexibly to pursue the path of duty wherever it may conduct me."

Holt did work tirelessly to secure the trust of all employees, and worked for the interest of the common citizens, always trying to give his best effort to make the postal system self-sufficient. In large part he succeeded. After Holt had taken over the position as Postmaster General, following the death of Governor Aaron V. Brown, Americans all across the country read articles from newspapers expressing how the nation felt secure and gratified having a public servant such as Joseph Holt protecting the interest and future of the country, as well as saving over $1 million to the United States Postal Office, providing better and faster service, illuminating handling the mail too many times causing delays, resulting in higher prices. Holt read newspapers as well.

On returning to his home on New Jersey Avenue and C Street, he picked up the evening newspaper that had arrived from Paulding, Mississippi. Editor S. R. Adams spoke of how President Buchanan had appointed Joseph Holt, the late Commission of Patents, to be Postmaster General, in place of Governor Aaron V. Brown, deceased. The editor's appointment would be recognized throughout the country by anyone who had ever heard of Holt as a most excellent one, and perhaps the greatest that could possibly have been made.

Over and over, Joseph's quite massive talents were recognized. A skillful business man and one of the most eloquent men in the United States, he had gained power with the Democratic Party, and the President who realizing this had placed him head of the Patents Office, and now Postmaster General.

With standards set extremely high by the press and with the weight of this responsible position, Holt realized his past career with the bar where he acquired fame as an orator and jurist in the southwest meant that now he was starting over again.

Holt enjoyed working, and felt it his duty to serve his country, to find errors of the system, and to root out abuses in government. He possessed high levels of energy and displayed the highest integrity in the task before him, with knowledge that he alone must bear responsibility. No political party would be able to sway him to defer from anything conflicting with the public interest. He was his own man.

It was not easy making a commitment to serve the nation, realizing your job many times meant being separated from the ones who were dear to you. Joseph missed sharing the rays of sunshine, touching the windows with the curtains of lace that gave bright patterns of roses, which Margaret had decorated upon their move to Washington, but with Margaret suffering with tuberculosis, she had moved back to Kentucky, to be close to her family, trying to regain her strength.

Empowered by the work of the Post Office, Joseph seemed to escape the pains of loneliness, while taking moments on his way to work enjoying nature, as Margaret and he once did together. As gentle breezes guided the swaying trees, they brought back happy memories for him as he remembered carriage rides around Washington, and strolling through beautiful formal gardens with her.

Letter writing helped Holt stay in touch and share his personal thoughts with Margaret. Her father had served as Postmaster General under President Tyler, and often sent positive encouragement to Joseph for the excellent work he was accomplishing for the country. Unfortunately, Holt found corruption within the United States Post Offices. His mission had been to clean up the Post Office and restore the public faith in the system once more, while saving taxpayers money. He would find much work to do.

One widely publicized case during Holt's term as Postmaster General involved Gideon G. Westcott, postmaster at Philadelphia. In the second quarter of 1857, Mr. Westcott discovered a deficit in the cash in hand compared with the accounts of the receipts of his office of over $1,525.00. He did not know if the money had been stolen by clerks or by others. However, Westcott held the clerks and the others responsible for the loss and withheld the amounts from the salaries of fifty-seven employees. He did this, concealing it from the department, by having clerks sign receipts blank and afterwards filled in the sums that amounted to the loss. He thus covered up the deficits while deceiving the department, and punishing innocent clerks for the offence of the guilty.

The cover-up stayed concealed until it was discovered deep in the archives of the Post Office in Philadelphia two years later, in 1859. President Buchanan quickly removed Westcott from office. This brought charges against Buchanan that he had removed Westcott on political grounds, without sufficient cause.

Postmaster General Holt, supporting President Buchanan and the United States Post Office, published an answer to complaints made by Westcott and his friends. On May 17, 1859, the response explained that his removal came after finding a deficit in the cash in hand compared with the accounts of the receipts of his office. Mr. Westcott, not knowing who had taken the money, held all the employees and clerks responsible, and had held amounts from salaries of fifty-seven employees.

As one paper noted, "Mr. Holt showed there was no justification upon the innocent and guilty, to cover up a loss for which the Postmaster was responsible, rendering himself liable to a prosecution under the act of Congress, declaring that any officer accepting, receiving, or transmitting to the Treasury Department, to be allowed in his favor, any receipt or voucher from a creditor of the United States, without having paid the full amount shall be, on conviction, sentenced to not less than six months or more than two years, paying a fine equal to the amount embezzled." With those facts the President had Westcott removed.

Holt exhibited stern virtue. When he published the letter about Westcott, he discussed the code of official morals, which the integrity of the government demanded:

> Sir, since my communication addressed to you on the third in relation to charges prepared against Gideon G. Westcott, he has filed in this department various affidavits and a printed argument in his

> defense, which have been thoroughly examined and considered. The case is now regarded as closed.
>
> The inquiry did not result in attaching suspicion to any one employee of the office more than to another. Mr. Westcott, in his letter to this Department of the 9th February, 1859, speaking of the deficit, used this language, 'It then became clear that considerable sums had been abstracted from the tills, but whether by the clerks in charge of them or by others it was impossible to tell in an office where the money is necessarily much exposed, and where more than a hundred persons had free access to it before it was returned to me.'
>
> The transaction arresting attention is an act of official oppression. Mr. Westcott had no right legally to take money from the salaries which was enforced, until he knew who had embezzled from the post office. The clerks were not liable criminally or civilly for the peculation of one or more of their number, is a proposition clear, both in law and morals. The clerks continued work, without voicing this because they feared their employment.
>
> The position taken in the defense and urged by Mr. Westcott was he derived no benefit from the act—is signally fallacious. It had been misfortune to suffer a heavy pecuniary loss from theft or embezzlement, and for the amount lost he was directly responsible to the Government. However, he chose that the liability should be met from employees and not from his private funds.

"Westcott" Holt remarked, "was" an officer charged with the disbursement of public monies. However well the transaction may have been known to the parties immediately concerned, its true character was intended to be concealed from the government, and was so concealed for between two and three years. When, in the course of events, and from the irrepressible nature of the truth, the deception was exposed.

"This is a growing evil," noted Holt, "for the repression of which too much solicitude cannot be felt or too much vigilance exercised." From the 251st section of the Rules and Regulations of the Post Office Department, Westcott knew that he was entitled to no "allowance or remuneration for losses by fire, robbery, or theft." The Postmaster General concluded, "The whole administration of the Government reposes upon the integrity and truthfulness of the vouchers furnished by its disbursing officers."

"Neither the proofs nor the argument offered by the defense vary essentially the original aspects of the case. The clerks were his agents, and held their offices at his will, and he was liable for their conduct. Their receipt of the funds was his receipt, and their custody of them his custody."

When the department communicated to Westcott the charge against him, he responded with a stout and emphatic denial. His letter to Postmaster General Holt, dated February 2, 1859, opened with the following language, "I content myself today with a prompt denial of this allegation as affecting the integrity of my accounts."

Holt's response noted:

> Soon after he abandoned the ground thus badly taken, and assumed that of confession and justification, which he has continued since to occupy. The investigation sufficed to disclose to him the existence of an amount of testimony with in the reach of the Government which rendered this acknowledgement as prudent as his former denial had been rash and ill-advised.
>
> The final transaction was free from the usual badges of fraud: Being open and understood by all who participated in it, and by those who were its victims. A few of these who volunteered their affidavits pronounced the vouchers which they signed false. They were too dependent to demonstrate when the outrage was perpetrated on them, and they are now too conscientious to permit themselves to be used as instruments for its vindication.
>
> It is the mission of the Post Office Department, above all others, to inspire and to deserve the complete confidence of the public, which it can only accomplish by discarding from its service those whose lives and characters are not above all reproach and all suspicion.
>
> All of which is respectfully submitted.
>
> I have the honor to be your most obedient servant,
>
> J. Holt
>
> To the President.

Joseph Holt operated as a servant for the people, and conducted his services accordingly. The mail service provided a very important aspect linking the country together, coast to coast, with new territories and the

West. Communication between countries, Congress, families, and businesses helped make the United States stronger, and more proficient.

Holt continued delivering his best, balancing office duties and helping with many details of his wife's illness while Margaret resided at Wickland, her childhood home. Holt lived and conducted business for the Post Office, but the absence from his wife hurt.

In a letter written to Holt from his wife dated September 9, 1859 she stressed, "Eddie Brown says we have the best Postmaster here in the United States, but he does wish Mr. Holt would look after that Louisville fellow. Pa says go on with your good work and do not give up the office."

How I Became Secretary of War

(by Joseph Holt)
(Manuscript Division of the Library of Congress)

Jno. B. Floyd having resigned the Secretaryship on 31 December, 1860, the President on the following day placed me in charge of the Department as Secretary ad interim and I at once entered upon the duties of the office, continuing at the time entered upon the duties of the office, continuing at the same time to perform the duties of Post Master General. A day or two afterwards the President expressed to me a wish to appoint me permanent Secretary, but I urged that he should not do so, saying that it would probably lead to an angry and fruitless debate, and that I thought I could serve the administration quite as well under the provisional appointment which I held. In this view, after some conversation, he acquiesced, though apparently with reluctance. On the 9th of January, 1861 Mr. Slidell of Louisiana offered the following resolution and asked the immediate consideration by the Senate":

> Resolved that the President be requested to inform the Senate whether Jno. B. Floyd, whose appointment as Secretary of War was confirmed by the Senate on the 6th of March, 1857, still continues to hold said office, and if not whether said office has become vacant; and further to inform the Senate how and by whom the duties of said office are now discharged, and if an appointment of Acting or provisional Secretary of War has been, how, when and by what authority, it was so made and why the fact of said appointment has not been communicated to the Senate.
>
> The consideration of this resolution having been postponed, it was taken up by the Senate on the 10th of January, and at the close of Mr. Slidell's argument in its support, he said, "We want to know who is Secretary of War, & if the Secretary of War is the person whom the public prints suppose to be exercising those duties, I say & say that Gentleman never could have obtained the approbation

of the Senate. We would not be Secretary by and with the advice of the Senate.

The resolution was adopted, yeas 35, nays 17. Those voting in the negative did so doubtless, because they regarded the resolution as frivolous and as touching upon the rights of the Executive in demanding the reasons of his action.

The resolution was replied to by a message from the President on the 16th of January to the effect that by the Act of the 5th February 1795, provisional appointments of this class were expressly authorized, not to exceed six months, and that this appointment had been made on 1st January, to fulfill the duties of the office made vacant by the resignation of John B. Floyd. The message was accompanied by a tabulated statement showing how all such provisional appointments had been made since 1829. The president also protested against the claim of the Senate to know the grounds of his action, as being unsupported by law, precedent or practice.

On seeing in the Intelligence the remark of R. Slidell as quoted, I carried the paper to the president and drew his attention to the offensive declaration in regard to myself. After he had read it, I said, "Mr. President, I have heretofore, as you know, opposed my name being sent to the Senate for permanent Secretary of War, but in view of what Mr. Slidell has said, I am now perfectly willing that this shall be done and we will then see what foundation there is for his affirmation that I could not be confirmed."

The subjoined official record will show what followed:

In the Senate of the United States
Executive Session
Thursday, January 17, 1861

The following message was received from the President of the United States, by Mr. Glossbrenner, his Secretary:

To the Senate of the United States:

I nominate Joseph Holt, of Kentucky, to be Secretary of War of the United States, in the place of John B. Floyd, resigned.

(Signed) James Buchanan,
Washington, 17 January, 1861

Friday, January 18, 1861

It was Resolved, That the Senate advise and consent to the appointment of Joseph Holt, agreeably to the nomination.

The vote on the question, Will the Senate advise and consent to the appointment of Joseph Holt?

It was determined in the affirmation.

Yeas 38 Nays 13.

On motion by Mr. Mason.

The yeas and nays being desired by one fifth of the Senators present.

Those who voted in the affirmative are Messrs. Anthony, Baker, Bigler, Bingham, Cameron, Chandler, Clark, Collamer, Crittendon, Dixon, Doolittle, Douglas, Durkee, Fessenden, Foot, Foster, Grimes, Hale, Harlan, Johnson of Tenn., Kennedy, King, Latham, Morrill, Nicholson, Pearce, Powell, Pugh, Rice, Sauisburg, Seward, Sirmons, Sumner, Ten Kyok, Turnbull, Wade, Wilkinson and Wilson.

Those who voted in the negative are Messrs. Bayard, Benjamin, Braggs, Clingman, Green, Hemphill, Hunter, Iverson, Lane, Mason, Polk, Slidell and Wigfall. So it was, RESOLVED, That the Senate advise and consent to the appointment of Joseph Holt, agreeably to the nomination.

*I at once resigned the office of Post Master General & the Hon. Horatio King was appointed as my successor.

*In recalling the subsequent traitorous career of the men who voted against my confirmation, it is difficult to determine which was the more complimentary to me, their vote or condemnation or the approval of the loyal, true men who gave me their support.

A Member of President Buchanan's Cabinet

(Pittsburg, 1860)

The ***Pittsburg Chronicle*** published a letter, stating that a much esteemed clergyman of Pittsburg had received a letter from a member of President Buchanan's Cabinet a truly Christian gentleman and patriot, the Hon. J. Holt.

Joseph Holt wrote he had little hope the President's message would accomplish anything in curbing the madness that ruled the hour of the country.

Some Free States said, "Let the South go! Given that there has been bitterness between the North and the South for the last thirty years." The nation wants response and some seem willing to buy it at any sacrifice. "I doubt not from the temper of the public mind that the Southern States will be allowed to withdraw peacefully," he wrote.

"We will soon grow up a race of Chieftains who will rival the political bandits of South America and Mexico and will carve out to us our miserable heritage with the bloody sands," he predicted. Mr. Holt mentioned his brother was reading in Mississippi to become a lawyer and is really a cotton planter and has never had any experience with politics. "I asked him to try and persuade the people against this brutal war" His response, "Because of the slavery issue it is in the heart of the southern people and their only choice to overthrow the government." Joseph's brother stated, "On the success of this movement depends my every earthly interest the safety of my roof from the fire band and of my wife and children from the poison and the danger."

Joseph stated in his letter that he supported the Union still because he has faith that the North will do the right thing and give justice to the South and save the Republic before the wreck is complete. Action had to be prompt to be effective.

"The people know nothing of Civil War," he offered," but it could be a war that darkens every fire side, and wrings every heart with anguish."

His letter foretold the situation addressing America just prior to the Civil War. Joseph Holt's words relayed the story soon lived by Americans experiencing a nation torn with sadness as the fearful time divided the nation, families, and states.

Encampment at Wickland

The Civil War changed the south forever and all families were affected in some way. Joseph Holt's wife's family was affected with the North and the South being on Wickland's grounds at the same time. Margaret had died in August 1860, after being married only ten years to Joseph Holt. After a year of war, Margaret's family decided to move to Canada, during such turmoil and unsafe times. As the war separated many American families, so, too, did the Wickliffe and the Holt family become distant. The family home symbolized the divisions.

Fog settled mysteriously as it arrived. Dew refreshed the earth as the family prepared to depart from the only home they had ever known. Just like leaving an old friend, Wickland stood majestically like a lady in waiting, but now waiting could possibly be grimmer.

She had known many social functions and entertained balls and family dinners. The threat of Wickland being totally destroyed seemed very real, after a skirmish had occurred a few months earlier.

Julia, Margaret's youngest sister, stood alone recollecting many glorious times she had witnessed at Wickland, the summer weddings, picnics, afternoon strolls across the enormous grounds. She visited one last time the view from her window outside the Georgian Mansion.

Many memories she had shared with her four sisters: Nannie, Lydia Ann, Mary, and Margaret. Julia relived times when Pa returned from Washington City and all the girls ran to hug him. She remembered his deep, strong voice echoing across the lawn and his unusual laugh.

She recalled the supper that almost burned down the house when the cook left food unattended for a moment.

Facing the plantation, she wondered, "Will I ever see Wickland again as it is now? Will she be burned by those deceitful Yankees?" Many questions would be unanswered for the months to come. Julia read scripture in the Bible telling not to fret, to be patient, and to let God's angels protect you and defend your safety. Surely angels' wings would be welcome to escort the small troop scampering with only a few reminders of home.

Julia must be reserved to make the trip easier for Ma and Pa and the rest of the family. Skirmishes were occurring all across the commonwealth and movement must be kept quiet. You could not be too careful.

As the carriage wheels started moving, Julia felt torn apart, like her life was being taken from her. It wasn't fair. Why did people have to have wars? Why couldn't they continue as they were? Life had been good, but now uncertainty was creeping in with each new day.

Traveling to Canada was a scary endeavor the family knew they must endure in order to protect the woman and children since most of the men were away at war. Julia, looking back, experienced a tearing of love of home and family, and faced the unknown, dusty, indiscriminating trip without the comfort of sleeping in a bed.

The pain left her spirit empty, for she also left her two sisters behind. Nannie and Margaret slept their last sleep in the St. Joseph Cemetery. The splitting of the family was a sickening feeling. The only comfort Julia felt was that her two sisters might be as angels watching over their beloved Wickliffe family.

This war was tearing families apart. That fathers and sons fought against one another seemed unspeakable. The way of life as they knew it did not exist any longer. This was the day the Old South died. It would never be as grand as she had once been!

In some ways being naïve and sheltered seemed commonplace in the South. Society sought to protect younger women from unsightly scenes and rough unpolished men. Ladies expected gentlemen to show them respect and admire their fragile ways and notions. The Wickliffe woman had been reared as wealthy, aristocratic children of a stern father who had sent his girls to the boarding school, "Science Hill for Girls," and only accepted success for his family.

To Julia's knowledge, the Wickliffe family had never run away from anything. It seemed so odd to be heading north, just because the southern and the northern soldiers had appeared at the same time at Wickland.

Julia's mother Margaret had such patience, showed such lady-like qualities. Her history of toughness and her family, the Crepps who were brave Indian fighters in the early days of bloody battles in Kentucky, came through in all she did.

Julia recalled the day both the Yankees and the Rebels came to Wickland. Ma had heard a slight tap on the east side of the house. When she went to answer the door she found a young man in grey uniform, with a stressful despair in his eyes. Panting like an old dog out of breath, the man asked Ma to please help him and another young comrade, until they rested and got stronger. Ma, seeing he could move only by dragging his feet, obliged to assist him. "I guess it was the wisdom of Grandpa Crepps coming out of me, to know when to put my trust into a complete stranger," said Ma. With the help of the servants, she rushed the two young men in rapidly and hid them secretly behind the cupboard in the kitchen.

At the exact moment a continuous pounding sounded at the west entrance of the house. The pounding continued for quite some time. Finally, Ma collectively and gallantly answered the door. A lieutenant from the Union army told Ma his troops wished to camp on the grounds. Ma responded calmly, expressing they could rest their horses at the barns but she expected the men to respect her family. She thought if she was kind to them they might spare the house and livestock.

Ma instructed the cook to prepare food and fed the men for two days. The men seemed to be exhausted, spending most of their time resting. Ma bravely served them, as there were only a few slaves remaining, mainly house servants. One older slave named Tom helped with the horses.

Only three horses remained in the barn because Pa, with the help of brother Robert, had taken the purebred livestock used for breeding and hid them out in a nearby cave. They went twice a week to feed and water the horses, and sometimes stayed over night. Fresh horses, especially like these, were worth a great deal and Pa did not want the Yankees getting his prized horses.

Julia whispered to Ma, "it was indeed lucky for Pa and Robert to be absent when the Yankees arrived because you know how Pa is. He would not permit any Yankee getting use of anything at Wickland."

"Julia, you might even say it was a great blessing. Thank goodness your father was not here. I only hope Robert and Pa don't return until the Yankees are out of sight," spoke Ma being careful not to be heard.

The two-day encampment of Union soldiers seemed to tarry on forever. Pa and Brother Robert were camping about three miles from home. As they were returning, one of the neighbor's warned Pa and Robert about the soldiers. Being stubborn, Pa was hard to convince to hide out, but he realized that if they returned the Yankees would question them and investigate their absence. He thought they might force him to tell where he had been and cause injury to the family, as well as stealing the entire line of horses he had raised.

As the lieutenant pulled his troops out of Wickland, he went to the big house and thanked Ma for the food and explained they would have to take the three horses with them. Ma, being persistent, convinced them to leave the family one horse belonging to her.

As the dusty cloud followed the battered soldiers, Julia wondered what would happen to her state when troops like this took food, horses, and heaven forbid anything they chose. What would be left? Nothing. Nothing would be left of this great commonwealth. How awful for a nation to fight among its own citizens!

Only last week Julia had received a concerned message from Mr. Holt. The brief message relayed concern he had for the family's safety with the moving of Union troops marching across Kentucky. Mr. Holt urged the family to stay close to home, never leaving without the protection of men escorting the women.

Reality set in and caused the family to believe what happened just months earlier could destroy their lives if it occurred again. Pa gathered everyone around the dinner table and spoke with his deep southern accent, "This family is lucky to be alive. God must have a purpose for us or we would not be together tonight. Everyone must gather important family heirlooms quickly, pictures, silver, precious things money cannot buy, and I will have Tom help me hide them in the cave where Robert and I have hidden the horses. It is dry and no water reaches it. After the war when we return from Canada we will retrieve these items we must now leave behind. It would put our lives in more danger when traveling if we take things of value. We must only take necessary items to make it bearable for the horses," spoke Pa in a firm voice.

He spoke slowly, "My beloved family, gather your belongings quickly, with food to last us until we reach Canada. Robert will stay behind with Tom and a few Negroes, hoping Wickland will be spared. I feel it necessary to take the woman to Canada to protect them from the raids of the nightriders: It is not safe to have them here."

Pa had traveled the roads many times back and forth to Washington. He had mapped out the way the family would travel. Fifteen miles away from home Pa stopped the carriage near the stream and told everyone to get out, and rest for a few minutes. He told us to listen and to remember this in our hearts.

Julia opened her journal and began writing: "Water is running in an unspoiled land but soon this creek could be filled with the blood of the soldiers who felt they were doing the right thing. Fighting for a way of life, a southern life of proud ownership of land, extended over hundreds of acres their ancestors had worked, died and passed to the next generation, who would carry on the tradition of tending and caring for the land, for the land is the worth of the south. It lives on after things die. The land survives and keeps giving to those clinging to it."

The stillness reflected the way Grandpa Crepps must have felt when he came to Kentucky many years earlier, and he too saw a place of beauty with the reflection of sun touching the colored rocks in the bottom of the creek bed, the deer wandering the paths beaten down by buffalo treading a steady way to the salt licks, the settlers pushing westward, exploring Kentucky, and the hunting grounds of many Indians. All this had been Kentucky.

Now people were supposedly more civilized and seventy-five years had passed, changing the way people lived. With the advance of civilization, refinement occurred over time, bringing with it institutions of higher learning, helping to better the quality of life.

Julia said to Elizabeth, "I believe in his own way Pa wanted us to remember this scene. To instill in our memory as if an artist had painted the scene."

"Hear the whooperwill's call out into the vast darkness?" said Mary.

"Yes, that is the night letting us know we are not alone," smiled Julia.

"Pa said our traveling will be mostly at night. We will move discreetly through the night and at daybreak find a reclusive place to stow away until late afternoon," stated Julia.

"And what about cloudy nights?" asked Mary.

"You have to have faith and believe that Pa can guide our path on cloudy nights," Julia voiced with confidence.

There would be little sleep for the Wickliffe family. Some would sleep while others watched for soldiers. Pa wisely brought only the best stock. Four horses would pull the carriage and two would be tied to the end giving needed relief as the other horses tired from the journey.

Eating the dust and grinding it between their teeth became part of daily life. The woman became sore from the jarring and bumpy ride across the back roads.

Before leaving home Ma had said, "Leaving your home place when war is surrounding you is not pleasant. For your heart of memories is instilled within your soul. But you must be strong."

Driving with the reins in his hands, Pa turned and smiled at his girls saying, "Life is living each day with the awareness of making the day successful." How could this day be successful saying goodbye to home, to two dead sisters, witty Lydia Ann and beautiful Margaret and to all the material things dear to all? Now the family traveled in a dangerous time where they could be robbed or killed by war criminals.

Julia thought Pa must be right because today she felt she must get her child John to Canada safely to ensure his future, if he was to have one. The fear of someone stealing him, in the night haunted her dreams. Julia recalled the time Ma had warned Pa about traveling to Shepherdsville and she begged him not to go. She told him he would have a dangerous accident. Pa being as stubborn as always went anyway not listening to Ma's vision. A storm sprung up suddenly with fierce winds and out of nowhere a tornado appeared downing trees all around Pa. He barely escaped injury by lying flat on the ground and holding dearly to a tiny bush. The horse was blown away and he was quietly shaken. After that Pa did not take so lightly Ma's ability to see future events.

At night as the family traveled, Julia took her turn at catnapping. Continuously she had the reoccurring dream about someone dressed in dark clothing trying to steal John, her son. She recorded in her traveling journal, "Morning brought sunshine with gentle breezes, a little chiller than the day before. Preparing for a long extended day, Ma made fresh coffee and we ate flat cakes with maple sugar."

"Pa and Mary gathered fresh water by the stream and filled the wooden buckets placing them in the bottom of the carriage. Little John helped me gather the quilts as we prepared for today's traveling. The weather is nice, bright and beautiful. Things seemed to be normal until we met Negroes traveling the roads searching for a place to call home."

"Our family would have to be careful with the food supply until reaching Canada. Flour had become so expensive it was outrageous. We brought flour from home, hoping it would last. Everyone had traveling clothes and extra shoes. The last store we stopped at shoes were two hundred dollars a pair! The day was lost by watching the horses prance as the carriage wheels turned hundreds of times."

There was nothing to see except the fall foliage of trees. Only small sections of fields were tended because no one cared for the crops except women and the elderly. Many slaves either fled to other farms, went to fight in the war, or if elderly they remained at the only home they had ever known. Many house servants did not know how to raise crops. Most women raised enough vegetables to keep food on the table. Lucky for his family, Pa left the legislature to help provide for his family with all the husbands away at war or Congress.

In a year's time the Wickliffe family's lives had changed dramatically. The North was using its strength to destroy the South's economy. Our way of life was gone. How would we survive without slaves to raise the tobacco? How would we care for our families? It took a great deal of money to keep slaves, Pa always told us. He said, "By the time you care for all the Negroes, their medical bills, food, clothes and extra blankets, it narrows the profits greatly."

By now most all the slaves were gone. Pa, being good-hearted, set the slaves free just after the war began. He said, "You now must choose your own path in life. You are free to move on if you wish, or you can remain on the plantation for as long as you live." Most chose to move on but parted with tears because the Wickliffe family had always been kind to them. Brother Robert would stay at Wickland with the few slaves who remained and try to save what was possible.

Mary looked at Julia, "What are you thinking about now, little sister?" Julia responded, "My thoughts drift back to the telegram we received several weeks back from Joseph, our dear beloved sister Margaret's husband. He cautioned us about this journey and thought we could fare better remaining in Kentucky. Mr. Holt stated this journey was too dangerous and he felt we were risking our lives out on the road like this. But you know how darn stubborn Pa and Ma can be at times. There was no changing their mind, and finally they convinced us both to come along."

"Mary, do you think Wickland will be spared through this Civil War or will it only be a memory of our past childhood, marriages, funerals, celebrations on the fourth of July, Christmas, and Spring Balls?"

"You are asking me questions only the Lord knows, Julia. We will pray and depend on the Lord to protect us and our heritage at Wickland," replied Mary.

"Decisions are hard to make especially with war surrounding and everyone having family fighting for the right cause," voiced Mary.

Pa said, "If we travel from midmorning carefully, getting only a few hours of sleep, we could make Canada in six weeks."

Julia spoke up, "but the animals need rest and so do we."

Caution set in when traveling at night. Deserters and raiders, as well as night-riders, roamed the lands "A family must keep watch continually," said Julia. "I'm glad Pa had me to practice shooting the rifle before leaving home, just in case the need arose. I believe I could hit a live target," Julia proudly bragged.

Ma, an understanding person, always cared for the neighborhood children. This move would be difficult on her. She recently designed two money belts for Mary and Julia to wear in their undergarments. The money was rolled and placed in the belt. She sewed it nicely to their dark traveling pants.

Ma said, "It is down right frightful to conceal money in such a matter."

"You all will think it's a good idea if someone tries to rob us and we are left with nothing to live on except what we have hidden to live on until this miserable war ends," Pa remarked using his authoritative voice.

What a change this represented for Pa, missing work with the legislature to make sure his family reached Canada safely. "This reminds me of my younger days when your Ma and I first married."

Winding down on her writing, Julia stopped for a while to relieve Pa from driving because he was getting older and his health had been poor for several years.

The days now grew shorter and the nights cooler. The dampness put a chill in the air. Julia dreaded night, not knowing who was wandering around in the dark. Would there be slaves, thieves, and robbers lurking out in the open country waiting to grab the first likely candidate?

"Thank goodness Pa convinced everyone to move to Canada," Julia said whispering, as the leaves rustling made her more nervous than she already was.

Traveling on moonlit nights and hidden days, the Wickliffe family reached Detroit, Michigan, where the family would spend several days with Pa's sister before continuing to Canada. Aunt Bess would be delighted to see Pa, Ma, Mary, Julia, and Little John.

Clean sheets, warm water, and washing ladylike never seemed more glamorous. "Sometimes you don't miss things until there gone," said Mary.

After three days of resting, bathing, and refreshing themselves and their horses, the family endured the hardship of traveling as commoners.

Traveling with Pa, Julia felt safe. He knew how to survive even if the food became short. The nickname of The Old Duke was tough and he knew survival techniques, insuring the family's safety. Julia took after Pa, being a real tomboy growing up. Recollecting, Julia thought how different she and Margaret had been. Margaret was strictly an English-bred, lady like beauty.

Julia amazed at new inventions like the Prarie Plow, had following Pa around, learning how to handle teams of horses. That would come in handy with the long tiring trip in the buggy.

The days passed quickly as the month of November approached. Pa said, "With a few more days we will be close to the Canadian border, but we must continue to remain cautious. We have been lucky so far."

Before dusk the carriage brought in sight a small town of Jackson, Michigan. Being low on food Pa thought stopping at a General Store would be safe enough. Anything would taste better than beef jerky.

Pa and Julia walked in the store together and the remaining family stayed put in the carriage. A voice called, "How can I help you?"

Pa answered, "We need a small sack of flour and some sugar."

"Well, we don't have any sugar. And I don't know when we will get any," said a big red-faced woman. The flour is thirty dollars for a small sack."

"All right, we will take it," said Pa.

"This is the first sack of flour I've sold in three weeks No one around these parts has any money. It sure is nice to have a paying customer, instead of someone wanting credit. Where you folks headed?" asked the big woman with muscular features.

"We are on our way to visit relatives," said Pa calmly.

"Sure seems like a dangerous time to be traveling with a family such as yours." By this time the woman was stretching her neck looking everyone over through the window.

"You need a place to stay tonight?"

"No, we'll be moving on now." replied Pa.

Pa and Julia climbed back in the carriage in rather a hurry. "What is all the rush?" spoke Ma.

"That woman seems rather odd, Ma, and she asked a lot of questions," said Julia quietly.

"Pa and I thought it would be best to move on," cautioned Julia.

Five miles past the General Store a wheel on the buggy broke, tilting the buggy dangerously. Pa called to the team of horses. "Woo, woo, easy girls, woo." The horses finally came to a halt. Now Pa would have to repair the wheel and the family would camp close to the nearby woods. Pa being wise had everyone to dismount the carriage and slowly drove it with the broken wheel a short distance into the woods to hide it for safety.

The horses would be hidden a little distance from the carriage in a thicker part of the woods, and the trees would catch the falling dew making the night seem warmer for all. Supper was better than usual with bread, maple syrup, coffee, and beef jerky. After a tiring day, the family began resting quietly.

Riders could be heard in the distant. One man was shouting, "They must have gone this way because it is the closest route to the border."

"They had a lot of money. I'm sure they were wealthy," said a coarse woman's voice. A rough growly voice responded.

"Why didn't you stall them then, ask more questions, and find out where they were headed?"

"I tried, I told you ten times already. They were closed mouth, couldn't get anything from them. They didn't think nothing about paying thirty dollars for flour," the woman was becoming angry because she was now shouting at the man.

"Well, there's more where that came from if we catch them," said the coarse voiced man.

The family laid snug to the ground. Each breath seems to make more noise. The reality hit at once. These people were out to make a quick buck at the expense of the Wickliffe family, no matter what the cost. Were they dangerous and wanted by the law? Would they possibly want to injury the family besides trying to rob them? Could they only be desperate merchants who needed cash immediately and this was the only means? Surely not!

Pa handled the horses gently. He had a special touch with animals. He had worked these horses from young colts, and they would move with any command he had taught them. They had learned how to hide and move without bringing attention. This was the only way Pa had managed to save the best breeding stock because he would stay, sometimes days at a time, in the cave hiding the horses from the armies who took whatever they desired.

Before leaving the family, Pa gave instructions on what to do. He said, "I'm going to move the horses to higher ground. Ma, John, and Mary crawl without making noise, and that will not be easy because of the dried leaves on the ground, but you have to do it. Remember to stay low to the ground, not rising to cause a shadow that could possible give you away. Julia, you linger afterwards pausing for a few seconds occasionally to listen with your ear to the ground and that will let you know if the robbers are close."

The riders came closer and they heard the sound of three horses. Two men were shouting at each other both blaming the other one for not catching the family. Julia heard one of the riders scream to the other saying, "You take the Old Stone Trail Road, and I'll Take the Pike Road, we can't miss them one way or the other." The woman must have backtracked to town, thinking the family stopped along the way to sleep.

Ma, Mary, and John continued following the narrow, winding path through the woods. It was difficult to maneuver through all of the underbrush and rocks. One of the horses lost its balance, almost falling to its knees, but Pa managed to retrieve it.

Julia continued to stop from time to time and listen for sounds like Pa had explained. It seemed like there was mass confusion on the road, and all the sounds started to sound the same. Julia decided to circle back closer to the road and, as the moon shone brightly through the trees, she caught sight of the huge woman they had seen at the store earlier.

Gasping, "Oh," Julia hoped the woman had not heard her. Maybe the hoofs of the woman's horse had covered the gasp. Frightened beyond panic, Julia remembered Grandpa Crepps telling her of a story of survival. Julia began crawling quietly in the night.

She continued to crawl slowly, and her knees ached from tearing some of the flesh off due to the steep route she had taken. The pain felt like a knife poking her and her hands felt numb from pulling herself up the steep cliffs trying to reach the other family members. Julia heard hoofs of horses echoing like bullets hitting a frying pan on the small road below the cliffs.

Strong willed and determined, Julia maneuvered, finally reaching the rest of the family. After a few hours, Pa gathered the horses nestled at the top of the steep ridge. Riding bare back definitely would not be comfortable, but the family had no choice. The Wickliffe family entered Canada at dusk the next evening, without stopping to eat.

Could the dreams of someone snatching little John have been the big coarse woman who tried to rob the family or was this dream the unknown future for the family? Would Ma foresee this event to warn the family? Was this inheritance of seeing into the future a trait Julia had received from her mother, and would it help her to save her young son?

As soon as Julia could make a trip to the telegraph office, she would send a telegram to her former brother-in-law, Joseph Holt, letting him know the family had reached Canada safely. However, it was done without Pa's knowledge, knowing how he felt about Union men, and Joseph Holt the Judge Advocate General in President Abraham Lincoln's administration.

The Lincoln Years

James Speed and Joseph Holt in the early years were good friends, attending college together, but later in life they chose different avenues. President Lincoln first offered the office of Attorney General to Joseph Holt. If Holt had accepted the position, James Speed's importance would have been significantly less.

Both men were born and raised knowing the importance of honor and of being a true southern gentleman. That meant being faithful to your friends as well as yourself and your country. Many *Washington Post* newspaper articles tell about Holt's patriotism. They discussed his dedication to the country and his fairness. Articles tell how he cleaned up Louisville, putting criminals behind bars when he practiced law as the county attorney.

Holt owed no one political favors, for he was his own man. Rough times had come for Holt in the Buchanan administration when the Confederacy was formed. Numerous cabinet members resigned. True to his character, antislavery and a strong supporter of the Union, Holt was promoted to Secretary of War with the resignation of John B. Floyd. He became one of the first strong leaders to assist in the Civil War and served as Secretary of War until President Buchanan's term ended.

Lincoln had much confidence in Joseph Holt as well. Holt joined the army as a colonel but on September 3, 1862, President Lincoln appointed Holt as the first Judge Advocate General of the Union Army. During 1864 Lincoln offered two positions, Secretary of the Interior and Attorney General, to Holt, but Holt declined. Judge Holt was one of many considered for the Republican Vice-president ticket. He never ran for an office, but was offered many.

Holt had been present the day Lincoln took the oath of office. The sky was as cloudy as President Lincoln's presidency would be. Awakening early, President and Mrs. Lincoln heard loud sounds as wagons, soldiers marching, and hooves of horses pounded the streets near the Willard Hotel on Inauguration Day. Precautions had been taken at every angle.

Notes across the nation warned the president-elect of dangers in the capitol, ranging from Baltimore schoolteacher Henrietta Phelps who wrote on January 14, 1861 she heard a young lawyer say, "3,000 men were to come to Washington, and that the capital would be taken before the 4th of March, 1861."

George W. Waite of Illinois wrote that J. Merrick wrote to Chicago lately that, "Washington would be seized. That men from Maryland armed by the Government would desert to the other sides."

James Henderson of New York told revolutionists at work in the northern and southern cities plotting the seizure of the city of Washington! "What they are fearful of General Scott's ordering militia to Washington. Recommends a strong force to be placed in Washington to prevent mischief." On January 29, 1861 Winfield Scott wrote Secretary of War Joseph Holt, "It is not necessary to be an alarmists to believe that the federal metropolis will be at the next inauguration, nay, on the 13th of February, and even much earlier, in great peril, and I am obliged to add that without a considerable augmentation of troops, I do not feel that I can guarantee its safety during the next five days." Respectfully submitted to the Secretary of War.

As Secretary of War, Holt worked endless hours, with a tireless effort keeping the country moving with turmoil at all corners. Numerous memos came daily across Holt's desk. Each note, each telegram, each letter and personal interview was taken in stride. All correspondence was carefully examined, professionally answered, in quick response to the concerns of the day.

General Scott wrote Holt proposing that on February 22, 1861, regular troops in Washington should march past the President's Mansion once, paying the Chief Magistrate a marching salute. If the Secretary approved this request, he was asked to name the hour.

On March 4, 1861, 25,000 people came to Washington, for the inauguration, many without lodging. The well-dressed crowd covered Pennsylvania Avenue. President Lincoln appeared dressed, in complete black with a matching top hat, new suit, and boots, with a cane in hand.

Along the route Winfield Scott quelled away problems or threats to President Lincoln. Federal rifleman covered commanding houses with instructions to watch the crowds, as the President's horse-drawn carriage was escorted by a company from West Point marching in front, while around it marched infantry from the District of Columbia. A battalion guarded the area near the capitol steps, as the carriage with President Buchanan, and newly elected President Lincoln approached. Quietness marked the ride between the two presidents. Because of rumors of the platform being blown up while Lincoln was speaking, soldiers carefully guarded underneath while Lincoln delivered his speech.

President Lincoln had reviewed his talk many times, revised it with suggestions from Seward and Browning, who suggested deleting from the address, "You can forbear the assault upon it [the Government]; I can not shrink from the defense of it. With you, and not with me, is the solemn question of "Shall it be peace or sword?" Seward suggested words of cheerful, calm, confidence, and words of affection. Lincoln wanted his speech touching the peoples' hearts, giving them hope, given the fears before the country.

On a brighter note, the Union ball seemed to brighten spirits for a while. Those present hoped for the country to heal, with the new administration.

President and Mrs. Lincoln spent their first night in their new home with the spirits of the past. Realizing what lay before him, Lincoln understood the tasks facing him and the help he would need from his new cabinet.

Only two months later the nation would be at war. The Civil War broke out in April of 1861, with Joseph Holt being instrumental in preventing succession for his beloved Kentucky, where he diligently worked giving speeches, writing and publishing the "Policy of the General Government the Pending Revolution, Its Objects, Its Probable Results If Successful, and the Duty of Kentucky in the Crisis."

At the beginning of Holt's pamphlet is a letter written to a father from his son, who speaks of the immediate future looking dark. The only hope of future peace, he predicted, would be for the triumph and victory of numerous troops. He writes his father and explains he is sending a copy of Mr. Holt's letter to the government. This letter was published in 1861 in Washington. It efficiently aided President Lincoln in his attempts to keep Kentucky Union.

Joseph Holt helped establish a recruiting station across the river from Louisville, in Jeffersonville, Indiana called Camp Joe Holt. Camp Joe Holt set the stage for signing up Kentucky troops, as the steps in which it declared itself neutral. The Kentucky Unionists, encouraged by Joseph Holt, meanwhile worked to keep Kentucky from succeeding.

A farmer, Blanton Duncan gave his farm for the establishment of Camp Joe Holt. Holt was honored by having the camp named after him, the first Secretary of War for President Abraham Lincoln. Many Kentuckians, many of them from Louisville, left to join the Union Army. A simple pine board was used with words Camp Joe Holt to lead the recruits to the location.

Washington, May 31, 1861

J. F. Speed, Esq:

My Dear Sir: The recent overwhelming vote in favor of the union in Kentucky has afforded unspeakable gratification to all true men through the country. This voice indicated that the people of that gallant State have been neither seduced by the arts nor terrified by the menaces of the revolutionists in their midst, and that it is their fixed purpose to remain faithful to a Government which, for nearly seventy years, has remained faithful to them. Still it cannot be denied that there is in the bosom of that State a band of agitators, who, though few in number, are yet powerful from the public confidence they have enjoyed, and who have been, and doubtless will continue to be, unceasing in their endeavors to force Kentucky to unite her fortunes with those of the rebel Confederacy of the south. In view of this and the well know fact that several of the seceded States have by fraud and violence been driven to occupy their present false and fatal position, I cannot, even with the encouragement of her late vote before me, look upon the political future of our native State without a painful solicitude. Never have the safety and honor of her people required the exercise of so much vigilance and of so much courage on their part. If true to themselves, the stars and stripes, which, like angel's wings, have so long guarded their homes from every oppression, will still be theirs; but if, chasing the dreams of other men's ambition, they shall prove false, the blackness of darkness can but faintly depict the doom that awaits them. The legislature, it seems, has determined by resolution that the State, pending the present unhappy war, shall occupy neutral ground. I must say, in all frankness, and without designing to reflect upon the course or sentiments of any, that, in this struggle for the existence of our Government, I can neither practice, nor profess, nor feel neutrality. I would as soon think of being neutral in a contest between an officer of justice and an incendiary arrested in the attempt to fire the dwelling over my head; for the Government, whose overthrow is sought, is for me the shelter not only of home, kindred, and friends, but of every earthly blessing which I can hope to enjoy on this side of the grave. If, however, from a natural horror of fratricidal strife, or from her intimate social and business relations with the South, Kentucky shall determine to maintain the neutral attitude assumed for her by her Legislature, her position will still be an honorable one, though falling short of that full measure of loyalty which her history has so constantly illustrated. Her executive, ignoring, as I am happy to believe, alike the popular and legislature sentiment of the State, has, by proclamation, forbidden the government of the United States from marching troops across her territory. This is, in no sense, a neutral step, but one of aggressive hostility. The troops of the Federal Government have a clear constitutional right to pass over the soil of Kentucky as they have to march along the streets of Washington, and could this prohibition be effective, it would not only be a violation of the fundamental law, but would, in all its tendencies, be directly in advancement of the revolution, and might, in an emergency easily imagined, compromise the highest national interests. I was rejoiced that the Legislature so promptly refused to endorse this proclamation as expressive of the true policy of the State. But I turn away from even this to the ballot box, and find an abounding consolation in the conviction it inspires, that the popular heart of Kentucky, in its devotion to the Union, is far in advance alike of legislative resolve and of executive proclamation.

But as it is well understood that the late popular demonstration has rather scotched than killed rebellion in Kentucky, I propose inquiring, as briefly as practicable, whether, in the recent action or present declared policy of the Administration, or in the history of the pending revolution, or in the objects it seeks to accomplish, or in the results which must follow from it, if successful, there can be discovered any reasons why that the State should sever the ties that

> unite her with a Confederacy in which councils and upon those battlefields she has won so much fame, and under whose protection she has enjoyed so much prosperity.
>
> For more than a month after the inauguration of President Lincoln the manifestations seemed unequivocal that his Administration would seek a peaceful solution of our unhappy political troubles, and would look to time and amendments to the Federal Constitution, adopted in accordance with its provisions, to bring back the revolted States to their allegiance.

Holt continued, in this powerful work, to describe events occurring with the Border States. He voiced the feeble conditions at Fort Sumter, explaining how the Confederate authorities realized that only a few days remained before starvation would take place. With the fall of Fort Sumter, the property of the United States government continued to be taken by force. Announcements were made, echoed with taunts that Washington City would soon be flying the Confederate flag over the capitol. Should nineteen million people permit five or six million to overthrow and destroy institutions which are common property of all?

If asked to protect the nation, citizen soldiers will march to points of rendezvous if called, he predicted. Such a large amount of social position, culture, and character, has yet to be found in an army so numerous in any era or country. The mission is of peace unless men of the South use swords across the path. "We impose no burden which we ourselves do not bear."

> Equally vain is it for them to declare that they only wish to be let alone. And that in establishing the independence of the seceded States, they do those which remain in the old confederacy no harm. It is easy to perceive what fatal results to the old confederacy follow should the blow now struck at its integrity untimely triumph.
>
> While a far more fearful responsibility has fallen upon President Lincoln than upon any of his predecessors, it must be admitted that he has met it with promptitude and fearlessness.
>
> The vigorous measures adopted for the safety of Washington and the Government itself may seem open to criticism, in some of their details, to those who have yet to learn that not only has war,

like peace, its laws, but that it has also its privileges and its duties. They have noted the course of public affairs to little advantage who suppose that the election of Mr. Lincoln was the real ground of the revolutionary outbreak that has occurred. The roots of the revolution may be traced back for more than a quarter of a century, and an unholy lust for power is the soil of which it sprang. A prominent member of agitators in a speech in last November or December stated that they had been occupied for thirty years in the work of severing South Carolina from the Union.

Revolutionists broke up the Democratic Convention assembled to nominate a candidate for the President, securing the election of Mr. Lincoln. Having achieved this–the election of a Republican president would be the cause for dissolution of the Union. When the election of Mr. Lincoln was announced cheering was heard in the streets of Charleston, the dramas progressed as one state after another succeeded from the Union, and withdrew their members from Congress.

The profligate ambition of public men, in all ages and lands, has been the rock on which republics have been split. Such men have arisen in our mist men who, because unable permanently to gasp the helm of the ship, are willing to destroy it in the hope to command someone of the rafts that may float away from the wreck. The effect would be to degrade us to a level with the military bandits of Mexico and South America, who when beaten at an election, fly to arms, and seek to master by the sword what they have been unable to control by the ballot-box.

Is Kentucky willing to link her name in history with the excesses and crimes which have sullied this revolution at every step of its progress? Can she soil her pure hands with its booty? She possesses the noblest heritage that God has granted to his children; is she prepared to barter it away for that miserable mess of pottage, which gratification of the unholy ambition of her public men would bring to her lips? Can she without laying her face in the dust for every shame, become a participant in the spoliation of the commerce of her neighbors and friends, by contributing her star, hitherto so stainless in its glory, to light the corsair on his way? Has the war whoop which used to startle the sleep of our frontiers, so died away

> in her ears that she is willing to take the red-handed savage to her bosom as the champion of her rights and the representative of her spirit? Must she not first forget her own heroic sons who perished, butchered and scalped, upon the disastrous field of Raisin?
>
> The object of the revolution, as avowed by all who are pressing it forward, is the permant dismemberment of the Confederacy. The dream of reconstruction used during the last winter as a lure to draw the hesitating or the hopeful into the movement has been formally abandoned. If Kentucky separates herself from the Union, it must be upon the basis that that separation is to be final and eternal.

Mr. Holt's letter discussed how the 1860 Fugitive Slave law had been successful over the last ten years. Under practices of the government, even slave states remained peers of the free. Seven out of fourteen presidents chosen by the people had been citizens from these states, he noted, and three of the remaining seven stood for southern principles of free states. Has the South been deprived from powers of government? Rulings by the Supreme Court had declared that slave owners could take their slaves to all places in the United States, and this has never been interfered with in any cases.

Mr. Holt wrote that Kentucky should carefully think about where she was going. If the state decided to go with the South, it would abandon a strong government able to protect it. Kentucky must think about safety and its central position in the Union, protected from the scourge of foreign wars. Becoming a part of the southern Confederacy, she might become a victim of border feuds that had happened during history.

Holt explained how the people sleep safely now at night in Kentucky. However, those in Virginia were not as fortunate with alarms and threats of war making each day a terror. Kentucky would become weak if attached to the southern Confederacy and would not be protected and safe as now.

Noted Holt: "Scarcely feeling contributions made to support the government now, if she becomes a part of the Southern Confederacy her taxes would have direct taxation for the newly creation of forts, a navy to protect, and customs houses protecting several thousands miles. She now enjoys her protection enforced by the government of the Fugitive

Slave law. Not being able to carry this law into the Confederacy, slavery will rapidly disappear in Kentucky."

Joseph Holt asked these questions: "Does Kentucky want to see a set-back of a century where others will see her winner of the African slave trade? Is Kentucky ready to leave with all her honored and safe positions to an unknown ambition leading a nation to perdition?" Holt demanded Kentucky to study the laws and the Constitution.

He requested Kentuckians to think back a few months before when the nation was free and prosperous, but now with war, the nation's thirty million citizens had their hearts darkened with anguish.

Joseph Holt's voice was heard across Kentucky as he delivered speeches encouraging Kentuckians to stay in the Union, giving them insight into the consequences they might certainly find themselves. His elegant voice helped capture the serious mood of the commonwealth. His words made people think, as families became torn apart, even his own. This Civil War was dividing not only a nation, but the basis upon which it was built, the family. He asked the people of Kentucky to appeal to their neighbors, to protect their patriotism and to protect their country's flag, the flag of freedom, in life or death.

Joseph Holt was instrumental in Kentucky with his letter, and his speeches, speaking to the hearts of Kentuckians. Would they listen? Would they support the flag that had always protected them? Would they keep Kentucky from being a battleground of the South? Would her famous sons stand proud and save the land so loved from doom in this great Civil War?

On September 22, 1862, Lincoln issued a preliminary proclamation of emancipation. Lincoln believed that the fate of world democracy was the central issue of the Civil War. He felt the breakup of America would be a tragedy, and all mankind would suffer. He understood the United States was being viewed by the world to see if our people could rule themselves.

After the Union army was defeated at Bull Run on July 21, 1861, the North knew the war would be long. And after enthusiasm worn down, Lincoln had a difficult job of arousing people's support for the Union army. Lincoln knew that to be successful he needed the support of Kentucky, Missouri, Delaware, and Maryland. In a letter dated August 22, 1862, Lincoln said, "My paramount object in this struggle is to save the

Union, and it is not either to save or destroy slavery." By having a moderate position, Lincoln kept all of the Border States in the Union.

President Lincoln could not afford a happy life while residing in the White House. Being president, he felt there could be no higher ambition for an American. He carried the weight of the nation, having a tiny staff, composing most of his letters and speeches continuously. He made decisions on thousands of military and political appointments, and turned no one away who came to see him.

While some of Lincoln's cabinet members gave him more headaches than help while in office, Joseph Holt was one person who worked diligently serving Lincoln. He was in charge of military court-martials.

It seemed as if a violent wind had swept over our nation to hug away hopes of a brighter tomorrow. Would this great nation stand, overcoming the violence of hatred, the sickness, the wondering day to day if there would be enough food? Families waited for letters bringing good news and some type of hope that the misery everyone was living would soon end.

Most families, wealthy or poor, now dealt with each day as a challenge. People struggled daily, trying to provide for their families. That summer of 1862, Lincoln felt the time had come when the policy for slavery should be changed.

Lincoln's decision about issuing a proclamation freeing the slaves came without the advice from his cabinet; however, they were briefed on Lincoln's intentions. With Steward's advice, Lincoln waited for an appropriate victory that came with the Battle of Antietam, fought on September 17, 1862. With the Emancipation Proclamation of January 1, 1863 slaves held "are, and hence-forth shall be free."

By 1864, Lincoln was losing popularity. He was quoted saying, "It seems exceedingly probable that this administration will not be re-elected." Then came the two great northern victories with the Battle of Mobile Bay and Sherman's capture of Atlanta, the great city of the South, helping him win the election of 1864.

All that time, Judge Advocate General Joseph Holt worked for the nation's success. In a letter addressed to President Abraham Lincoln on November 30, 1864, Holt discussed the consideration he had had for the appointment of Attorney General. Holt spoke about the generous offer and encouragement he had received from the president to take the office but explained to President Lincoln that he could serve him better in the position that he now had in his hands. Holt begged the president to be assured that he was most grateful for the distinguished token of the president's confidence and good will. Judge Holt said, "In it I cannot fail to find renewed incentives to the faithful and zealous performances of the public duties with which you have already charged me."

With the re-election of President Abraham Lincoln in 1864, the nation faced numerous challenges. Lincoln, a master politition, also experienced the people's needs, felt their pain, and lived their misery, serving the people who had instilled their faith in him.

Sadness succeeded as the nation tried desperately to mend the wounds so pressed in the hearts of its fallen soldiers, widows, and separated families. In the South, lost fortunes, and the lack of laborers, spelled doom for the plantation system.

Much damage was done to the South with the battle scars that war brings. Even Unionist Kentucky saw numerous losses with property, livestock, and looting.

Judge Holt's beloved home state of Kentucky received federal funds for damage done by Union soldiers. Later, this helped to some degree to build a new capitol in Frankfort.

The end of the Civil War brought relief to the people but also brought challenges to a tired nation, a nation that had been broken apart, and now faced a reconstruction that would test its people. The North rejoiced as some fighting ended on April 9, 1865, with Lee's surrender to Grant.

But little did the country know what the future would bring when Judge Advocate General Joseph Holt was asked to deliver an address in South Carolina on the evening of April 14, 1865, at the Charleston Hotel. Invited by the Secretary of War to witness the ceremony of raising the United States flag on Fort Sumter on that day, the former Commander, Kentuckian Robert Anderson, made a warm tribute to the Secretary of War, Major General Dix, and the Honorable Joseph Holt for the support they had given him while in command of that fort.

Judge Holt began his part of the program by saying he was most grateful for the kind words and the generous reception, which they had received. Holt said he felt little able to speak as the audience had encouraged him to do so. He spoke about the ruins of Sumter pressed at his feet and viewing the historic surroundings, "I experienced emotions too profound for utterance, and was deeply conscious that silence would best express the awe, and wonder, and ambition, and the thanksgiving with which I was filled, and so I feel now."

Holt in his talk said, "We all thank the President of the United States for the delicate and earnest appreciation of the craving of hearts which instructed him to order the flag which for four long years was lowered before the treacherous foe would be today flying once again among the breezes, with salutes and the honor restoring to the nation." That same night, Holt received a telegram saying that President Abraham Lincoln had been shot.

Sadness of Seclusion

The cool breezes on a September morn brought the arrival of Fall. The stillness of the days lingering moment after moment reminded Joseph Holt of what use to be.

Once he had arose each morning with a thick, inspiring agenda, but now only noise from the busy streets of Washington City faced him. Making a daily attempt to rise, he studied the commission report over and over again seeing if any evidence overlooked had taken the life of Mary Surratt.

Joseph thought, "I truly miss the conversations with folks arriving for meetings and the busy hustle and bustle of normal routine." After years of having a title as the Honorable Judge Holt, now the new reality made living difficult. Who wished to live isolated from the rest of the world, in drab light with the curtains drawn tight, with only the company of faithful servants, or visits from close friends and family?

Passers-by stared into what use to be a grand home. The house on New Jersey Avenue & C Street in southeast Washington had been quite magnificent in earlier years. But now it seemed unmanageable, a web of forbidden landscape.

The roses became tangled and weeds out grew the blooms of the manicured flower garden. The public now rarely saw Mr. Holt. He would give health reasons when he declined invitations from friends and family. However, some still visited Holt's residence and he received them with warmth. When it grew too dim for his weak eyes to see, he instructed others to compose his thoughts. The ivy that crept over his steps gave a hushness of how life was, like gravity in the world he had lived.

Joseph responded to his long-ago friend from Elizabethtown, Kentucky, A. M. Brown's letter. "It is with my regrets I cannot make the long journey at this time. I do however appreciate the thoughtfulness of you to include me on this recent invite. I dearly miss the opportunity to spend time with my deserving, close friend who has always stood and backed my words and actions as well as believed in the principles of serving the people of this great nation."

Joseph had been appointed Postmaster General in 1859. His appointment as Secretary of War came on December 31, 1860, and he held the post until the inauguration of Abraham Lincoln.

Shortly after President Lincoln took the oath of office, Holt, then Secretary of War, backed the new administration. Holt denounced Kentucky's neutrality in the beginning of the Civil War and thus became an ardent unionist. Lincoln then appointed Holt Judge Advocate General of the Union Army on September 3, 1862. His career to that time had been full of accomplishments and bright with promise. But the tragic incident of Lincoln's assassination forever changed the life of Joseph Holt, who probably would have achieved everlasting recognition had not his name become linked with incidents surrounding the death of Lincoln.

As Judge Advocate General, he prosecuted the people accused of being responsible for Lincoln's assassination in Ford's Theater. Mary Eugenia Surratt owned the boarding house, where actor John Wilkes Booth lived while he plotted to kill Lincoln. Booth had already been shot by a band of men who had pinned him in a barn in Virginia about two weeks after the president's death.

On June 29 the officers of the military court went into closed session deliberating the future of Mary Surratt and her fellow defendants. The first task was to decide the guilt or innocence for each defendant. They convicted all but one of the main charges of "treasonable conspiracy." Ned Spangler, who was found guilty on the lesser charge of abetting and aiding Booth's escape from Ford's Theater where the murder took place.

Spangler received six years in hard labor, while Dr. Mudd, Arnold and O'Laughlin received imprisonment for the remainder of their natural lives. Dr. Mudd escaped receiving the death sentence by only one vote. The court decided that Powell, Herold, Atzerodt, and Mary Surratt would be put to death.

After the commission finalized the investigation, five of the members of the commission signed a recommendation for a lighter sentence for Surratt, because of her age and sex. Both the verdicts and sentences were kept away from the public in secret until President Andrew Johnson could examine and sign the requisite papers. Five of the nine men on the commission signed the petition and it was fastened, face-to-face, to their investigation of the assassination. Then Judge Holt delivered the papers to President Johnson in person.

With the illness of the president from bilious fever, it was not until July 5th did President Johnson receive Joseph Holt, who quietly and without attention, slipped into the White House through one of the side doors.

Holt brought an abstract of the proceedings from the trial. Exactly what happened at the meeting will never be know except by the two. When the session ended President Johnson, did approve the death sentences of Lewis Powell, David Herold, George Atzerodt, and Mary Surratt. Execution day was then planned for July 7th , only two days later.

Not long after Mrs. Surratt's hanging, evidence came to light that threw doubt on her conviction. With public pressure, President Johnson, through friends and others, charged Judge Holt "had, on with the proceedings of the military trial commission, suppressed and withheld from him the petition for clemency in Mrs. Surratt's case, signed by five members of the commission." And that he had signed the death warrant without the knowledge of the existence of the petition.

It seemed finished. Yet there would be a sickening aftermath. Time passed, life went on, and two years later Mary's son, John Surratt, was captured on suspicion of being involved with the assassination. During his trial, his defense lawyer spoke about rumors of a petition of clemency for Mary Surratt that had been included in the papers Holt had shown to President Andrew Johnson.

When that became known in the trial, President Johnson ordered the War Department to send him the important documents. Surprisingly, Johnson said the petition was among the papers. President Johnson made a statement remarking he had never seen the recommendations, but he remembered his grave reluctance when he had approved her death.

Joseph Holt, for the rest of his life, insisted the President had read, had discussed, and had refused the petition. The petition had been signed on June 30, 1865, and taken to President Johnson by Joseph Holt on July 5. *The New York Times* knew the existence of the clemency petition on the execution day, informing the public that the newspaper correspondent knew, as had Johnson, about the petition but chose to do nothing to stop the execution of Mary Surratt.

Soon after Mrs. Surratt's hanging, evidence surfaced that questioned the decision. Afterwards in two publications, Judge Holt refuted President Johnson's accusations, noting the mass of proofs presented by Holt. Statements of William H. Seward Secretary of State, and Edwin M. Stanton, Secretary of War, seemed to support Holt, stating, "This statement of clemency was before the President and considered by him before the sentences given."

Attorney General Speed stated, "After the trial and before the execution, President Johnson had seen the record of the military trial in the president's office and no plea had been offered for her behalf, except she was a woman and this interposition would possible license female crime."

The prisoners did not know their fate until the morning of July 6th, when, to their surprise, just before noon time Major General Winfield Scott Hancock, the respected corps commander who commanded the district, and General John F. Hartranft, Prison Commandant, appeared at the cells of the four condemned to read their sentences.

The dire news of Mrs. Surratt was heard on the streets by her attorney as a newsboy was shouting the headlines, outside their office. "Guilty, Guilty, Guilty, Going to the Gallows." On the afternoon of the scheduled hanging, hardly knowing what else to do, her attorney Clampeth accompanied Anna Surratt, daughter of Mrs. Surratt, to the White House, where the young lady desperately would try to persuade the President to save her mother's life from the gallows of a cold death.

As reported all over Washington by the President's friends, Miss Surratt went on the eve of her mother's execution to plea for her dear mother, and the White House staff told her to go see Joseph Holt.

After reaching Holt Anna said, "The President was immovable," and Holt spoke to Anna in a sadden tone, "You might as well attempt to overthrow this building as to alter his decision."

However, in a letter written to General R.D. Mussey in July of 1873, Judge Holt told his side of the story:

> Washington July 1873
> General R. D. Mussey,
> Dear Sir:
>
> You are doubtless aware that soon after the execution of the assassins of the late President, it was by certain persons sympathizing with them, and seeking to relieve President Johnson of his proper

responsibility for his action in the matter reported in Washington and through the disloyal journals of the country, that the petition signed by five members of the court, asking the president–in consideration of her age and sex–to commute Mary E. Surratt's death sentence, had never been received by him, but had been withheld by me, when laying before him the record of trial, to which it was attached. This accusation being wholly false, I venture to ask of you such information as you may possess, tending to illustrate the issue of fact, thus raised under circumstances so unjust to myself.

As showing how prolific is the subject of detvaction, it was also reported that I had prevented Miss Surratt from seeing the President, the morning of the day on which her mother was executed, and in the wildness and silliness of popular credulity, this ridiculous story is said to have received considerable credit at the time.

Please state what you know as to the circumstances under which Miss Surratt was denied the interview with the president. She is alleged to have sought on this occasion reference to. On the night before, she, with two friends, as now recollected, called at my house, bringing with them certain papers appealing for clemency, on a resprite for her mother. I listened patiently to all they had to say, received the papers from their hands, and promised to deliver them to the president the following morning, which promise was faithfully kept. As I ascended the stairs of the Executive Mansion, on my way to the president's office with the papers, I saw Miss Surratt in the Hall below, but nothing was either said or done by me, seeking or tending to influence the question whether she should be received by the President or not. It was a matter with which I had no move to do than had any other citizen of the country. The decision of the question belonged to the President with his constitutional advisors and door keepers and certainly I was neither of these. It would have been sheer impudence in me to have obtruded a suggestion on the subject. You were on duty at the Executive Mansion at the time, and enjoying, as you did, intimate personal and official relations with President Johnson, you probably had opportunities of knowing either from your own observations or from conversations with the President, whether the petition referred to was seen and considered by him before the sentence was carried into execution. I shall be much obliged for the statement of any information bearing on the subject, which your recollection many enable you to make, and for any declarations made by the President, as to the appeal to him in behalf of Mrs. Surratt on the grounds of her sex.

Very respectfully
Your obedient Servt.
J. Holt

Only hours before the executions were scheduled, once again, a frantic Anna returned to the White House. She climbed the stairs to the second floor office of the President and found her way barred by New York Senator Preston King, a close acquaintance of Johnson, and Senator James Lane, veteran of Kansas Missouri guerrilla wars.

Anna, weeping and crying so loud that sobs could be heard ringing through the White House's vast halls, called out, "Oh, please sirs, please let me see the President. I have to talk to him face to face. I must stop the execution. Help me, I beg you! My mother is a good, decent mother. She must not die for something she did not do." Screaming loudly, Anna became hysterical. She threw herself on the stairs as the President's daughter, Martha Johnson Patterson, came by saying, "My poor dear you break my heart, but there is not a thing I can do."

"You can do something. You can convince your father to see me and maybe it will not be too late for my mother." Walking away shaking her head, the President's daughter did not give any comfort to Anna. She did not even try to get her past the blockade.

Now, Anna felt the pain of a heart aching for relief. She lived with a constant, tearing tearful sorrow, weeping with sadness, and begging for comfort. With eyes that would not cry anymore, Anna had a numb body and a tormented soul, abandoned in a world that seemed cruel without mercy.

With sand in the hourglass running out, there was one chance left. At 2:00 A.M. the lawyers of Mary Surratt had awakened Judge Alexander Wyler of the District of Columbia Supreme Court and begged for an order stopping the execution. With considerable spunk and courage, Wyler issued a writ of habeas corpus. However, President Johnson declared the writ suspended for this case.

The courtyard became overcrowded as on-lookers gathered outside the Washington Arsenal. Around 1:15 P.M. on that dreaded afternoon a condemned woman went to the gallows, despite questions about her involvement in the conspiracy.

Mrs. Surratt had to be supported by soldiers, not being able to walk on her own. The eyes of the entire condemned saw their freshly dug graves, as they passed by in disbelief. Raw pine coffins rested beside the small graves. Climbing the scaffold with the last minutes of life, they faced death, passed from this life to the next, and satisfied the laws and the consequences of being found guilty in a court of law. Justice for a fallen President came from a nation that wanted results, and to see the conspiracy finally put to rest.

Even though Joseph Holt had carried out the responsibilities of his office during the trial, his name would be linked with the conviction of a condemned woman. Holt had high ambition at this time when he had been seeking top run, up the political ladder in Washington. On March 13, 1865, Joseph Holt became Major General of the United States Army for his distinguished services during the Civil War, but the lingering questions about his role in the assassination articles and court rulings about Surratt ended any hope of advancement.

At his request, he retired on December 1, 1875, but he continued to write, to read, and occasionally to travel, never seeking bids for a higher office.

In that time, Joseph told his faithful servant Rose, "Memories pass, but as I trod the trail tread before me, I go where footsteps have touched the edges and center of the cobblestone streets. Lingering solely, it is difficult to face each new tomorrow for the pain I feel, and endure, hurts beyond explanation. To be excluded within your circle of friends, is worse than the dust of death, for without hope what does life bring?"

After eight years of humiliation, Judge Holt was finally vindicated of the dishonorable accusations made by President Andrew Johnson.

In another letter to Holt dated July 1873, General R.D. Mussey wrote:

> President Johnson told me of that recommendation (for Mrs. Surratt's clemency). I had seen this attempt to stigmatize you, an act for which Andrew Johnson was then proud, and which now repudiate, with deep pain and still deeper shame.
>
> I am pained because it is unjust and untrue, and because it seeks

to acquit him by charging a fearful crime, of violated trust and of inhumanity, to you.

I am so ashamed because there has joined in the attempt, a man who was once President (or acting President). Should you desire to make any public use of the whole or any portion of this letter, you have my most cordial permission to do so.

Yours, very truly,
R. D. Mussey

Holt's life's work had been put into words, sealed with faith, for future scholars to visit daily, revisiting with a clear, unbiased, open mind the work of a lifetime dedicated to the people.

Remaining Judge Advocate General until 1875, Joseph Holt retired but continued to live in Washington D.C. until he passed away on August 1, 1894.

As the centuries have long passed, questions still remain unanswered: Why was President Andrew Johnson in such a hurry to tear down the prison where Mary Surratt and assassins were held? Why were they buried in the night, and why was a building built over the gravesites? This all took place before President Johnson left office. Was he trying to make a wrong right? Was he trying to make his term as president less devastating and less remembered for the terrible tragedy of a condemned woman in the gallows? Did President Johnson use the power of the office in the right way or was he shadowing the office of the president?

It seems almost strange that both men who blocked the stairs from the daughter of Mary Surratt would commit suicide shortly afterwards or did the President, too, hear the cry and plea of a daughter, trying to spare the life of her mother only to be turned away?

Why could not have the President at least listened to Anna Surratt instead of having her forced from the premises? Mary Surratt was not even allowed last rites by a priest. Should a person tried, convicted (innocent or guilty), be denied the opportunity to get their life right before the final judgment?

The trial took place rapidly without delay. What was the rush to hush the public? If it is meant to be, the truth will rule in the end, even if it takes several centuries to unravel. Conversations, diaries, and letters of witnesses may yet surface, despite a nation who wishes to seal them away. Goodness will prevail over evil.

The case was closed, or so it seemed sealed away, as if in a time warp. A lifetime would have to be lived out before people seriously began to question the actions of the President. After all, who then dare to say unkind words about their highest leader?

Punishing a less political person filled the public speculation. Holt had not signed the clemency papers but still, because of his professionalism, had carried out his duty to President Johnson, and presented the petition witnessed by twelve powerful men.

The nation wanted quick results. Was Joseph Holt used as a scapegoat? Did he serve the life sentence of being imprisoned by public opinion, by President Andrew Johnson in stating he had never seen the clemency papers that could have spared Mary Surratt's life?

How long must a person be punished for the unjust of the powers that be? Why would a kindred heart work the rest of his natural life trying to clear his name if he was not innocent? Truth wins out over evil, eventually.

Day after day, year after year, people arrive daily to the city of Washington. At the Library of Congress, they can examine the over twenty-thousand items in the papers of Joseph Holt. Each individual can decide who told the truth and who lied for selfish reasons. America deserves to hear the story and revisit it because it is part of its heritage.

Reading the "Vindication of Hon. Joseph Holt," the public can revisit the slander against a worthy Kentuckian, Judge Advocate General of the Lincoln Conspiracy Trial, and dedicated servant of our country. It was published for Joseph Holt in 1873, by The Chronicle Publishing Company, Washington.

A Kentuckian's Steadfastness

After the death of someone, many stories surface, some true and some partially true. Whatever the case, this story was told about Judge Advocate General Joseph Holt shortly after his passing on August 1, 1894.

In Judge Holt's early life he married Margaret Anderson Wickliffe, the beautiful daughter of Governor Charles Anderson Wickliffe. The Wickliffe family was delighted by the union of marriage of their Margaret to the brilliant lawyer, Holt.

After many months of sickness and the dreadful disease of consumption, Margaret, though young in life, was taken by death. Her body was laid to rest at the St. Joseph Cemetery by the shadows of one giant pine, standing majestically, watching over other family members.

In that age family members often waited three days before burying the deceased, in part to make sure the loved one was dead, not just unconscious or sleeping. In some instances graves were left open in case a family member came to or were revived. Sometimes at funerals individuals lying in the casket would rise during their funeral, scaring those present.

A wake was held for Margaret Wickliffe three days after her death. Fresh flowers were brought into the mansion to give the home a fresh smell, because of the body lying there for days. A family bathed the body dressed it and laid the body on a long beautiful table or decorated casket. Under the casket huge pieces of ice helped preserve the corpse until after the funeral.

Margaret's family prepared the home as well as the grounds for family and friends. It took all of Joseph Holt's courage to prepare himself for Margaret's funeral and parting. He chose to give a short account of her life and living as she requested. This would be one of the most difficult challenges for him. How would he get through this tragedy once again, of burying another young wife? Did he really have a shadow following him through life as he had once said, or was it simply fate? Margaret's eulogy would be about living instead of sickness and dying.

Joseph portrayed his Maggie as he called her, as his sweet earthly angel, a young woman, independent and loving, who cared about the world. Afterwards the quietness was broken only as Joseph, her brothers and sisters, with parents and close friends talked quietly and gave condolences.

A small hearse drawn by two horses waited in front of the beautiful mansion. It seemed so strange that Margaret was not attending the funeral of someone else. She had her favorite blue dress on with a black cross Joseph had given her. She appeared to be sleeping, as if ready to arise at any moment to speak. But today her world had grown silent, for there would be no more words spoken from her lips.

Joseph had been present with Margaret as she had taken her last breath. He had promised her he would take care of himself. As family and friends gathered closer, the small walnut casket was carried to the hearse and gently laid in safely. The other carriages lined behind the hearse following to the St. Joseph Cemetery, on the outskirts of town, to Margaret's final resting place.

Joseph was riding behind the hearse with Margaret's youngest sister, Julia and her husband. The widower solemnly looked slowly around the grounds of Margaret's home place and remembered, "It has been only ten years since we married. Margaret's youth is still present, and it seems still like a dream, that she is gone, out of my life forever. She should be running across the yard to greet us, Julia, not being taken to the grave."

Julia answered, "It breaks my heart Joseph, for on this day, the fourteenth of August, I am losing not only my sister, but my best and dearest friend. Oh Joseph, what will we do without Margaret?"

"I really don't know but the happy memories also bring sadness knowing you can never again have what you once loved. I'm lucky, for I did truly love Maggie, and she tried so diligently to give me a child. She was so young and had a difficult pregnancy, losing the baby before it developed. We were going to name her Margaret Millicent Wickliffe Holt," said Joseph with his head bent down.

As Joseph departed from the eight-hundred-acre plantation, with its rolling fields and meadows, his eyes viewed the creek they would cross. He remembered how in summer not many years ago the little ones loved to wade out into the cool water when the heat beat down on the hot days of summer, much like the temperature of today.

As the carriages moved up the hill toward town, fellow citizens stood in respect as the funeral procession continued. There were many following, as the Wickliffe family was looked upon highly by the state, as well as the community. Joseph was feeling pain, but how could parents bear to lose their child, only thirty-nine years old?

Next, Julia pointed out the courthouse, where so often she and Margaret had visited, but now it seemed as though an eternity had passed since they were young girls, skipping along carefree and enjoying the adventure of having a great day!

Julia remarked, "I believe the servants and the field hands were crying today as if their own child had died."

"No wonder, Julia, many of them have nursed Margaret as a child and watched her grow into such a beauty," said Joseph with a small smile of gratitude.

"Pa always worried over her because she seemed to be fragile, and so delicate," said Julia.

"I guess that is one of the reasons I fell in love with Maggie, her delicate and soft features. She was so refined, and she made me feel alive once again after I had suffered such depression. She was vibrant, and energized, entertaining, and had so much grace at social events. She always knew what to say, and how to say it. Maggie has given me ten wonderful years of marriage that most men would only dream about," spoke Joseph proudly.

"Well, we are here Joseph. I never thought I would bring my dear, beloved sister to St. Joseph Cemetery except to place flowers on our grandparents' graves," said Julia.

"Here Julia, let me help you down," said Joseph.

As the family exited the carriages and friends gathered closely, "Amazing Grace" was being played on bagpipes. The sunshine beat down, scorching the small shelter of a majestic pine hovering over the Wickliffe family as if the wings of God were sheltering their sorrow.

On the outskirts of Bardstown, not far from Margaret's home, the hearse had traveled the path many times to the graveyard, but seldom for such a young beauty.

A vacant spot beside Margaret waited for Joseph, her love. But many times young married wives were buried with their family because the husband might remarry and the family wanted to be sure their loved one was cared for properly. Joseph respected the wishes of Margaret's family by giving permission to let her be buried with her family at Bardstown.

The gravesite ritual began, a prayer followed, the minister said a few words, and the sisters of Margaret placed flowers on her coffin. The Wickliffe family had gathered to say good-bye to Margaret. Weeping mixed with sobs as tear-lined faces showed the sadness for all those present. Friends left the gravesite, heading back to Wickland for food and fellowship after the funeral. Next, the family members loaded into their carriages with tears and red eyes. Julia stood beside Joseph the entire morning, but realized that maybe he needed to say good-bye alone. Finally, everyone left, and only Joseph remained beside his Maggie.

Joseph asked the grave diggers to please leave and to give him some time alone. They obliged.

After the sisters, brothers, and parents left, Joseph lingered to have private time alone with Maggie. How sad it is to say good-bye to someone so beautiful, so vibrant, and so enthusiastic?

How could Joseph go on with life? This was not the first, but the second time, of the torture of loss of his loved one forever. Both wives would never know the suffering Joseph would live with, taking to his grave an unresolved injustice of fate.

Five years later, Margaret's father old Governor Charles Anderson Wickliffe, decided to make a return visit to Margaret's grave. It must have been a difficult journey because he was troubled with many elements of old age, legally being blind, he needed assistance from a faithful servant, driving his carriage to St. Joseph Cemetery.

As Gov. Wickliffe arrived at the family cemetery, he noticed the added name of Margaret to the list of names engraved upon the shaft. "Margaret Wickliffe Holt" the inscription read, and then later, came the Surratt trial, when Judge Holt became the focus for abuse by the "Copperhead" organs throughout the North and the unreconstructed South. But that lay in the future.

The servant helped the aged Governor Wickliffe out of the carriage. He slowly made his way to Margaret's grave. Governor Wickliffe said, "Margaret, your deep sleep is peaceful, and sadly the grave yard has grown since your departing. Your dear Papa has traveled today the small road to see you for I fear my health is worsing, and this may be the last time I can talk to you before I die," said the former governor.

"Master, be careful, the fence is sharp and Margaret's grave is very close to it," said Big Tom.

"Leave me alone, just guide me to Margaret's grave," spoke Governor Wickliffe.

He felt the grave, wrapping his long arms around the tombstone as a father would his child. He fell to his knees weeping, "Oh, my Margaret, why did you leave me and your Ma? You had so many years before you. You were always delicate, and fragile. You would have been fine if you had not married that stranger, Joseph Holt.

"Five years have passed since you have died Margaret. Our country is in a dreadful war. It is tearing families apart, even ours. Maybe it is best you are not here to see the pain and what is happening to the South."

Governor Wickliffe moved his hand across the monument until he found the name Margaret. There were tears in his sightless eyes. His hands trembled remembering happiness of that name, Margaret's happy, guarded youth, growing into a beautiful southern lady. Wickliffe, a proud honorable name given in marriage to a stranger, leaving all things behind for Joseph Holt. And on that dark day of her last homecoming, when he had seen her body committed to the embrace of her native soil, Margaret Wickliffe lived alone in memory.

Next Governor Wickliffe found Holt. The fingers traced the four letters, not trembling anymore. The face softened by emotions a few minutes ago, now grew stern and angry. For now he could not remember a time when he loved the bearer of that name. He now felt the name was only a blot on the tablet. Feeling the name Holt caused sadness to the old governor.

"Big Tom, go over to the carriage and bring me that chisel," said Governor Wickliffe in a demanding tone.

"Whatever for do you want that old chisel master?" said Big Tom.

"Never you mind why I want it, just fetch it," said Gov. Wickliffe.

The old governor, almost totally blind and bothered with all signs of old age, had been bitterly offended by the actions of his son-in-law. With his own hands he wielded the mallet and chisels, effacing the hated name, Holt.

The judgment of the world may not accord with that of Governor Wickliffe. It may believe Judge Holt performed a most unpleasant duty with loyalty and dignity of a great lawyer, deserving gratitude from his country for this service and others so grandly performed. Some will admire the steadfastness of the old man to his convictions, even if they were mistaken.

In the shadow of Margaret's grave, a soft flowing breeze blows, sending comfort to those stopping by to visit, and looking above a majestic picture, dusted clouds contain touches of angelic sweeps, portraying a painting of natural elegance. The bagpipes strike up once again for another family, to remind them they are saying good-bye for now but not forever.

The uniquely constructed Victorian fence serves as a protector of family; however memory lingers even now, centuries later. All is quiet except the beating of a distant drum. Butterflies land on the small metal fence surrounding the family graves, as if remembering life as it use to be. In the distance whippoorwills call persistently, as if saying, "Come out and play just one more time."

Today on the left side of Margaret's grave the inscription reads, "Blessed are they which do hunger and trust after righteous for they shall be filled." On the right side it reads: "For I know that my redeemer liveth."

Headlines Read: No Will Found for Judge Joseph Holt

Did Joseph Holt have a will? Was it destroyed by servants before nephews arrived from Breckinridge County to Washington, D.C.? Did Judge Holt believe and trust his nephew, Washington D. Holt, to take care of his fortune? Was the will burned when his two nephews destroyed papers they testified later in court were only letters written from family to Judge Holt and nothing of importance?

Could it have been Judge Holt's nature to completely neglect the promise he had made his first wife Mary on her deathbed to always provide for her Cousin Elizabeth Hynes? Was it strange that many relatives' letters never reached Holt when Washington D. Holt became more involved with Judge Holt and promised his estate? Was it not usual for a nephew to offer someone in the Register of Wills Office $40,000 to locate a will for the late Joseph Holt?

Judge Holt had always taken care of first wife Mary's cousin Lizzie, Elizabeth Hynes, raised by Mary Harrison (Holt), and her father, Dr. Burr Harrison, until Mary's marriage to Judge Holt. When Mary Harrison married Joseph Holt, she asked him always to treat Lizzie as their daughter. Joseph kept his promise by including Lizzie on the many trips he took. He also gave Lizzie fifty dollars a month to live on, later a bond in the amount of $10,000, and sent smaller amounts later.

Elizabeth Hynes had communicated with Judge Holt for over forty years and was one of his favorite people who came to visit him. Josephine Throckmorton, a godchild named for Judge Holt, the daughter of Major Charles B. Throckmorton, and cousin to Judge Holt's second wife, also received favors from him.

After the Civil War, Judge Holt continued living and working in Washington. During that time no family reunions took place at Holt's Bottoms in Breckinridge County. Even though Judge Holt was kind to his nephew, Washington D. Holt, it did not help relations with other family members.

Judge Holt was saddened by family members being active with the South, and would not receive some of them when they came to visit him in Washington. It was not until those old wounds begin to heal that Judge Holt read letters from some family members without returning them unopened. However, the Judge's love of his own home remained deep in his heart, and many times he traveled back to his boyhood home in the spring and fall staying months at a time, enjoying sitting under the majestic trees collected from his travels around the world.

Judge Holt enjoyed relaxing by the beautiful bottomlands nestled by the scenic Ohio River his family had homesteaded in 1811. He loved his home place and stated that there would not ever be a place he loved more. His three-story home sat on the same site where his parents had homesteaded in 1811. The former structure of logs was destroyed by fire and he rebuilt the house in 1850.

Deeply stirred with Judge Holt's death on August 1, 1894, family members wondered who would inherit the fortune. Servants repeated conversations heard while Judge Holt was still living. He mentioned he would not worry about his last wishes, knowing, his nephew Washington would take care of his final affairs. The servants told of how Judge Holt had made a statement to Mary Holt, Washington's daughter, stating she needed to learn French for upon his death Vanda Holt and daughter, Mary, would be able to travel to Europe and Mary needed to be proficient in French.

Immediately upon Judge Holt's death, his nephews, Washington D. Holt and William G. Sterrett, came to his late residence in Washington, and the keys were delivered to them by one of the servants. A strict search was made for Judge Holt's will, but nothing was found. While both nephews were searching for the will, they also burned and destroyed papers, as Judge Holt's cook watched from a window behind the kitchen area. They later testified the papers had been wholly unimportant, and were only letters from relatives of Judge Holt to him, and that no papers destroyed were of a testamentary character.

Washington D. and Vanda Holt were very restless as they arrived at the depot. "I knew we should have visited Uncle more often," said Vanda.

"We made at least one trip a year and communicated by telegraph often. Remember, Uncle said everything was taken care of and we would be better off than before," spoke Washington assured.

"That is easy for you to say but we have not seen any will, and I will worry about it until we know Uncle's last wishes," said Vanda with hesitation in her voice.

"I am sure Uncle Joseph has his business arranged as he has always been very careful about keeping records and putting things in the right order. We must have patience!" William Sterrett assured her.

As the three pulled under the huge oak trees in the driveway, other carriages hovered near the home. As Washington, Vanda, and daughter Mary ascended the steps to the beautiful old mansion, it somehow seemed different with the master of the house no longer present.

Things seemed to have been ransacked before their arrival. They searched, Judge Holt's desk, closets, and every suitable place, however, the resemblance of a will never surfaced.

With the absence of a will, nephews and another named John W. Holt, filed a petition in the Supreme Court of the District of Columbia, holding a special term for orphans' court business, in which the fact of intestacy was stated and the appointment was asked. Pursuant to the petition on September 28, 1894, the National Safe Deposit, Savings & Trust Company was appointed administrator of the estate and continued until August 26, 1895.

With news of Judge Holt's death, a funeral was planned in Washington. The flag was ordered at half mass at the Department of War until the funeral was completed. Judge Holt had told Lizzie Hynes that his will had instructions for his final wishes and funeral. Once while visiting the judge, he asked Lizzie to go upstairs and find a flag in which he wanted his body to be wrapped. Judge Holt wanted to know if the flag was motheaten, but to Lizzie's surprise the flag was in good shape. That final wish was granted, but the other requests were never known. Judge Holt's body then traveled by train to Cloverport where the funeral home conducted the most famous funeral in Breckinridge County, at the Holt Church, the same church Judge Holt had built years earlier for his beloved mother.

Judge Holt was laid to rest in a small cemetery containing several graves. His grave is surrounded by a thick brick wall with a rounded concrete top. In the center of the wall is a double iron grate with an arch over the top. Trailing over the arch and wall are vines in a solid mat of green. In the center of the cemetery towers a large pine tree brought from the South on a boat and carried from the landing by slaves. Above the wall can be seen the tops of several stones. The largest of these is Joseph Holt's. The tombstone has a bronze eagle on two crossed cannons. Beside the cannons are three cannons balls. Engraved on the stone are the words, "Joseph Holt, born January 6, 1807, died August 1, 1894. Orator and Statesman, Held successively these office: Commissioner of Patents, Postmaster General, Secretary of War, Judge Advocate General during the Civil War."

In the distance can be seen the red brick church built by Joseph Holt. On the sides are windows to many shaped glasses with one large round window near the top over the vestibule. The roof consists of slate shingles. Inside the church are swinging lamps suspend from the ceiling. The brescord ceiling and seats are in the old English style. Hanging on the wall beside the pulpit is a marble slab on which is written, "In memory of Eleanor K. Holt, who died as she lived, a consistent member of the Methodist Church."

With the dilemma of two nephews not finding a will, a petition was filed in orphan's court in Washington. The first year after Judge Holt's death only $25,000 dollars was distributed to members of Judge Holt's family, and things seemed to be moving in a positive direction until, one year later, when a mysterious will suddenly appeared at the Registry of Wills in Washington D.C.

With this news, reporters flocked to Washington to get their own version of the highly discussed case. Multiple copies of the will were made by a photographer, so it could be studied to examine the authority of the handwriting.

The arrival of the mystery will caused an emotional stir within the family of Judge Holt, once again, and the case continued in the courts. What Judge Holt had worked for his entire life even small items, would be fought over by family whose company the judge had not enjoyed or received in his Washington residence for most of the time since.

Notices appeared in national newspapers with the urgent find. Two young ladies mentioned as recipients of Judge Holt's estate Lizzie Hynes and Josephine Throckmorton began their journey to Washington.

Lizzie Hynes was around sixty years old, but only appeared to be in her fifties. Mr. Holt had promised the first Mrs. Holt to care for Lizzie as their child when they first married, and then once again on her deathbed.

Lizzie testified in court during the time of trying to prove the will of 1873 that she had communicated with him for over forty years.

Josephine Throckmorton, around thirty years old, was the other young lady named in the mysterious will. On the first day of the will contest on Monday, May 18, 1896, Miss Throckmorton made her entrance into the courtroom. She exhibited unusual beauty, having bright and dark eyes, and light brown hair. She dressed plainly in dark colors, and looked very becoming in black, showing good taste and refinement.

Holt's ex-coachman and butler George Johnson spoke about Judge Holt. He testified Judge Holt said, "None of his relatives who abused him for taking sides with the Union should be benefited by his death." He continued to say that Judge Holt liked Washington D. Holt and his wife Vanda and Lizzie Hynes, and that during his lifetime did a great deal for Washington and Vanda. Johnson said he took calling cards from women who said they were relatives of Holt, but the judge refused to see them.

The coachman of Judge Holt told in court about the relations between Judge Holt and the Throckmortons, covering the period in which the estrangement began. For eight years, George Johnson was Judge Holt's coachman and he recalled several incidences. He remembered Judge Holt in 1884 or 1885 speaking of a will made for the benefit of Washington D. Holt and his wife, and Elizabeth Hynes, and that no other relatives were included in its provisions. The judge frequently expressed that none of his relatives who had abused him for taking the side of the Union during the war should be benefited by his death.

Johnson left about 1886 before Col. Sterrett and his wife arrived in Washington, and had no knowledge of the judge's sentiments toward Washington. Johnson said he never learned the cause of the estrangement between Judge Holt and the Throckmortons, but believed it was something Mrs. Mary Throckmorton had said about Vanda Holt when Judge Holt visited Washington Holt in Kentucky. The judge and Throckmortons were very close friends at the time.

When Judge Holt went to Kentucky, he had ordered Johnson to be in charge of his mansion, and to look after the comfort of Mary Throckmorton, Miss Josephine's grandmother, and to leave nothing undone. Mrs. Throckmorton had use of Judge Holt's carriage while Judge Holt was away as well. When Judge Holt returned from Kentucky, he seemed in a good mood when he went in to see Mrs. Throckmorton, but was in rage when he left her house. He told George to never admit Mrs. Throckmorton to the house again and even the two little children were denied admittance to his presence.

Joseph Holt's fondness for Washington Holt and his wife found expression in acts of benevolence and kindness. Johnson was summoned to the house after Judge Holt's death and saw them. They had been looking for a will and had not found it; Mrs. Holt declared that someone must have ransacked the house before they arrived. She was apparently much disappointed, supposing that a will would be found among the effects of the deceased. An old friend of the judge heard him say just a year earlier that he had named Washington Holt his heir and executor.

The public continued wondering why the sender of the will did not come forward. People clung to the theory the will was a forgery. Many theories arose as to why the mysterious will arrived at the Register of Wills. One very possible motive was that the will was found by someone who bought one of the judge's books sold after his death.

There was no penalty in the case for a person mailing a mutilated will to the register. Thus, the sender could go to the register, make a full explanation of the facts for the benefit of the heirs, and save them from the expensive law suit in trying to determine the validity of the will. It was believed the will was burned purposely with a cigar, not an accident.

A news release was printed in the August 22, 1894 issue of the *Breckinridge News*:

> Washington, August 20 (special), John Holt of Texas, Washington D. Holt of Kentucky, and William G. Sterrett of Kentucky, as heirs of the late Judge Joseph Holt, have filed a petition in the probate Court praying for a settlement and distribution of the estate of the deceased who is stated to have been an uncle of the petitioners. It was supposed that Judge Holt left a will dividing his estate between his favorite relatives, but so far no will has been found.
>
> The petitioner's state that the real estate of their uncle amounted to between $30,000 and $40,000 and that the personal estate was even larger, $66,000 of the latter being in the District of Columbia. Three hundred and sixty-five bonds were discovered in an old satchel in Judge Holt's Washington home. Other personal estate

included 2,600 of 5% percent bonds of the city of Louisville, 5,000 of 4 percent.

U. S. Supreme Court Throckmorton v. Holt, 180 U. S. 552 (1901)
Josephine H. Throckmorton and Luke Devlin, Piffs. In Err.
v.
Washington Holt et al.
No. 21
Argued December 7, 10, 1900
Decided March 25, 1901

A proceeding began in the Supreme Court of the District of Columbia for the purpose of proving an alleged will of the late Joseph Holt a distinguished lawyer and for many years Judge Advocate General of the United States Army, who died at the age of eighty-seven, in Washington on August 1, 1894. The proceedings resulted with testimony after testimony trying to establish the authenticity of the paper on the ground that it was or was not the will of Judge Holt or was it a forged document. Washington buzzed with gossip, as this became one of the most talked about cases in the history of Washington.

Luke Delvin had been administrator in the mysterious will. But who was Luke Delvin and why would Judge Holt put him as executor of his will? Delvin was a young man who had worked at the War Department and had been a messenger for Judge Holt. Delvin also collected autographs of famous people.

Register of Wills McGill testified to the conditions of the will. Attorneys for the heirs-at law put on the stand a very important witness, Colonel Thomas Barr, from Governor Island, New York, and the Assistant Judge Advocate General, who knew Holt well. He had reported to him until April 1, 1870. Colonel Barr testified that he daily saw Holt's handwriting and signature and knew its style and manor of composition. The will was then handed to him as he examined it long and carefully. Then in a reserved manner he stated, "My impression is Judge Holt never wrote that paper. The paper is similar in some responds but as a whole although unlike anything I have ever seen of his."

Colonel Barr said, "Judge Holt had the cleanest power of expression I have ever known and was the finest rhetorician I have ever met. He gave great care of reports prepared by him and no one ever read an incorrect expression."

Emma S. Briggs met Judge Holt at Andrew Johnson's inauguration. She was a correspondent, and journalist, during her acquaintance with Judge Holt, and had exchanged letters with him. He had also visited her home. She admired his style of writing and continued that she did not believe the signature and the will was Judge Holt's.

Ex-Postmaster Horatio King said, "In 1861 I was appointed Postmaster General serving from March 7 that year until Judge Holt resigned with the Cabinet. I was the first assistant under Judge Holt, when he was Postmaster General.

"We were often in conferences on official matters and I became familiar with his handwriting. I remained very close to Judge Holt until near his death. During the judge's illness four or five years before his death, hardly a day passed that I was not a caller at the Holt house chatting with him.

"I had much correspondence with him and have twenty letters signed by Judge Holt." Unquestionably, he said, "The whole thing is a fraud!" With this outburst the crowd of spectators stirred a commotion, causing the court officer to rap for silence. "Order in this court, Order in this court," shouted the officer.

Upon General King's examination of the will of last year with Washington Holt, he too believed the will a forgery. He stated that Judge Holt would have used over fifteen commas.

As the spectators of the courtroom listened carefully, different witnesses relived small segments of the life of Joseph Holt. One such account was the testimony of Emma S. Briggs whom Judge Holt had written a letter of introduction for with her present at his home. Briggs was the first woman engaged in newspaper work as a Washington correspondent. Her connection to the press dated back to the Civil War. She became a frequent visitor at Judge Holt's house for the purpose of drinking in the beauties of his rhetoric and loving herself in the fountains of his diction. From this association of Judge Holt, Briggs declared she came to be known as a great writer.

Presently an old lady dressed in black silk, she remembered asking Judge Holt about the whereabouts of Mrs. Throckmorton. "I do not know the Throckmortons," was Judge Holt's reply. In conversation with Judge Holt about another will, cautiously she suggested he be careful. Judge

Holt replied, "In my own case, my nephew, my brother's son Washington Holt will attend to my affairs, and I know it will be done right."

She discussed Judge Holt's writing style. The chief characteristic of Holt's style was forcefulness. He never used a word that could be omitted, but wrote in a cramped, scratchy hand. His composition had accuracy, and his style of expression was marked by great care. Both in speech and in writing, his composition was a little formal and a little florid, marked by emotion, although he illustrated a good deal.

One witness who quieted the courtroom was Miss Willie Green Sterrett, a young woman of thirteen. She replied to all questions, without the slightest reserve, and sometimes the innocence of her answers brought smiles even to the faces of the litigants on either side, who had been sitting all day absorbed in evidence, making an occasional sarcastic comment when it did not meet with their approval. First, Miss Sterrett gave account of her brothers and sisters, and what she knew about the relatives of her own family with Judge Holt.

She said, "I live on H Street, and Judge Holt lived on New Jersey Street. My sister and I always had fun visiting Judge Holt. He played with us and took us upon his knee. We could always talk to Judge Holt, and enjoyed eating delicious food at his home. Sometimes the judge gave us money, sometimes 50 cents, sometimes a dollar, once he gave us both two dollars and fifty cents.

"Judge Holt use to come to my parents' home in his beautiful carriage taking my mother, sister and me driving. He always treated our family very nice."

At the Judge's house a few days after his death young Willie continued, "I was looking for postage stamps because Judge Holt always had plenty of stamps, but instead of finding stamps I found a small piece of paper in one of the closets in the Judge's room." Mr. Worthington then asked, "Could you read what was on the paper?"

"Why of course," she answered with a rising reflection.

The piece of paper had been placed in a valise belonging to one of the heirs, and the valise was stolen while Judge Holt was on his way from the South to Washington. The papers were burned by the thief. The paper was inscribed: "Will Jan.1, 1886, and there were two names on it, one of which was Roundtree, without any initials while the other could not be deciphered."

"I was looking for stamps and found the paper. They all looked the papers over and were through with them."

Then Miss Sterrett was asked, "Who looked them over?"

She said, "The heirs, they were trying to find the will."

"Where did Judge Holt keep his papers when he was alive?"

Miss Sterrett replied, "I couldn't tell you to save my life." She bore up well until the ordeal ended and when she returned to her mother she began to cry. (She was attending school at Staunton, Virginia at this time.)

Next to testify was Emma Board, who had been a servant, in the family of Washington Holt, at Holt's Bottom, Kentucky. Miss Board began, "Judge Holt visited his nephew every spring and fall until his health got bad. He has always treated the family members very kindly and frequently sent the two daughters presents. One time I was fastening the judge's collar and he told me he would not live long, advising me to remain with the family of his nephew. Judge Holt said I would be taken care of, as he had provided for Washington's family in his will."

Albert L. Smith testified that Luke Devlin was a messenger for Judge Holt when he was Judge Advocate General. Questioned to whether Devlin kept autographs, Smith replied, as all present craned their necks, "Yes, Devlin kept an autographed album."

Then a deposition of Robert S. Holt of Tacoma, Washington, a nephew of Judge Holt was submitted for the heirs-at law by Mr. Worthington. The deponent simply testified to the warm relations existing between his father and Judge Holt. A large number of letters from Joseph Holt to deponent accompanied the disposition to show friendly relations were continued with the son.

Mrs. Iglehart, sister of the deponent, Robert S. Holt, was sworn in. Mrs. Iglehart testified to her first meeting with her uncle. "On my wedding trip in 1874 I was joyously entertained at my Uncle's home. He took me riding, and I enjoyed being entertained all over Washington. Once again ten years latter I visited with a most welcomed feeling making me feel as if I had always lived with Uncle. We corresponded before and after my marriage. I found it quite amusing that Uncle tried to give me advice on how to make my husband happy," stated Mrs. Iglehart.

The letters of correspondence written to Mrs. Iglehart between 1870 and 1887 were entered into evidence. Mr. Worthington noted that at the close of each letter, after your affectionate Uncle, J. Holt, he had a jab to the J. But Judge Holt had stopped making jabs and the person writing the will did not know it.

Mrs. Iglehart said, "The writing does not look familiar at all. I wrote to Uncle complaining to him he had never visited me."

The next witness was Martha Scott, a servant, in Judge Holt's house from 1881 until his death. "Mrs. Throckmorton called on Judge Holt's house once a week. I would give the judge her name and the judge always told me to tell her he would not see her. This continued weekly, but Judge Holt never saw Mrs. Throckmorton," remarked Mrs. Scott.

Probably no case in the history of the local bar had had as much excitement and more widespread interest than this contest of Throckmorton v. Holt over the alleged will of Judge Holt in Judge Bradley's Court. The mystery surrounded the appearance of the will and its mutilated condition of charred paper, torn, without a seal, and witnesses such as President Grant, and General Sherman and Mrs. Sherman.

The irregular paper had bequeathed everything to Elizabeth Hynes and Josephine Holt Throckmorton. Holt died on August 1, 1894 leaving $180,000, no will was found, and the estate was being administered in the interest of certain blood relatives including Washington D. Holt. Some $9,000 dollars had been divided among the heirs–at law, when unexpectedly, within a few days of the legally constituted limit, the mysterious will of 1873 naming Luke Devlin, a clerk in the War Department executor, made its appearance in the Office of the Register of Wills in a large white envelope addressed in a disguised hand.

The will had been burned in places, but had not destroyed any vital part of the writing. The place where the seal should be affixed had been torn off and the part bearing the signatures apparently separated from the body by long wear, the whole having been pasted on a new sheet of paper to hold it together.

Edges were burned while the document was folded. The fire marks on the face of the will were made while the paper was face open or only partly divided. The letter containing the document was put in the mail Saturday afternoon August 24, 1895. The letter bore the post office stamp at 6:00 P.M. and it remained in the office until Monday morning when it was delivered.

Enclosed in a large white envelope, was a fitted piece of cardboard to protect the will. Two two-cent stamps had been carelessly or hurriedly attached.

Both sides had distinguished legal talent engaged. Attorneys for the legatees under the will were J.J. Darlington, Ex-Congressman Ben Butterworth, and Blair Lee. The other side had A.S. Worthington, Jere M. Wilson, J.C. Heald, James C. Poston of Louisville, and attorney McCord of Kentucky, the personal representative of Miss Hynes.

On day two of the proceeding, Mr. Worthington stated there was more reason to believe that Luke Devlin wrote the will than Judge Holt. The court decided the council for the beneficiaries must produce full evidence in support of the validity of the will, and strained relations between Judge Holt and the Throckmortons was brought out into the open.

Mr. Luke Devlin, named executor, a short, stout, middle-aged man, was Judge Holt's private secretary from 1862 until sometime in the 1870s during the time Holt was Judge Advocate General of the United States. Devlin was regarded as a man of high integrity, employed in the record and pension division of the War Department. Through the proceedings he had a sharp, nervous interest. His full face seldom changed with expression.

On May the 20, the third day of the proceedings, Darlington, one of the attorneys for the legatees, tried to establish the genuineness of the writing.

Attorney Wilson wanted to know if the will had character of Judge Holt, and. Darlington objected. Worthington said, "It is not a question whether the handwriting was Judge Holt's but whether the handwriting was Judge Holt's last will and testimony and to prove that they might have to go deeper than handwriting."

Clarence F. Cobb, thirty-two years clerk at the War Department, compiled correspondence between General Brice and Judge Holt, examined the will last January and believed Judge Holt had written it. Rev. Butler was asked to examine the handwriting, (he had written to Joseph Holt in 1865 about the Surratt Trial) and he thought the writing was in Judge Holt's handwriting.

Back on the stand Miss Throckmorton was asked when you wrote Judge Holt did he answer your letters. "He most certainly did," she said triumphal.

Judge Bradley ruled on Thursday May 21 that the testimony showing the character of the relationship between Judge Holt and the Throckmortons toward the close of his life was admissible as evidence. That turning point in the case afforded the attorneys assailing the will a full opportunity to prove that the relationship existing in 1873, the year in which the will in evidence was alleged to have been drawn in favor of Miss Josephine Throckmorton and Miss Lizzie Hynes, no longer existed during the closing years of his life, at least to the first two beneficiaries.

People on the streets of Washington wandered by the street where Judge Holt had lived. The fine old mansion at the corner of New Jersey Avenue and C Street Southeast, opposite the Varnum Hotel, now had been neglected since the death of the man who had entertained Washington, including the President. The judge owned a fine piece of property but weeds now grew in blissful innocence of a scythe or mower, as ivy vines now crept over the front steps of the home.

Judge Holt lived many years with his servants after the death of his second wife. Two servants, man and wife, Charles and Frances Strother, occupied the rear of the mansion, and showed strangers the house by appointment of the real estate agent, for the mansion was for sale.

Frances Strother, a woman of about thirty, had long served Judge Holt. Her mother, Ellen Christian, was Judge Holt's cook for fifteen years. Housekeeper Martha Thomas had served Judge Holt for fourteen years. Coachman Strother diligently cared for Judge Holt for eight years and two years earlier married Mrs. Christian's daughter Frances. This constituted the judge's household for many years.

As the trial continued, Lizzie caught herself daydreaming. She thought about the many trips she went abroad with Judge Holt, and she could still remember his great speaking voice. How strange things seemed. How would Judge Holt feel about this mess, being such a talented lawyer how would he have conducted this trial, and what would his defenses have been?

Lizzie remembered one afternoon when she visited Judge Holt.

"Lizzie, Lizzie," called the judge.

"Yes, what did you want," answered Lizzie?

"I want you to go up stairs and find a flag for me, look and see if it has been moth-eaten, and report back to me," said Judge Holt.

"I climbed the stairs, thought Lizzie, wondering what the judge wanted with his flag that had been carefully put away years ago. I searched through several dresser drawers before finding the stars and strips. I then hurriedly went down stairs to where the judge was setting by the window letting the light shine through."

"Uncle, the flag looks just like it was placed inside the paper tissue yesterday," smiled Lizzie.

"That's magnificent," the judge said, as he shook his head. "Listen carefully Lizzie, when I die I want that flag to be wrapped around my body and all other funeral arrangements are in my will. As you know I always keep my closets in the library and my desk locked. However, when I die I want you to take charge of my watch, and the ring of keys I keep in my trouser pocket. Keep them until Washington arrives here and telegraph him for all of my business is in Washington D. Holt's hands."

Momentarily awaken from daydreaming, Lizzie heard a bell ring. It must have come from a passing carriage in the streets. It definitely caught Lizzie's attention as Judge Holt always kept a bell close at hand when he had become sick.

Refocused, Lizzie listened as the efforts of counsel for the heirs-at-law had been directed toward proving by reading many letters during the trial from Judge Holt that the old gentleman devoted the greater part of his life during his later years to making his relatives happy.

Ellen Foster then was asked to take the oath to testify and she began,

"Judge Holt thought more of Washington Holt's family than anyone else in the world. Judge Holt had special cups and saucers for them and no one else was permitted to use them."

Next Miss Mary Holt, daughter of Washington D. Holt, first saw her uncle in 1876. Miss Holt, eighteen-years, old, began, "When I was only eight years old I came to Washington with my parents and stayed at Uncle's house for several weeks. Uncle took me out driving and to the theater. He gave me fruit and candy and we never went without him buying me a present. I visited Uncle in 1881 and 1882. He always paid my school bills and told me I could study in the United States or Europe. My parents did not want me to go to Europe."

Mr. Worthington asked, "What did Judge Holt do to beautify the place when he came there?"

"Oh, he had the house built, besides summer houses and carriage houses, and other things.

"What if anything did he say he wanted done with the old homestead?"

"I heard him say many times that he never wanted it to pass out of the family. That it was the only place he loved, and the only place that was home to him," said Mary, teary-eyed.

Next some letters were read out loud that had been written to Washington D. Holt and his wife. As Mrs. Holt read the letters, the courtroom watched her movements, for she was a very attractive woman.

"The great desire of my life is that the dear old place shall be kept in our family from generation to generation. I hope that in 1911 you will celebrate the centennial of the settlement of our family in the Bottoms." This referred to the old homestead at Holt's Bottom, the present residence of Washington Holt. Joseph Holt had built the dwelling, standing in the same spot as a former log dwelling, which had housed his family when his parents were still living but had been destroyed by fire.

The case continued with testimony after testimony. The closing hours of what had been one of the most remarkable trials in the history of the Circuit Court of the District, were dramatic. The crowd in the courtroom throughout the day was dense, but when time came for Judge Bradley to deliver his charge to the jury, many members of the bar strained their ears in efforts to hear everything.

Judge Bradley said, "There are four issues which have been submitted by the Orphans' Court, and to each of these issues you must return an answer, and that answer will be yes or no, save with respect to the fourth issue. The answer to that issue may be, if the evidence justifies it, more than the simple affirmative or negative. The first issue is, 'Was the paper executed by the said Joseph Holt?' The second is, 'Was the execution procured by fraud practiced upon Joseph Holt?' The third is, 'Was it secured by undue influence?' The fourth is, 'If it was executed, has it been revoked by the testator?' Your deliberations will be confined absolutely to the first and fourth issues which have been on trial."

It was 4:20 P.M. when the court completed the charge, and both Darlington, and Worthington called attention to minor points to which they took exception. They were all straightened out without difficulty, and at 4:35 the jury filed out of the courtroom.

Judge Bradley left orders to be notified at any time before 10:00 if a verdict was reached. He was back at the court very soon after 8:00 upon notice that the jury had agreed. Washington Holt's family sat motionless, and the two young ladies waited patiently, as if they wished the whole thing would soon be over.

Lizzie Hynes wondered, "Was this finally going to be settled? Would Judge Holt's estate have closure with all parties being satisfied?" She remembered earlier what Judge Bradley had said,

"If we had been enlightened by the testimony of any one of these witnesses, probably this question of whether this will, as well as the signature to it, was written by Joseph Holt. If any one of these subscribing witnesses, General Grant, who was at the time of this alleged execution President of the United States, or General Sherman who I believe was General of the Army at that time, or his wife had testified, I hardly think that any one of you would have a question as to the genuineness of the signature of Judge Holt. If a reputable witness had testified that he had seen Judge Holt sign the paper, or had heard him acknowledge the signature, this question this would have been almost absolutely foreclosed.

"If we were enlightened as the source from which this paper originated just before it made its appearance in the office of the Register of Wills, doubtless that we would throw a great deal of legation upon this question. The difficulty is that this paper was deposited in the mail by some person where for some reason, deems it necessary to be quite, for he does not come forward and indicate that it was deposited. Who that person is, is no direct evidence in this case. Who that person may be is claimed by counsel for both parties, is indicated by circumstances in this case. Who the person is you may be able to determine, measuring these circumstances by your experience as men and understanding the motives which ordinarily influence them. And if you do reach the conclusion as in all probability sent this paper to the office of the Register of Wills, you will probably have your hands on the key to this situation."

Fading back to the present, Lizzie gazed upon the single gas lamp throwing a dim light upon the final scene in the great drama. The figure of Judge Bradley was only a dark outline upon the bench, and a few indistinct shadows scattered over the room representing the lawyers and public.

After waiting until 8:20 P.M., when some of the lawyers made their appearance Judge Bradley announced that he did not feel justified in keeping the jury waiting any longer, and ordered that they be summoned to the courtroom. They filed in and stood in a straight line in front of the bench. The foreman handed the clerk the paper on which the questions they had decided upon were typewritten, and after each man had answered to his name, the clerk read the four questions.

The whole verdict hinged upon the first question: "Was the paper, bearing date February 7, 1873, and filed in this court August 23, 1895, written and executed by the said Joseph Holt as his last will and testament? Your answer to this question is--." And the clerk paused, and the foreman answered, "No." The answers to the other three questions were the same, but they were all read and the proper replies made.

On the points of law, principally rulings on evidence, the verdict was sustained in the Supreme Court of the District (1898, Throckmorton v. Holt 12 D.C. App. 552). But in the Supreme Court of the United States, the judgment was set aside, three judges dissenting (1901, Throckmorton v. Holt 180 U. S. 552, 21 Sup 474). No second trial took place; the parties settled the case by compromise."

Time passes but the focus and conversations remain still drawn to the unsolved will, never found except one perhaps forged in 1873 by someone other than the late Joseph Holt. How could a gentleman so gifted and prepared for life with such timely management not plan the destiny of the fortune he had worked a lifetime to gain?

Epilogue

By the river, sounds of snow geese circling can be heard chanting a praise of the sleepy earth, waiting to be awakened on a cold, sunny winter morning. The sun dazzles brightly as puffy, white, blotched clouds float by in haste. The crow gives his morning serenade to other birds of flight.

Water from snow-melted lawns, covered with fallen leaves, press in the high winter grasses. The trees overlook a frosty morning in the South.

The freshness of air causes the soul to relive energetic moments of winters past. The magical moments of spring at last arrive, raising spirits, opening hearts to the adventures ahead when spring pounces jubilantly, bringing life and living once again. To those who listen, they can hear the words:

"Over two hundred years ago I was born, and over two hundreds years have passed. Great occurrences have progressed in history. Leaders and successors have brought both pain and strength, allowing our country to proceed into today's destiny."

In order to progress with great dignity, people must first understand, appreciate, protect, and carry the past in their hearts. It is only fair to speak of every man's story to get the truth, sometimes lost in the heart and soul of those who fought as well as lived to preserve a wholesome way of life and to strive for goodness over evil and power.

Searching the records, skimming the archives, and visiting the past, show that Judge Holt's work still encourages the nation to stand for its beliefs to work together instead of dividing the power of togetherness, to unite a nation to work for a solution, to heal a nation to join together their talents, continuing the good works the world desires.

Today, sitting beside Judge Holt's grave in Breckinridge County, Kentucky, the only place he loved and the only place he really called home, the wind is blowing, and leaves flying. The train's whistle moans in the distance, over a path covered before in different centuries when Judge

Holt traveled back and forth to Washington. The engine roars behind the grave of Joseph Holt, now silent. The screeching of the wheels is heard as they grab the rails. The whistle blows three times as a signal to the past.

The yellow-colored moss embraces the red brick encasing the graveyard of seven visible gravesites. A black gate sealed by a rusty chain has a key to let visitors view what was.

The bronze eagle is no longer majestic. The years have turned it to green. The indention on the left side of the entrance of the Holt family cemetery served a purpose in the past. The bricks are crumbling but still waiting. The inside wall of the small graveyard has lost over a yard of bricks. The top of the post made of cement is beginning to crack. Joseph lies next to his mother, as close in death as in life. The outside part of the wall has a layer of bricks with another inside layer of bricks. The gate is cemented into the edge of the bricks when entering the graveyard. The Holt House in Breckinridge County, Kentucky can be seen in the distance from the grave.

Recalling the words of Judge Joseph Holt, "It is encouraging to know that behind every cloud the sun still shineth, that if we are patient every cloud shall see its light again." The brilliant light of the sun covers the dark graveyard, and extends on the inside and outside as leaves tumble around on the foreground. The sky is clear, with a few feathery clouds decorating the sky. In the background, extending over the top of the brick fence trees can be seen in the distance across the Ohio River to Indiana. The train passes, but no passengers step off today.

Walking in the yard, tracing the footsteps taken long ago by Judge Advocate General Joseph Holt, visitors can still hear his voice if they listen to stories of the past, the grandeur of life that once was.

As the light house of Summer Seat sent out its beacon and welcomed strangers, so does truth that speaks out to all those who care to know it. "So have I lived my life to nurture a torn nation desiring to unite. Such is the destiny of people who need assurance, relief, and a feeling of worth and protection by a strong and united country, proud of the early documents of this nation."

Studying and carefully examining history, learning about those who lived, worked, and developed a national government, shows the power of the past and of people. What matters is the strength of knowledge, the truth tested and tried over time.

The country deserves to know the whole story and have the complete picture, not images written by an unkind pen. The good in life lifts spirits, and transforms personalities.

Life as it was will never be again. The forgotten moments must be recaptured. Joseph Holt's spirit can rest only when the world knows he did make the world a better place and lived life to the fullest. His fate was changed forever by a broken promise of a president. But to the end, Joseph Holt loved Kentucky.

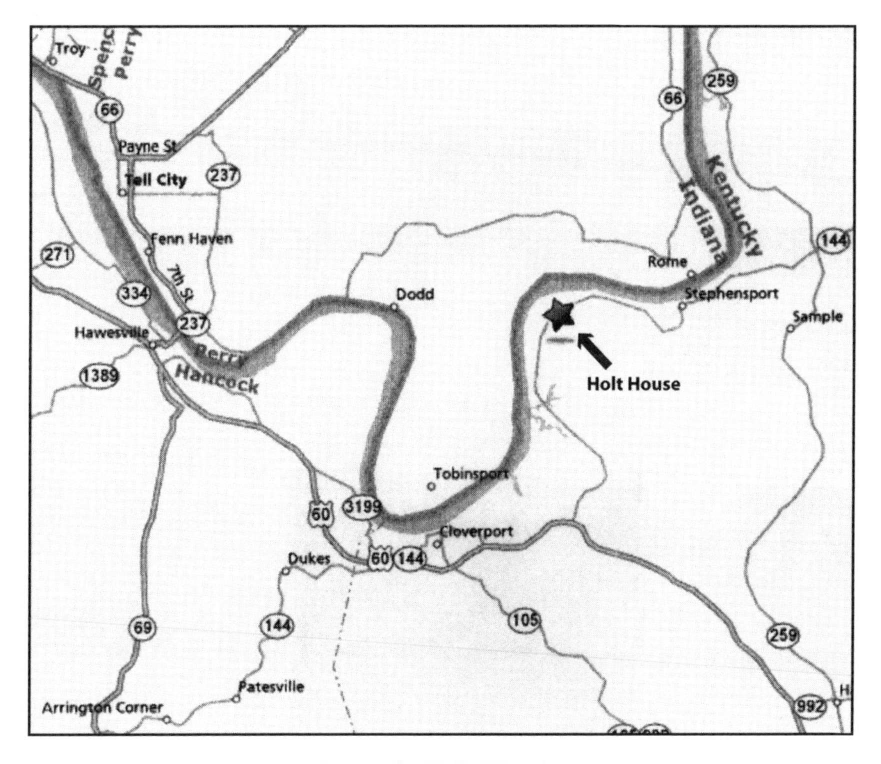

Map to the Holt Mansion.

About the Author

Born at Fort Knox, Susan Dyer was educated at Western Kentucky University with a B.S., M.A., and Rank I in Education. Formerly a Language Arts teacher, Susan has been included numerous times in *Who's Who Among America's Teachers*.

Dyer lives in Breckinridge County, Kentucky, with her husband. They have two sons. Undertaking two projects at the same time, she has written the sensational story of Judge Joseph Holt, Judge Advocate General under President Lincoln, while working with various groups to save and restore Holt's boyhood home as part of the Lincoln Bicentennial Celebration.

Susan has received the following honors in relation to her work with the Judge Joseph Holt House: Outstanding Citizen of the Commonwealth, by the Kentucky House of Representatives, 2008; Volunteer of the Year, Breckinridge County Chamber of Commerce, 2008-2009; Cooperative Hero, *Kentucky Living Magazine*, March 2010; and most recently, an Ida Lee Willis Memorial Foundation 2010 Service to Preservation Award.

Index